The Drowning Nets

THE DROWNING NETS

Bill Knox

HUTCHINSON

LONDON SYDNEY AUCKLAND JOHANNESBURG

This edition first published in 1991 by
Hutchinson

Random Century Group Ltd
20 Vauxhall Bridge Road, London SW1V 2SA

Random Century Australia (Pty) Ltd
20 Alfred Street, Milsons Point, Sydney, NSW 2061, Australia

Random Century New Zealand Ltd
PO Box 40-086, Glenfield, Auckland 10, New Zealand

Random Century South Africa (Pty) Ltd
PO Box 337, Bergvlei, 2012, South Africa

British Library Cataloguing in Publication data
Knox, Bill *1928–*
    The drowning nets.
    I. Title
    823.914 [F]

ISBN 0–09–174458–X

Phototypeset in Baskerville by
Input Typesetting Ltd, London
Printed and bound in Great Britain by
Mackays of Chatham PLC, Chatham, Kent

For my son, Captain Michael Knox, who flies jets.

In *The Drowning Nets*, as in all previous Webb Carrick stories, I extend my sincere and grateful thanks to the officers and men of the Scottish Fishery Protection Service. At both their administrative headquarters and aboard ship, their patient assistance and background guidance were once again freely given and they are much valued.

I have taken the liberty of making a few, mainly minor alterations to Fishery Protection procedures.

Theirs is the skill and the seamanship.

Any errors are mine.

Bill Knox

Prelude

It was a night with no wind, and the sea was a glassy calm. Somewhere overhead, bright stars were singing in a blue velvet sky. The moonlight was the special kind that shines over the islands of the west coast of Scotland.

It was not that way at sea level. An eddying band of damp grey fog had drifted in from the North Atlantic, born where the warmth of the Gulf Stream met the chill currents coming down from the Arctic. It was the kind of thick fog in which it was easy enough to wonder if the rest of the world really still existed.

The patrol launch had state-of-the-art radar and satellite navigation. But she was moving at little more than steerage way through the water and her triple exhausts produced only a whisper. There was the merest sound of a rippling against her hull.

She was hunting. Not a light showed aboard, no orders were given, and none were needed. Her crew were a good team. They'd been trained that way – and they knew they weren't alone in the lazily swirling sea-mist.

Another vessel was somewhere near, and they were getting nearer. They could hear the idling thud of an engine and the occasional high-pitched yowl of a power block. Most recently, there had been sounds that might have been voices.

Briefly, the fog thinned and moonlight probed down from overhead. In the patrol launch, the helmsman barely noticed. He was too intent on watching the hand-signals being given by the vague silhouette of a crewman stationed on deck near the bow. Another lookout was stationed aft. The port and starboard doors of the patrol launch's enclosed and wide bridge had been clipped open to improve hearing.

1

It had to be soon.

As another swirl of mist came in, the helmsman slightly shifted his grip on the big, thin-rimmed steering wheel. The wheel was big and it was thin because that way the slightest rudder alteration could be sensed and translated. Deliberately, he made his fingers relax then tighten again. Then he gave a sideways flicker of a glance at the shadowed figure of the man seated beside him in the command chair.

'Soon,' agreed the shadow. He paused as they heard the power block scream again out there across the water. Then he spoke again, his voice soft and deliberate. 'Any time now.'

The helmsman nodded, mostly to himself, saw their bow lookout signal again, and obediently eased the steering wheel a fraction to port. A fraction, no more. That should be enough. Briefly, he caught himself wondering at the way the other vessel's engine note seemed to have changed. The rhythm seemed to have varied a little, and so had the direction. But a sea mist could play tricks on the senses.

The figure in the command chair rose, prowled across the tight, black confines of the little bridge, and peered out of the starboard door. Then he returned to his chair.

'Another point to port – no more.' The order anticipated another hand-signal from the bow lookout. 'Steer small.'

'Steer small,' repeated the helmsman in an automatic murmur. 'Aye, skipper.'

Briefly, the swirling grey blanket wiped out his view. Then he saw them again . . . the long quivering line of spaced, yellow fishing floats that ran less than a stone's throw away to starboard then vanished ahead, just as so many others had already vanished astern.

For the moment, they were what mattered.

The patrol launch had come across the line of floats twenty minutes earlier, exactly as the sea mist came drifting in from the west. They had been following the floats ever since, knowing what they meant. Radar had located another vessel ahead, another vessel which was maybe twice their size and at about two miles' range.

Then the contact had gone, lost among an electronic jumble of other contacts. They were too near the coast of Lannair Island for radar to do much more. Lannair meant 'A Glitter of Swords' in the old Gaelic tongue of the islands, and Lannair's swords were raw reefs of weed-encrusted rock which possessed unusual magnetic abnormalities.

Going to silent running, the patrol launch had crept on.

The whole reason for her being in the patrol sector or anywhere near Lannair lay under these endless floats. Long, killer drift-nets, made of a fine monofilament nylon, were tough and almost invisible. Already they had seen some of the haul of big Atlantic salmon that had been trapped. Some of the large steel-blue and silver shapes were still thrashing helplessly, others hung limp. Fish could drown when caught by the gills.

A net two miles long was normal enough. One found south-west of Barra had been four miles long. Any kind of deep-sea net fishing for salmon was illegal, yet it took just one night, one good run, and a poacher crew could earn as much money for that night as an ordinary crew could earn in a year.

The quivering along the floats had been growing. They were visibly jerking in the water, another sign that the patrol launch was closing with the other vessel. The helmsman even thought he could make out the tight line of a head-rope.

Yes, they were very near, and the other vessel was hauling in her net. He corrected the thought – nets. It was called a fleet, a string of several nets each attached one to the other.

The casual thought died there. Suddenly, unexpectedly, the patrol launch had broken out of the fog into a large clear gap of sea which glinted in the moonlight. The stars twinkled –

And the patrol launch skipper was already on his feet, yelling orders, grabbing to open their throttle levers.

For a few seconds, no more, the rest was like a frozen cameo. Their quarry was ahead but was two vessels instead of one. The nearest, which had the silhouette of a small trawler, was still hauling in her nets. The second vessel was about the same size and type but didn't seem to be fishing.

Then the patrol launch had come to life with a roar of engines and a lancing beam of white light from the searchlight on the pulpit mount above the bridge. Gathering speed, a vast churn of wake appearing at her stern, she began to race towards the poachers. She was taking a curving course, the kind that would take her in astern of the other vessels, into an ideal position to board them.

The trawler hauling in her nets had stopped work. The figures on her deck stood as if frozen, staring. But the other ship seemed to have different ideas. She was also moving, gathering speed, her black bow coming round to target on the patrol launch. That happened. The patrol launch bucked and danced round on the water, widening her curve to avoid the challenge. Spinning his wheel again, the helmsman grinned as he felt the whole hull around him vibrate with gathering power. He always enjoyed a chase.

But there was something else out there, something very small and moving very fast. The patrol launch skipper saw it first and rapped a warning from his command chair as the new factor raced towards them. Previously hidden from view by trawlers but now no longer masked, there was no mistaking that fast-moving white wake streaking towards the launch. The searchlight swung again. This time, it caught a rubber raider-style boat full in its beam. Two figures were crouched beside the big twin outboard engines howling at the stern. Both of them wore black rubber wet-suits and had black wool ski-cap

4

masks with slits cut for eyes and mouth. One hugged the raider's tiller, bringing the little craft almost shaving down the side of the patrol launch. The other straightened, braced himself, then threw something aboard the patrol launch. It looked about the size of a school satchel and it landed somewhere aft. At the same moment the satchel landed, the small attacker was already swinging away.

An instant later, the whole world seemed to explode for the people aboard the launch. A terrible red-white blast bathed her length in a flash of searing heat.

Engines dead, half a dozen small fires raging aboard, the patrol boat became motionless in the water. The helmsman discovered that he was still on his feet. A splinter of some kind had cut him badly across the head and the blood was almost blinding him. It registered that his skipper hadn't been so lucky and was lying on deck, halfway out of the starboard bridge door.

Then he saw the trawlers again, and cursed long and bitterly. One seemed to be picking up the raider boat. Behind them, the fog was rolling in.

In less than a minute, the trawlers had been swallowed up again by the fog. But they no longer seemed to have any interest in the patrol launch, and the helmsman had other things to think about.

Like dealing with the skipper's duffel jacket. It was still smouldering.

1

It was ten days later, a mid-morning in early September, and a stiff breeze was blowing from the north-west, where the Outer Isles lay beyond the horizon. Overhead, only a few stray wisps of cloud chased across the sunlit sky. The sea was a steady, lumping swell that broke white and roaring below the dark cliffs of Ardnamurchan Point, the most westerly part of the Scottish mainland.

Two grey patrol launches lay at anchor in the shelter of a little bay near the Point. The bay was a hidden place where the sea came in gently, foaming like cream across undisturbed silver sand and empty shoreline. The launches were fast and broad-beamed, their names were *Tern* and *Puffin*, and they flew salt-stained Blue Ensigns with the Scottish Fishery Protection Service's gold crown and thistle crest. But the stiff breeze couldn't reach into the bay and the flags showed only an occasional flutter.

The Scottish Fishery Protection Service was unique in Europe, probably in the world. The men who served under that Blue Ensign were sea-going police officers whose remit began with enforcing the law in the multi-million pound, multi-national fishing industry all round the Scottish coast, then went on from there 'as the Service required'. That could mean working side by side with land-based police or taking part in search and rescue operations. Their warrant cards described them as Sea Fishery officers.

Their job was policing the sea.

That was why the two patrol launches had come to the bay. Three men were meeting aboard the gently swaying *Tern*, seated round the small table in her tiny wardroom. Two were Fishery Protection officers. They watched in silence while the third man, a middle-aged civilian, continued spreading a collection of colour photographs in front of them.

The photographs showed a scarred, blackened hull. That it had stayed afloat seemed almost a miracle – disaster had come very close to overwhelming their sister patrol launch *Pippin*.

'One more view, from aft,' said the civilian. He wore a blue suit and a Royal Naval Reserve tie. His name was John Kennan and the helicopter which had brought him to the rendezvous had landed on the beach. It was still there. *Tern*'s Zodiac boat had ferried him out from the shore. 'As you can see, the worst of the damage was aft.'

Producing the last photograph from his briefcase, he laid it in line with the rest.

The two men sitting opposite him each took a long look at the photographs and then exchanged a grimace. This was very personal to them. Patrol launches rated as a Chief Officer's command, with the courtesy title of Skipper. Webb Carrick, the dark-haired younger man of the pair, commanded *Tern*. The pudgy-faced, slightly older Johnny Walker commanded *Puffin*.

'We heard it was bad,' said Carrick softly.

'But not this bad,' grimaced Walker.

John Kennan nodded.

For a variety of reasons, he knew them both. Webb Carrick, aged thirty-one, might be slightly younger but rated as senior of the two skippers – partly because he had slightly longer service, partly because Headquarters were happier with it that way. Five feet ten inches in height, he had dark eyes, a broad-boned face, and a weather-tanned complexion. He wore a white rollneck sweater under his dark blue uniform blouse. He had the slightly thin lips of a man who could occasionally be short on temper – but for balance he also had the first few signs of some crows-foot lines of humour around the eyes.

Johnny Walker was very different. Smaller as well as fractionally older, he usually looked the way he did at the moment – almost in need of a shave and almost in need of a clean shirt. That pudgy face could be sulky and his personal file with Fishery Protection showed that he fell in and out of trouble with monotonous regularity. Mostly, the thing that saved him was the bottom line that he was a skilled seaman – perhaps not as skilled as he believed, but skilled enough to cling to his small command.

'This.' Carrick touched the nearest photograph with a fingertip and looked directly at Kennan. 'So much damage. How did it happen?'

'Mice?' Walker made a forced, acid attempt at humour.

'We asked the Royal Navy – they've the experts. They found enough remnant traces to identify what was used.'

'Semtex?' asked Walker.

It would have been Carrick's choice too. Anyone with terrorist connections could get hold of some Semtex, originally Czech-made, distributed happily by Libya's Gaddafi.

'No, a lot more basic,' said Kennan. He shrugged. 'The Navy say two commercial underwater blasting explosives were used – Geophex and Cordtex. They calculate it was a satchel charge of about two kilogrammes, mostly Geophex with Cordtex detonator.'

'Doesn't help much,' grunted Walker. 'Hell, half the marine construction and salvage firms on this coast use Geophex or Cordtex. What most of them call security is a joke.'

'I'm aware of that,' said Kennan with an icy patience. 'The Navy also say that *Pippin*'s people could have had it worse. In the right place, that satchel could have sunk them without trace.'

'Should we call this luck?' Carrick stared again at the photographs. They had been taken after *Pippin* had been towed into harbour. Grim reality had been captured in fine-focus detail.

'Nobody died,' said Walker warily. 'Hell, that's luck.'

'Luck or a small miracle,' murmured Kennan.

One or the other. What had happened to *Pippin* had been near disaster. The photographs made it hard to believe she had stayed afloat, might even sail again some distant day.

Each patrol launch was sixty-five feet long, forty-five tons of glass fibre hull and modern maritime technology, with a replacement value of about one million pounds. Russ Donald, *Pippin*'s skipper, was a man Carrick regarded as a friend. All three crews mixed well together when they were ashore. That was natural enough – patrol launch crews treated one another like family. Part of it was pride. Their little craft might look like waterfleas beside the big Fishery Protection cruisers that operated far out into the Atlantic, yet patrol launches could run fast rings round their big relatives when the weather was right.

Now, the photographs showed *Pippin*'s broad-beamed hull, her upperworks scorched and deeply scarred. Bridge windows had smashed, deck rails had vanished. The pulpit lookout, her searchlight mount, all of her high, familiar clutter of radar and radio antennas had been reduced to a tangle of scrap. Part of her stern was missing, and the davit-mounted Zodiac boat she carried aft had simply disappeared.

Two of her people were still in hospital. Russ Donald had cracked ribs and carried several stitches in a head wound. His second officer, a new arrival named Galbraith who had joined only three weeks before, was detained with burns and had had a long, shrapnel-like piece of metal removed from his stomach.

'The latest from the hospital is that Russ Donald should be discharged home in a couple of days,' said Kennan, as if reading his audience's minds. 'Second Officer Galbraith doesn't make the doctors quite so happy. Before he's finished, he may need some plastic surgery.'

'Do we know who we're chasing?' asked Walker. 'Do we have names?'

'The perpetrators? No. Little more than we started with – two small, ordinary-looking trawlers were seen. They were using a high-speed raider skiff as a guard-boat.'

9

Tern's visitor's voice had hardened. John Kennan might sometimes describe himself as a Department errand boy, but he was senior management, running one of the operations desks in the Fleet Support Unit headquarters in Edinburgh, the Scottish capital. 'But whatever it takes, we'll find them.'

'Amen,' said Walker gruffly.

The patrol launch had been swaying gently with the light swell, giving only an occasional tug at her anchor. That changed as a rogue wave which had found its way in from beyond the bay suddenly broke hard against her side. *Tern* lurched, they saw an edge of foam dash like a brief curtain outside the wardroom porthole.

There was an indignant, muffled curse from the other side of the partition door that separated the wardroom from *Tern*'s compact galley. Then as the lurch settled again, the door opened and a large ginger-haired seaman appeared in the gap. Chief Petty Officer William 'Clapper' Bell had a face like a friendly, well-worn brick and came in carrying a plastic tray which held three mugs of slopping coffee.

'Thought that Mr Kennan might want a wet, skipper,' he told Carrick amiably, then managed a long, close inspection of the photographs while he placed the tray on the table. 'And I could get Gogi to organize some sandwiches.'

'Maybe later.' Carrick saw Clapper Bell's innocent blue eyes still lingering on the photographs. 'I'll let you know.'

'Do that, skipper.' The ginger-haired giant managed another interested glance at the photographs then went out, closing the partition door again.

'Your bo'sun, isn't he? The one who came with you from your last ship?' asked Kennan politely. A twinkle in his eyes showed he already knew the answer.

'Chief Petty Officer Bell,' agreed Carrick.

'Who sticks his nose into everything,' said Walker caustically. 'Webb, since when did that half-tamed thug know how to boil water?'

They each took a half-empty mug of coffee – the rest of it was swirling on the tray – and sipped for a moment, looking at the photographs again. Carrick could hear the soft, regular slap of water against *Tern*'s hull and the heartbeat background murmur of her generator. Then heavy footsteps sounded on the deck overhead and he heard Clapper Bell's voice without being able to make out the words. The other voice that answered probably belonged to Gogi MacDonnell, an ex-fisherman from the islands who also held chief petty officer rank – launch crews were structured as a skipper, a second officer, an engineer officer, and two chief petty officer ratings. As bo'sun, Chief Petty Officer Bell didn't normally volunteer for galley duties – partly because he knew better. The galley area was jealously guarded by MacDonnell. But when it mattered, Clapper Bell could always manage some form of minor bribery.

'Your boats haven't been involved in the *Pippin* investigation,' said John Kennan unexpectedly.

'That hasn't been our fault,' said Carrick dryly.

'We offered,' said Walker. 'We were told to mind our own business.'

'You were told to do the job you'd been sent to do up north,' corrected John Kennan. 'I drew up the orders. Maybe you've forgotten.'

Carrick glanced at Johnny Walker and knew that, just once, they felt the same way.

They had been working about as far north as patrol launches could be located, off the Butt of Lewis in the Outer Islands, when they had heard of the attack on *Pippin*. But they'd been left there, snapping at the heels of an invading fleet of about a hundred large Spanish boats that had arrived and were stretching the new European Common Market regulations to their absolute limit. Spanish boats and local Scottish boats had been involved in regular skirmishes, with some Norwegian shark-hunters also appearing in the middle of everything.

It had amounted to endless frustration, the Fishery

Protection wavelengths busy with distant orders and distant signals from the south-west, where the pursuit raged for the men behind the terror attack on their sister launch. They had listened to aircraft in sweeps, they had picked up radio traffic from at least half a dozen of the big fishery cruisers – each a ship with the power and size of a small naval frigate – and then there were other call signs, call signs which they knew were navy or coastguard.

But nothing for *Tern* or *Puffin* until last evening's coded signal, received at dusk, telling them to drop everything and get down to Ardnamurchan Point.

They had.

It would be a long time before any of the men aboard *Tern* or *Puffin* forgot that dash. They had stopped briefly to refuel at Stornoway on Lewis, then had come down through the islands in darkness, lumping seas and drenching spray. Dawn had found them off Skye, where they surprised a travelling family of blue whales. South of Skye, they had had to snake-track behind some of the smaller islands to avoid a scatter of radar contacts that were probably lobster boats.

But they had reached Ardnamurchan Point and the rendezvous bay with time in hand before Kennan's helicopter appeared.

'So.' John Kennan had been sipping his coffee again. The view through *Tern*'s porthole had altered as a changing tide began swinging her round on her anchor. Where before it had looked towards the empty sea, now it was towards the beach, gleaming silver sand, and the coarse grass of the shoreland. He brought his gaze back to them. 'Now it's your turn. First, I want to explain a couple of things – '

'Wait!' hissed Walker dramatically, rising from his seat.

Two strides took him to the partition door. He seized the handle, flung the door open, and glared out into the galley. No one was there. Disappointed, he went back to his seat and managed to collide with the wardroom table in the process.

'I'm sorry,' he said weakly.

'Can we get on?' suggested Kennan. 'We start with what happened to *Pippin*. When she found those salmon nets, it wasn't by accident. She'd been told to look off Lannair Island.'

'Told?' Carrick raised a quick eyebrow.

'Told. I'll explain that later,' said Kennan. 'The way the opposition reacted wasn't expected. Trouble, yes. A fight, yes. Not bombing. Which brings another puzzle. After the bombing, *Pippin*'s radio was knocked out. Yet someone, somewhere sent out an anonymous Mayday call for help, saying she was sinking and where. Again, that's all we know about it.'

'Someone with a conscience?' suggested Walker doubtfully, scratching a thumbnail across his stubbled chin. 'Or maybe someone who was scared to get involved?'

'I said we don't know,' repeated Kennan shortly. 'Now to the present. As of this morning, the search for the people who attacked *Pippin* is being shifted – apparently in total – about sixty miles north. It will also and genuinely wind down in size – we've got to resume normal patrol schedules, there's near mayhem breaking out in some sectors. At the same time, we have arranged for the rumour to spread that we now think that these two damned trawlers are either clean away or hiding up in one of the northern sea lochs.'

'I don't understand,' said Walker lamely.

'Good.' Kennan gave a wrinkled, humourless smile. 'Do you, Carrick?' Carrick shook his head.

'Then listen.' Kennan delved into his briefcase and produced a folded Admiralty chart, one of the new blue-and-yellow colour editions. Spreading it out on the table, he used two of the coffee mugs to hold the edges. He used a pencil as a pointer, stabbing it down at Ardnamurchan. 'We're here. You're not going too far – to Mull.' The pencil danced across to the big island, which was shaped like an old-fashioned boot. Then it moved carefully down the west side of Mull and stopped. 'Here's the place that matters – the village of Port Torquil. You remember Port Torquil, don't you, Walker?'

Johnny Walker flushed. 'That was a time ago – '

'Three years.' Kennan kept his attention on the chart and the pencil took another hop. 'The fleet of illegal nets that *Pippin* found began here, about twenty miles out from Mull. She followed them.' The pencil traced along an already inked line. 'Then she found the trawlers and was attacked here, off Lannair Island.' The pencil stopped at a neat, final cross. 'You both know the sector around Lannair. It's a devil's playground for anything that floats.'

'And Port Torquil?' asked Carrick.

'A team of marine biologists have a boat based there,' said Kennan. He tapped a pencil on the cross mark. 'They told *Pippin*'s skipper to try off Lannair if he wanted to put a stop to an illegal salmon netting operation. They believed it had to be big, they had no proof about anything – just some educated hunch.' He sucked hard on his teeth. 'The kind that damned nearly cost us *Pippin* and her crew.'

'What kind of hunch?' asked Walker suspiciously.

'One of their research projects involves keeping a watch on the numbers of Atlantic salmon in their area.' Kennan grimaced a little. 'There's an established, respected scientific theory about how salmon migrate across oceans at different times of the year. Coming and going, they always use the same routes like they were pipelines. The marine biologists at Port Torquil reckon one of the main pipelines to and from Scotland runs near Lannair Island. The salmon population had begun taking an unexpected nosedive. It seemed that something was happening near Lannair. Add one or two rumours they'd heard, and the best answer was that a major illegal fishing operation was going on.'

'Run by some madman ready to throw bombs to keep himself in business?' Walker came close to a jeer of disbelief.

14

'Why not? If the rest is true, the money might be good enough.' Kennan stopped. *Tern* was still being gently pulled round on her anchor by the tide, and the move had brought a ray of bright sunlight directly into the cabin through the porthole glass. As the hull swayed, the bright patch of light danced on the front of a locker. For a moment, Kennan's thoughts seemed elsewhere. Then he was back with them. 'I got Russ Donald's side of the story first. Since then, I've had someone speak with these marine biology people – but we've kept any kind of contact down to a minimum. That's for their own sake. They could be in enough danger already. Why add to it?'

Carrick gave a slow, slightly frowning nod of understanding. 'And now you expect something more will happen?'

'If it does, it will happen soon,' said Kennan flatly. He used the pencil like a pointer to circle an area which covered from Port Torquil out to Lannair and beyond. 'Somewhere around the same area. The Port Torquil people say that the salmon will stop running through this pipeline after another couple of weeks – then that's it finished until next year. End of season. Every day these trawlers lose is costing them money. They'll know it, and that's maybe how we can trap them.'

'They think everything is fine, they come back, then we charge in?' Walker showed one of his sudden swings of mood. 'I like it!'

'Do you?' Kennan was caustic. 'What else will you do? Toss a coin to see who gets blown out of the water first?'

'Sorry.' Walker sighed and scowled down at the chart again.

'The way you'll do it, your boats have separate tasks for a spell. But *Tern* remains command boat, as before.'

Walker nodded. He made no pretence at ever liking the situation, but he accepted it.

'*Puffin* first.' Kennan's pencil swept a new line. 'She'll patrol south and west of this which keeps you just below Lannair Island. You will advertise the fact that you're around. After a day or so, you can use Port Torquil as an occasional base – where I think they're likely to remember you.' Kennan glanced at Carrick. 'Three years ago, Skipper Walker made a rather spectacular arrival at Port Torquil. He misjudged his approach, he rammed a small long-line boat, he succeeded in sinking it in fifty feet of water, and he didn't win many friends. No one was injured, but the Department had to pay compensation. The boat owner's laments were a wonder to hear. True, Walker?'

Walker sighed but said nothing.

'So, we have the return of the Demon Skipper,' said Kennan sarcastically. 'You patrol your allocated sector. The salmon trawlers will accept you as the only known Fishery Protection presence anywhere near them. You're apparently leaving the door open for them to get to that salmon pipeline – but in reality you're doing a sheepdog act.' Pausing, he reached into his briefcase and drew out two large brown envelopes, checking the way each was initialled. He handed one to Walker and slid the other across to Carrick. 'Orders in writing.' Abruptly, he seemed to change the subject. 'Carrick, how do you rate your Second Officer?'

'Andy Grey?' Carrick blinked in surprise. 'He's young but he's good.'

'He can make decisions?'

Carrick nodded. 'I'd trust him.'

Kennan glanced at Johnny Walker. 'What's your opinion?'

'He's all right,' said Walker cautiously.

'He's also your brother-in-law, isn't he?'

'I'm married to his sister. That's not his fault.'

For a moment, Kennan allowed a wintry wisp of a smile to stray across his lined face. Then he turned back to Carrick.

'The computer says you've never worked the Port Torquil sector.'

16

'Never.' Carrick had a sudden suspicion about the sealed envelope in his hands.

'So you're not known. You'll arrive as a replacement for the mate aboard the *Dirk*, the marine biology craft lying at Port Torquil. The man you're replacing has gone off on sick leave and you'll be one of two seamen aboard her. She's a converted coaster, cargo space taken out and scientists put in.' Suddenly, the visitor got to his feet. 'Things are going to happen in Port Torquil. Your job will be to keep your eyes open and use your ears. You'll have *Tern* tucked away not too far distant for when things really happen. You'll stay in radio touch with young Grey, he'll keep in contact with Walker.'

'And when things happen?' asked Carrick. He and Walker had also got to their feet.

'By then I want names. Local names and other names.' Kennan was packing the chart and photographs back in his briefcase. 'We don't run unnecessary risks, but we round up these people. I don't like gangsters throwing bombs at Fishery Protection.'

'It's bad for the image,' agreed Carrick mildly.

Johnny Walker snickered, but Kennan's expression didn't change. He looked at his wristwatch. 'Your orders cover most eventualities. Meeting over, gentlemen – I've got to leave you.'

Carrick opened the partition door. They left the little wardroom and moved for'ard, along a narrow companion-way and into the patrol launch's cockpit bridge area. It ran most of the width of *Tern*'s broad-beamed hull and had more floor space than anywhere else aboard. Panelled in polished mahogany, it had thick glass down to chest level on three sides and a gleaming, aircraft-style mass of instruments, controls and dials for'ard. The aft area was storage lockers, and racks of radio equipment covering marine and aircraft VHF bands as well as MF and HF radio telephone and a telex link. *Tern* also carried satellite navigation equipment and the best radar that could be fitted aboard anything her size.

'Andy.' Carrick nodded to his Second Officer, who was standing beside one of the black control seats. 'Get the Zodiac ready. Mr Kennan is leaving.'

'Aye, skipper.' Andy Grey was in his twenties, with a lean, pock-marked face and spiky black hair. His blue battledress jacket had a single gold stripe on each shoulder. As usual when he was dealing with a stranger, he looked at Kennan with a reserved caution. When his glance moved on and reached his brother-in-law, his manner thawed only a little. Andy Grey and Johnny Walker might be related by marriage, but beyond that they simply tolerated one another. 'Will I radio Mr Kennan's helicopter pilot?'

'No. Not yet.' Kennan spoke first. He touched Carrick's arm. 'Skipper, I need a moment with you first. Alone.' With a bare courtesy of an apology, he turned towards Johnny Walker. 'A small matter. Nothing that affects your orders.'

Walker shrugged. Opening the bridge door, he thumbed Andy Grey through, then followed the black-haired Second Officer out on deck. The bridge door closed with an indignant thump.

'Temper,' mused Kennan. Taking a step forward, he looked for a moment at the array of instruments with what could have been envy. Outside, Walker and Andy Grey had moved out of sight. But a squat, hairy man in faded white overalls was sunning himself at the bow. Sam Pulsudski, *Tern*'s Engineer Officer, only really showed himself in daylight when the launch was at anchor. 'Carrick, I've a couple of things to add. For your own ears.'

'Sir?' Carrick waited, hearing the steady lap against their hull as the sea argued with the background murmur of the generator.

'Port Torquil.' The older man seemed to make up his mind about something, yet not completely. 'All right, you're going in with an arranged cover story. The chief scientist in charge of the marine biology project unit is a woman, Dr Margaret Steeven. She knows who you are.

18

It stops there. I've – ah – ' Kennan hesitated slightly ' – I've known Margaret Steeven for a long time. She is damned good at her job, but you may not find it too easy to get along with her. Try. She's worth the effort.'

'Try,' agreed Carrick. 'How does she relate with the local fishermen?'

'Call it armed neutrality,' said Kennan acidly. 'Some of them are scared of her. Mostly, they've been reasonably friendly and she'd like to keep it that way. Don't expose her people to – well, to any kind of risk. That could include another satchel bomb landing in their laps.' Pausing, he frowned down at a couple of instrument dials for a moment. 'We put someone else into Port Torquil three days ago. He's in the village. Margaret Steeven doesn't know who he is – just that there's someone.'

Carrick gave a soft whistle. 'Have you heard from him yet?'

'Once. Briefly. He's using the name Cormack. Leave it at that.'

'All right.' Carrick looked down at the envelope he was still holding. 'Any local police involvement?'

'The last police station at Port Torquil closed fifteen years ago,' said Kennan. 'To be more exact, it was burned down. As an economy measure it wasn't rebuilt. I think the theory was it would probably only be burned down again.' He gave a grimly humorous shake of his head. 'No police. I think a sergeant comes over from Tobermory once a month to make sure the place still exists. Until something positive happens somewhere ashore this stays our business – the police can do without it.'

An outboard engine fired to life outside, starting with an initial snarl then settling back to a low throb.

'My cue,' said Kennan. 'Good luck, Webb. Look for trouble, yes. But when you find it, don't do anything foolish. We'll send in the heavy brigade.'

'I'll try to remember that,' promised Carrick.

'Good.' John Kennan sighed to himself, thinking of the waiting helicopter, and of the kind of paperwork waiting on his operations desk at Fleet Support. The main computer at the Headquarters building in Edinburgh could reduce people to basic civil service printouts of information. Most people. It could tell him that Chief Officer Webster Carrick had been deep-sea Merchant Navy and had gained his master's ticket before he had switched to Fishery Protection. But there were other stories he'd heard, the kind that weren't in any printout. Suddenly, surprising himself, he offered his hand. 'Let's nail these devils.'

They shook hands. Then Kennan went out on deck and walked aft, where Clapper Bell had the Zodiac boat loitering alongside with a faint haze of blue coming from her exhaust. Johnny Walker made a considerable show of helping their visitor over the rail and into the inflatable.

'Good luck,' said Kennan again. 'All of you.'

He nodded to Clapper Bell, the outboard's throttle opened, and the little craft went screaming away from *Tern* towards the shore and the waiting helicopter while Kennan held his briefcase tightly on his lap. On the launch, the two skippers watched from the stern rail for a couple of minutes.

'I could use a beer,' said Johnny Walker at last. He raised a hopeful eyebrow. 'Your place or mine?'

Carrick grinned. They went back into the cockpit bridge, which was deserted.

'Wait,' said Carrick. 'I'll bring them.'

He went along to the galley, where a lean, sad-faced man was chopping up meat. Gogi MacDonnell always wore a wool tammy hat because he was totally bald underneath. He was dressed in his usual blue overalls, tucked into cut-down fisherman's boots. When Carrick entered, he glanced at his skipper with a suspicious interest then pointed the knife he was using at the chopping board.

'We could be eating a decent stew in an hour, skipper,' suggested MacDonnell in his soft West Highland lilt. 'Or are we going somewhere in a hurry?'

20

Carrick thought of the monotony of half-defrosted meals they'd eaten for days and gave way to temptation.

'Give it a try, Gogi,' he suggested. 'I'd like to use a plate again instead of a bowl.'

Opening the galley refrigerator, he removed two cans of beer and took them back to the bridge. Walker had opened the envelope containing *Puffin*'s orders and was glancing at them. When Carrick gave him one of the beers Walker opened it, took a gulp, then went on reading. Carrick used the time to open the other beer and sip while he watched the inflatable still heading across the bay but beginning to slow as it came in towards the beach.

'This is garbage,' said Walker gloomily, stuffing his orders back into their envelope. 'What it really says is I act like an idiot out there while you do the hopeful hero bit.' He took another long, noisier gulp at his beer. 'Webb, I'll give it a try. But I think it's crazy.'

'If I win a medal you can wear it at weekends,' promised Carrick woodenly.

Walker sighed then waved the envelope again.

'This says Margaret Steeven is running the team at Port Torquil. Do you know her?'

'No.'

'I do,' said Walker wryly. 'The woman frightens me. Margaret Steeven may look like somebody's granny, but when she feels inclined, she flays people alive!'

'Thanks for the warning.' Carrick's corner of the bridge was bathed in the warmth of the sun through glass. Enjoying it, he leaned back against the instrument panel and nursed his beer. 'What do you remember about Port Torquil?'

'Mainly, the collision that Kennan went on about.' Walker's plump face showed that the memory wasn't a happy one. 'All right, I was trying too hard – first-time arrival, showing off a little with lots of white water, lots of power. It would have been all right, except that the original ancient mariner chugs out in front of me at the last moment, with an old wreck of a boat. When we hit

21

the thing, it didn't so much sink as fall to bits.' He gestured with his can for emphasis and some suds of beer sprayed the bridge. 'Naturally, as soon as it sank, then that wreck became the most valuable boat in the western world!'

Carrick made a sympathetic noise. It usually happened that way. When a Government boat damaged anything around the Hebridean islands, local lawyers jumped out from under every stone waving writs.

'What about *Puffin?*'

'She dented her nose, we lay over in Port Torquil for about ten days sorting things out and making repairs.'

'And Port Torquil – as a place, Johnny?'

'In looks? Pretty much your average Western Isles fishing village – with some spectacular scenery around.' Walker paused and began choosing his words carefully, trying to be helpful for once. 'Boats? A reasonable number of locally owned, a small fleet of them. Others that come and go. There's good fishing a few miles out. As usual, every last one of them screams poverty every time they get a cutback in what the regulations allow them to catch.'

'The usual.' Carrick nodded. It wasn't too often they met fishermen who didn't feel that fish stocks should be preserved. They just wanted them preserved further along the coast. 'People?'

'Reasonable enough, most of them.' Walker grimaced. 'There are two fishing families to watch – tribes, near enough. One tribe is the Grants, the other tribe is the Stewarts. They don't like each other, and they prove it most Saturday nights.'

'Suppose you're an outsider?'

It was a reasonable question, but Walker shrugged. 'They don't like Fishery Protection. We rate about level with tax collectors. But usually it's still a case of don't worry them and they won't worry you.' He could sense where Carrick's questions were leading. 'The boat I sank belonged to a Grant, which made the Stewarts almost like me. I ran a check on both tribes at the time. A few of them had minor records – convictions for various things, but nothing serious. If they're involved in anything, how often do people want to give evidence against a tribe?'

'Illegal fishing?'

'What about it?' asked Walker stonily. 'The same scene. Minor convictions, nothing big. If we're talking salmon nets, you've found them floating, I've found them floating. But how often have you proved who put them there?'

Carrick sighed. Once. Even then, only because of a mistake. *Pippin*'s discovery had been a freak.

'Would your Grants or your Stewarts use a bomb?'

'And almost kill five people?' Walker took another gulp of beer and seemed surprised that he'd emptied the can. 'All right, if someone has hit a salmon pipeline the way Kennan claims, it could breed a lot of nastiness. But – no, I wouldn't label either the Grants or the Stewarts as killers. At least, not in any major kind of way.' He paused and chuckled. 'The local story is that the last time the Stewarts and Grants did anything together was when they burned down the Port Torquil police station.'

'Someone has to like us,' suggested Carrick patiently. 'Who might have sent that Mayday message that *Pippin* was sinking?'

'Whoever did, don't expect them to ever admit it.' Walker tossed his empty beer can into a waste basket and looked disappointed when Carrick didn't offer a replacement. 'For the Grants, talk to Sam Lawson. He's married to a Grant, he runs the chandler's store beside the harbour. Your best bet with the other crowd is Big Charlie Stewart – or it used to be, three years ago. He skippered one of the Stewart family boats.' He paused, remembering again. 'One person was reasonably friendly towards us, an old man named John Hill. But he was English, an outsider, one of the White Settlers who leave the Big City and move up to the islands when they reach pension age. He might be dead by now.'

'No one else?'

'No one I can remember, Webb.' Walker thumbed out towards the bay. Kennan had been landed, and *Tern*'s Zodiac boat was already on her return trip. 'Clapper can ferry me over to *Puffin* when he gets here. I've a schedule to keep – all those busy, important noises to make south of the Lannair line.' He gave a resigned grimace. 'So what have we still to sort out?'

There wasn't much. The two patrol launches had operated often enough as a team to have few real problems. But there were always small extras, extras that might matter if something happened that it wouldn't necessarily do anyone any good for Department to know about. That ranged from agreeing their usual private code of radio call-signs to an emergency rendezvous and the way *Puffin*'s crew would behave when they came into Port Torquil.

'I need a word with that brother-in-law of mine before I go,' said Walker as they finished. 'Do you mind?'

'Go ahead,' agreed Carrick.

They went out on deck. The Department helicopter had already taken off from the beach and was climbing fast, heading inland. The Zodiac boat was almost home again, steering in towards *Tern*'s stern.

'Hey, Andy!' Walker spotted his brother-in-law as he emerged from the aft companionway door. 'A minute!'

Leaving Carrick, Walker trotted along the deck towards Second Officer Grey. Walker reached him and spoke briefly and earnestly in a low voice. Grey listened, nodded, and *Puffin*'s skipper seemed satisfied. Turning away, he made for the boarding recess in the stern transom. Another moment, and he was in the Zodiac and the inflatable was away again, heading the short distance towards the other patrol launch.

'Get the inflatable aboard as soon as Clapper gets back, Andy,' called Carrick. 'Then I want everybody together in the bridge, ten minutes later.'

Grey grinned along the deck at him. 'Is it true I'm being left to run the shop, Skipper?'

Carrick raised an eyebrow. 'Was Johnny handing out advice?'

'Well – ' his Second Officer's grin widened ' – something like that. But nothing I'm going to worry about.'

Going aft, Carrick went down the steep internal ladder that led to *Tern*'s lower deck and along to his cabin. The cabin was small, but with plenty of locker space and a separate compartment which held a washbasin and toilet. There was an adjoining shower cubicle, which he shared with Grey, who had the next cabin. Each member of the patrol launch's crew had a cabin. The two chief petty officers were situated for'ard with their own messing area and shower. Sam Pilsudski lived midships beside his beloved engines.

Once in the cabin, the door closed again, Carrick hung his jacket on a hook where it swung gently. Lying full-length on his bunk, he opened the sealed envelope he'd been given by John Kennan, took out the surprisingly brief orders, and read through them. At the finish, he softly cursed the absent Fleet Support deskman, put the orders down and frowned up at the cabin ceiling.

In effect, he was to go in, find out what he could in any way possible, then act accordingly – but at the same time he was to give diplomatic weight to any advice given by Dr Margaret Steeven.

Carrick had worked with marine research people before. Sometimes they were easy to get along with, sometimes they had a mule-stubborn attitude to anything that didn't fit into their own precise ways of thinking. This time – he could only find out.

Resting back on the bunk, hands clasped behind his head, Carrick enjoyed the sheer luxury of letting his eyelids close for a few moments. There had been no sleep for anyone on the rush down from the north. Sooner or later, that caught up with anyone.

A raucous, angry screech came from a gull outside as it was chased from the deck. Gogi MacDonnell was houseproud enough to treat bird-droppings as an almost personal insult. Footsteps passed overhead, going towards the stern, and then there were other noises aft. The Zodiac boat was back. It bumped lightly against the hull, there were voices, more footsteps, then a whine as the electrically powered davit brought the inflatable back aboard.

Carrick smiled to himself. He was proud of his little command and her crew. He still thrilled each time that *Tern* came fully alive on her 'three by three' power package. Three massive turbo-charged V8 Detroit diesel engines, from a truck derivative, drove three big, full-feathering propellors handled by three slim, deep, spade-blade rudders. Close on sixteen hundred b.h.p was available in a highspeed hull that tackled all-weather duty. It was a vibrating hi-tech world that could test any seaman to the limit, that made her cramped engineroom a noisy, deafening hell even when wearing ear protectors.

But *Tern* could operate for up to seven days on her own resources, including diesel fuel and fresh water. Any possible problem was deliberately anticipated. Proof of that was in the way she had two totally separate electrical systems throughout and even duplicate fire protection systems.

It was that way with all of these unarmed patrol launches. It had been that way with *Pippin*.

Until someone heaved a bomb aboard her.

Carrick allowed himself the luxury of the bunk until his watch showed that nearer fifteen than ten minutes had passed since the Zodiac boat had returned. He heaved himself out of the bunk and to his feet, grimaced at his reflection in the mirror of the dressing table opposite, went through to the little washroom, splashed some water on his face, dried it off with a towel, then ran a comb through his hair.

It was time to tell the others what was going on.

Except they probably knew most of it already.

They were all there when he went through – even Sam Pilsudski. The Engineer Officer, with a ready smile of gold-filled teeth, sat on the sill of one of the bridge doors, smoking a dark cheroot. The rest of the pack, as usual, protruded from the top pocket of his faded overalls. For Pilsudski to be there meant he was interested – usually, he made a religion of arriving late. Andy Grey stood beside him, his young face set in what was probably intended to be an impassive expression. *Tern*'s two chief petty officers were over on the other side of the cockpit bridge, gossiping quietly on their own, content to let the world come round when it was ready.

'Good!' Pilsudski, in his late thirties and the oldest of the crew, beamed across at him. 'Words of wisdom time from our hero skipper!'

'Sam, in a happier age you'd have been flogged for insolence every Tuesday,' said Carrick mildly. He let the others chuckle. 'You all know about our visitor. Our job is to square the account for what happened to *Pippin*. We'll be working around Port Torquil.'

No one looked surprised. Clapper Bell and Gogi Mac-Donnell exchanged a fractional smile.

'But at first I'm going in on my own – ' That was different. As he went on, explaining the rest of it, his crew listened in a silence broken only by an occasional grunt of doubt from Pilsudski. One of the radio receivers was muttering in the background, but it was a routine trans-mission on a fishing frequency and they ignored it.

'What about *Puffin?*' asked Pilsudski as he finished.

'She'll be doing high-profile things, mostly away from Port Torquil. But she'll also be ready to give back-up.' Carrick nodded towards his Second Officer. 'While I'm ashore, Andy will be acting skipper. Mainly he'll try and keep out of trouble.'

'Prayer might help,' suggested Clapper Bell solemnly.

Andy Grey grinned, but still said nothing, which was wise. He knew, as they all did, that if there was a problem then Clapper Bell would be close by to hold his hand.

'Gogi.' Carrick turned to the thin West Highlander,

who had been listening to it all with his usual gloomy air. 'How well do you know the coast around Port Torquil?'

'Well enough, skipper,' said MacDonnell carefully. His home was a fishing village in the Outer Isles, he had been regarded by some of his friends as a traitor when, after an early lifetime around the islands, he had joined Fishery Protection. 'I had an aunt who used to live near there, years ago. Why?'

'We need a place where *Tern* can park. As near to Port Torquil as we can make it, yet well hidden. Nowhere that would dry out with the tide – when things do happen, she'll be needed in a hurry.'

'Aye, I can imagine,' said MacDonnell, frowning. He pushed the woollen hat slightly back on his head and scratched the extra inch or so of skin that became visible. 'How far away is "near", skipper?'

'Twenty minutes at the outside.'

MacDonnell sucked hard on his teeth. Then he gave a slow nod. 'There's a place, if a man knows the marks to steer by. When do we try it, skipper?'

'After dusk, this evening.' By which time Johnny Walker's *Puffin* would be in position and broadcasting the fact. 'Then you come back again after you've dropped me off somewhere else. Any problems in that?' He saw there were none as far as MacDonnell was concerned. 'Gogi, something different. Two families, Grant and Stewart – do you know them?'

'Most of them should have been drowned at birth,' said MacDonnell unemotionally. 'I know a few folk who would oblige.'

He stopped as a rumble of engines came from across the water. Like the others, he turned to look. *Puffin* was getting under way. A broad white wash was beginning to build at her stern, they could see a cloud of light blue diesel exhaust. Johnny Walker was indulging in one of his showman acts, taking her out on all three engines when most skippers would have been content to ease away on two.

28

'He knocks hell out of his transmissions,' Sam Pilsudski told the world in general with an engineer's disgust.

A siren bray of goodbye came from the other launch, as if in reply. Then *Puffin* was moving, the white wake still building, her Blue Ensign streaming straight behind her.

Carrick still found it good to watch; odd to watch, knowing that there would be times when *Tern* would look the same to an outsider. First, as she gained speed, *Puffin*'s bow came up. Then, as her diesels continued their bellow and speed still increased, that changed and gradually her bow came down again. Riding strangely flat in the water in a way that constituted a high-speed signature for her class, the patrol launch streaked her way out of the sea loch. Immediately she was clear, she used her rudders and that white wake swung in serpent style to the north.

In another minute, the grey hull had vanished behind the cliffs of Ardnamurchan.

'That one won't be happy till he finds himself a nice war somewhere,' said Clapper Bell sardonically. He caught Carrick's grin and winked. 'Maybe they'd make him an admiral, skipper.'

'And maybe he'd sign you on as cabin boy,' countered Carrick dryly.

They had formed the scuba diving team on *Marlin*, their last ship, and that kind of relationship built up its own blend of friendship and discipline. It was the reason why Clapper Bell had followed Carrick to *Tern* and they both knew it.

'Admiral Walker!' Bell said it almost under his breath. 'That's all we'd need!' Then he stopped, partly because of Carrick's warning frown, partly for another reason. He sniffed, his eyes widened, and he sniffed again. Urgently, he gave Gogi MacDonnell a nudge. 'What's that?'

'The stew!' MacDonnell could smell it too. His eyes widened in horror. 'It's burning!' He glared around. 'I warned you, all of you, the microwave isn't meant as a clothes dryer!'

'Just a pair of socks, Gogi,' said Sam Pilsudski warily. 'Hell I – uh – I forgot to take them out. Sorry.'

MacDonnell snarled. Then he went past them, clattering frantically towards the galley.

Pilsudski sighed. He smiled feebly at the accusing eyes all around, then took a sniff of his own at the burning smell drifting in from the galley.

'Goodbye, socks,' he said sadly.

Pilsudski drifted away, followed by Andy Grey. Frantic noises were still coming from the galley. Leaning his elbows on the back of the command chair, Webb Carrick glanced across at Clapper Bell.

'Andy will be all right,' Carrick said quietly. 'But keep an eye on him.'

'He's been offered help already,' said the Glasgow-Irishman dryly. 'Johnny Walker said to call him up any time he needed advice – and a little reminder that if we lose you, then *Puffin* becomes senior boat.'

Carrick chuckled. That sounded pure Walker.

'I'll try not to let it happen,' he promised.

'Good,' said Bell easily. 'I'd hate to have to break in a new skipper. You've been bad enough.'

The smell of burning socks was fading. Maybe they could still eat.

2

Webb Carrick had his first daytime view of Port Torquil a full twenty-four hours later. He was a paying deck-passenger on the little inter-island coaster *Duchess May* as she plugged a stolid way through a light swell off the west coast of Mull. It was early afternoon, and a moderate wind was pushing only a few clouds across a mostly clear sky.

It was being a reasonable day.

Or it was for most people.

'Over there,' said the girl beside him. Pleased, she pointed ahead. She had long chestnut hair and, wherever she'd been, she had lost very little of the Hebridean lilt in her voice. 'There – you can see the harbour.'

'I see it.' Standing beside her at the coaster's bow rail, Webb Carrick nodded a solemn agreement. A thin line of houses and the low trace of a harbour wall were beginning to show ahead. He looked at her again and made a guess. 'Home?'

'Home.' She nodded, a sparkle in her dark eyes.

'How long have you been away?' asked Carrick.

'Two years.' She was in her early twenties, slim and medium height. Her chestnut hair, being blown by the breeze, framed a pert-nosed oval of a face and she wore rust-brown corduroy trousers with black shoes, a black sweater and a lightweight red jacket. She had a large canvas suitcase lying in a sheltered corner aft, and the coaster's crew seemed to know her as a friend. 'Long enough.'

Carrick nodded, feeling the steady thud of the coaster's engine vibrating the steel deck under his feet. The *Duchess May* was only a year out of her birthplace yard on the Clyde, still new enough to look immaculate, but the rig-

31

ours of slogging inter-island cargo-passenger work would sort that out soon enough.

'Where for two years?' he asked.

'London. Nice people but too many of them.' She grinned as a brief mist of spray stung at their faces. 'I work in an insurance office and I've saved up holiday time – I'm due six weeks.'

'Then back to London?'

'I'll wait and see.' The girl brushed some loose strands of that chestnut hair back from her eyes. 'What's your name?'

'Carrick. Webb Carrick.' He waited quizzically.

'Let me guess.' She considered him. Carrick was wearing a blue open-necked work shirt, faded denim trousers, and a pair of old, rope-soled canvas shoes which had once been white. The ancient tweed jacket he carried draped over one arm had been borrowed from Sam Pilsudski and smelled of mothballs. Even Pilsudski didn't want it back. 'Seaman?'

He nodded. 'I'm joining a marine research boat based out here. The *Dirk* – someone went sick, so she needs a replacement mate.'

'*Dirk?*' She frowned a little. 'No, I don't know her.' The frown lightened. 'I'm Liz Lawson. Most people know me around Port Torquil – my father runs the chandler's store at the harbour.'

Carrick hid his surprise. 'Is your father Sam Lawson?'

'Guilty.' She nodded with a sudden small degree of caution. 'Do you know him?'

'This will be my first time in Port Torquil. I've heard his name mentioned,' said Carrick vaguely. He had certainly heard of Sam Lawson – head of the Grant tribe at Port Torquil, one of the names on Johnny Walker's worry list. 'A lot of people seem to know him.'

'My father?' She said it dryly. 'A lot of people do. But check his prices. If he can't remember a price for something, he makes what he calls a favourable guess at it – meaning favourable to Sam Lawson.' The thought made her chuckle. 'He sells just about everything from boat spares to cat food.'

'I'll remember.' Carrick chuckled. 'Will he be along to meet you?'

Liz Lawson shook her head. 'This is meant as a surprise. Yesterday, it seemed a good idea. Right now, I'm not so sure.'

'Like maybe he has rented your room to a lodger?' suggested Carrick.

'More likely he's got it stacked out with crates,' she said wryly. 'We live above the store. Until I was school age, I thought all houses smelled that way.' She glanced up for a moment as a new gust of wind sent some of the coaster's halyard blocks into a mad clatter overhead. 'Do me a favour, Webb. Check if your new boat has a spare bunk. I may come begging for a place to sleep.'

Liz Lawson left him, heading aft, then vanished through a companionway door that led down to somewhere between decks. Briefly, Carrick pursed his lips. Meeting Sam Lawson's daughter on this trundling little ship was a bizarre coincidence. He had already decided he liked her – and he had already started lying to her.

He switched his attention back towards the shore again then glanced at his black, plastic-cased diving watch, thinking.

It had been dusk the previous evening when he had last seen the west side of Mull, mostly as a grey haze in the fading light. Then, he'd been in the command chair of *Tern* as the patrol launch crept in.

There were five hundred islands in the long scatter of the Hebridean chain, only about one in ten of them now populated, but Mull was one of the largest. It measured thirty miles in a direct line from top to tail, but a rocky, broken shore eaten into by long sea lochs translated that into a coastline that measured over three hundred miles.

Mull's small population was thinly spread, most of it in the island's little town of Tobermory, to the north-east. Port Torquil, one of a handful of fishing villages along the almost empty lower west coast, was located on a great, isolated haunch of land that projected out into the sea. The harbour was small, but regarded as safe. That was partly because of the way it lay close under the shelter of a high, raw cliff of green-veined granite known as Torquil's Shield.

Torquil's Shield was a name that went back through Hebridean folklore to pre-Christian stories of a Celtic hero-legend. The green-veined rock sat as if raised ready to defend the little village against any attack that might come from off-shore – where a scatter of islands began and led out to the horizon and beyond.

Beyond, to Lannair, where *Pippin* had been bombed.

In that late dusk, with Port Torquil and Torquil's Shield less than a handful of miles to the south, *Tern* had come in with her diesels at a muffled murmur. She had steered in towards what appeared to be only beach and rock at a stretch of Mull shoreline marked on the chart as Sanna Head.

But then there was a narrow, unexpected twist of hidden deep-water inlet and Gogi MacDonnell had taken them in. MacDonnell had a habit of knowing similar strange and useful places around the islands, collected as a youngster when he had helped crew his family fishing boat. He didn't encourage too many questions about that time, or exactly what they had always done.

Getting in and out of the hidden deep-water inlet was a simple matter of lining up three markers in turn. Two were distinctively shaped pillars of rock, the middle key was the rusted skeleton hull of an old boat. Though the grey light had almost gone, Carrick could see that the inlet showed no sign of being used by anyone. It was shaped like a bottle, with enough room inside to allow the patrol launch to lie at anchor. Coming out again, Carrick decided against swinging *Tern* round and used his engines astern.

He was sweating by the time it was done. But it was an ideal hiding place, likely to go undetected for the few

34

days they needed – and no trawler even half the size of the pair seen by *Pippin*'s crew could have squeezed in where they had just been.

That was when he thumbed Andy Grey into the command chair, then made his suddenly dry-lipped Second Officer repeat the approach and exit.

Then they left, quietly easing out from the coast, able to see the flash of a couple of bobbing beacon lights marking the approach channel to Port Torquil, the rock mass of Torquil's Shield now swallowed up in the darkness but a faint glow of light showing where the fishing village was located.

Tern had turned north again, away from the glow. All three engines gathering speed, she began carving a great white wake under the moonlight.

By midnight the broad-beamed patrol boat had travelled a long way and was loitering off a black shadow of beach outside Oban, the mainland port and railhead for much of the West Highlands. Out of uniform and carrying a travel bag, Carrick was taken ashore by the Zodiac boat. He watched from the beach while the inflatable returned and was taken back aboard. Then *Tern* had slipped away again into the night, on her return run to the hidden inlet at Sanna Head.

He walked up the beach to a road where there were lights, houses, and passing vehicles. A few minutes brought him to an hotel, where he took a room. Other travellers were booking in, newly arrived by road or rail from the south, making an overnight stop before going for one of the early morning ferry services to the islands. It meant he had the luxury of a real bed for a few hours' sleep, then a leisurely breakfast before he went down to the harbour.

Only the coaster *Duchess May* had Port Torquil on her list of calls and she was still loading cargo when he joined the few passengers boarding. Her captain, an elderly, thin-faced man, ignored them all. About a score of blackface sheep were already penned on the open afterdeck, new breeding stock for some island farmer.

The *Duchess May* sailed with the tide, Port Torquil sixth on her list of stops. Carrick found himself a sheltered corner for'ard, away from the bleating sheep, and first noticed the chestnut-haired girl soon after they sailed. She was talking busily with one of the deckhands, looked round, saw Carrick, and gave him a casual smile but left it at that.

The coaster plodded on between islands. The sheep went ashore at the last call before Port Torquil. Afterwards, Carrick had left his sheltered corner and had moved to the coaster's rail. Studying the shore, trying to make it appear casual, he had been trying to spot the inlet where *Tern* would be concealed. Trying but failing and feeling pleased about it. That was when Liz Lawson had first come over beside him and spoken.

Now he saw her coming back along the deck again. She stopped beside him, leaning her elbows on the rail, carefully inspecting the nearing shore and the fishing harbour ahead.

'Everything look the same?' he asked dryly.

She considered, then nodded. 'So far.'

'That always helps.' He nodded solemnly.

'It does.' For a moment, the glint in her eyes was frosty. Then she grinned at her own enthusiasm. She had already hauled the canvas suitcase out from the companionway door and it was waiting on deck near the *Duchess May*'s roped-down gangway. The grin lingered. 'It seems your research boat could be a nice soft number.'

'Who says?'

'He does.' She nodded towards one of the coaster's crew, who had appeared beside some deck cargo which was also near the gangway. The man was checking labels. 'That's Jimsy. I went to school with his brother. I asked him.'

'And?' Carrick raised an untroubled eyebrow.

'He says the *Dirk* spends most of her time tied up in

harbour – or if she goes out, she seems to run back in again the moment the weather gets nasty.'

'And I should complain?' Carrick chuckled aloud at the idea. Inwardly, it matched what he wanted. 'I'll survive it.'

'Port Torquil is pretty quiet,' she warned. 'People don't exactly go out dancing in the streets.' The idea amused her. 'Definitely not.'

'Then what do they do instead?'

'The usual things.' She paused, as if at some memory, then shrugged it aside. 'If you want, I can introduce you to some people.'

'I'd like that.' He nodded carefully. Liz Lawson was pleasant, interesting and attractive. But his thoughts were mainly focused on the fact that she was Sam Lawson's daughter. 'Once I find my feet.'

'You know where to find – ' the rest of her words were lost under an unexpected bellow from the *Duchess May*'s siren. The harsh roar echoed back at the coaster a moment later from the rock face of Torquil's Shield. The coaster's sour-faced captain had appeared on one of the open bridge wings and was scowling ahead. The coaster's engine had begun to slow, then another long, indignant bray came from her siren and echoed back at them.

'Our captain isn't happy about something,' murmured Liz Lawson. She narrowed her eyes, frowning towards the harbour, then sighed. 'The man should watch his blood pressure. There's a dinghy working off the north quay, near where the coasters usually berth. She'll move – he knows it.'

Carrick nodded but said nothing. Looking around, he was taking the chance to have his first real view of Port Torquil. Even with the coaster slowing, the distance had shrunk. She had come in past the tossing, jerking buoy which warned craft clear of an underwater edge of the long, curving line of reef which acted like a natural breakwater across part of the mouth of the approach to the fishing village.

Ahead, cosily beneath Torquil's Shield, there was a beach of fine white sand, a narrow strip of green grazing land, a scatter of houses and shops, then a small harbour which was a dramatic gem even by Hebridean standards. Two long, broad-based stone quays constructed from blocks of that green-veined local material formed the outer arms. Inside, he could see that both were lined with fishing boats and other small craft. The sun was at just the right angle overhead to glint on wheelhouse brasses and to bounce off the windows of buildings at what looked like a boatyard and docking slip in the background.

The reason for the *Duchess May*'s siren blasts was clear to see. The main north quay ended in an exaggerated T-head. A scatter of vehicles was parked along it, among some outgoing cargo waiting the coaster's arrival. Several people were gathered at the edge of the stonework, but they were ignoring the approaching *Duchess May*. They were watching two men who were in a dinghy which was bobbing in the water beneath them. One was using a pair of oars, the other was bending over the stern of the little boat with his attention apparently fixed on something he could see beneath the surface.

'Maybe I was wrong,' said Liz Lawson quietly.

Silently, Carrick nodded and heard the coaster's bridge telegraph ring then her engine respond. The sea churned a brief, furious white as her propellor went astern, then the telegraph rang again, and the engine dropped down to a slow, lazy thud as the *Duchess May* waited where she was.

The little drama around the dinghy off the quayhead went on. First a scuba diver suddenly surfaced beside the boat. He brought a limp, sack-like shape along with him, then the man at the stern of the dinghy was helping. Between them, they dragged a fully clothed body out of the water and in over the stern. It lay over the stern thwarts for a moment, the clothes dripping water aboard, then the man at the stern had dragged it further in, out of sight.

'Damn,' said Liz Lawson softly. She gave a small shake of her head. 'Grief for someone, somewhere.'

'Welcome home,' said Carrick with a grim sympathy.

She shrugged. 'Where there's water, people drown. Just don't ask me to get used to it.'

The little drama was almost over. The diver had hauled himself out of the water and into the boat. Carrick could see he was a tall, thin man who was wearing a grey rubber wet-suit and had been using a twin-cylinder aqualung. Removing the breathing tube, shoving back his face mask, the diver sat at the stern and leaned back, obviously glad to relax. His dank-wet hair was very, very fair.

'Know him?' asked Carrick, nodding towards the man.

Liz Lawson shook her head. 'He's a stranger. But I've been away.'

Someone shouted a question from the quayside and the fair-haired man answered. It was the start of some kind of a conference between the quayside and the diver, then it ended. The diver nodded at the oarsman, who began pulling. The dinghy swung round, moving along the edge of the T-shaped head. As it disappeared, the diver was easing out of his scuba harness.

The *Duchess May* was already moving again. On the quayside, some of the figures were drifting away now that the excitement was over. Things could get back to normal. Looking down, Carrick could see deep, clear water under her bottom – and great dark-green streamers of waving wrackweed. He grimaced to himself. Working down among that kind of stuff was never easy and could be dangerous. The diver in the grey scuba suit had accepted a few risks.

In a very short time the coaster had eased in against the quay and her fenders were rubbing the coarse stone-work. Out on the bridge, supervising while two of his crew handled her mooring lines, the long-faced captain looked almost happy again. The for'ard line was caught by a fat harbour worker who quickly used it to haul the main hawser ashore before looping the hawser round one of the quay's iron bollards.

'Hey, Andy,' shouted the deckhand who had thrown the line and paid out the hawser, 'who got fished out?'

'Nobody local,' called the fat harbour worker reassuringly. 'Just a man over from the mainland.'

'What happened?' demanded the deckhand.

'He's too dead to tell anyone.' The fat harbour worker grinned at his own joke. 'People say he was drinking in the Pride of Mull until late last night, then just left.' He kept on in the same loud voice. 'A couple of lads on one of the boats thought they heard a shout for help later – around midnight – but couldn't find anything. A laddie who was fishing wi' a hand-line snagged him about half an hour ago.'

'Too much of the drink, eh?'

'Aye. Must have been, Jimsy.' The harbour worker ambled off, secured the coaster's stern hawser, then returned. He paused to light a cigarette. Then he delivered his verdict in the same loud voice. 'Terrible thing, the drink.'

'True,' agreed the deckhand sombrely. 'Too little or too much – terrible, either way. Right, Andy?'

The two men exchanged a dark twist of a grin. People who lived with the sea could develop their own harsh, partly protective attitude towards death from that sea. Carrick felt the girl beside him stiffen a little, but she said nothing.

Cargo had priority on a coaster like the *Duchess May*. Her for'ard derrick boom was lifting a first sling of crates from her hatch by the time her gangway was in place and the dozen or so passengers for Port Torquil began landing. Relatives and friends were there to meet some. A few new passengers formed a ragged queue, waiting to come aboard. Around the islands, little ships like the *Duchess May* were like local buses. Maybe safer. Not many buses carried lifejackets.

'Hey.' Carrick stopped Liz Lawson as she started strug-

40

gling towards the gangway with her bulging canvas case. 'I'll take it for you.'

She gave him a grateful grin and let him. The canvas case, he discovered, was even heavier than it looked. His own travel bag in one hand, the case in the other, he took a deep breath, lifted, and followed her ashore over the gangway. But as they reached the quayside a man who seemed to appear out of nowhere was suddenly blocking his way.

'I'll take that suitcase, mister,' said the man curtly. He was a squat, thick-set individual with greying hair, very broad shoulders, and a growl of a voice. The left side of his broad face was marred by an old, deep scar and his expression was impassive as he immediately switched away from Carrick to consider Liz Lawson. Apparently satisfied by the inspection, he nodded and the growl moderated. 'You look well, girl.'

'Thank you. So do you, Dad.' Liz Lawson's voice was carefully formal. Her dark eyes seemed to offer a challenge. 'This was meant to be a surprise.'

'You were seen getting on the boat at Oban. Someone phoned us.' Sam Lawson was probably in his late fifties and whatever he lacked in size it was obvious that most of his build was muscle. He turned a brief suspicious glance towards Carrick, his dark eyes so much like his daughter's. 'Who is this, then?'

'Someone I met on the boat.'

Lawson's eyes stayed on Carrick. 'You've a name, mister?'

'Webb Carrick.' Lowering the suitcase, releasing his grip on it, Carrick gave a friendly nod. 'Glad to help.'

'My daughter is obliged, Carrick.' The small, squat man thumbed at the travel bag in Carrick's other hand. 'Visiting, are you?'

'No.' Carrick shook his head. 'I'm joining the crew on the research boat.'

'The *Dirk*?' The scarred face became more friendly. Carrick had obviously been promoted to the human race.

41

'I was talking with Dr Steeven, your new boss. The woman told me someone was coming.' Lawson offered a handshake, a brief, bone-crunching squeeze of a grip. 'The man you're replacing left yesterday – he wasn't much good. I'm Sam Lawson. I run the chandler's store along the harbour.'

'He knows, Father,' said Liz Lawson patiently.

'The good and the bad?' Lawson showed the start of a pleased attempt at a smile. When he was young, before that scar, he had been handsome. The attempt vanished again. He shrugged. 'There might have been a better time to arrive.'

'We saw,' she said simply.

'Aye. You would.' Lawson sucked his large, strong teeth. Two were missing from his lower jaw, on the same side of his face as the scar. He didn't look a man who would fit comfortably behind a shop counter. The leather waistcoat he was wearing was over a faded army surplus khaki shirt which was tucked into moleskin trousers. His feet were in ankle-length green rubber fisherman's boots. Some ballpoint pens and a blackbound notebook bulged one waistcoat pocket, the carved bone handle of a large folded jack-knife protruded from another. He looked past his daughter for a moment, then the tooth-sucking ended. 'It wasn't a good way to die.'

'Who was the diver who got him out?' asked his daughter unexpectedly. 'A tall, thin man, very fair hair – '

'You mean near enough white,' corrected Lawson. He grunted. 'He's new here since you left, girl. That's Michael Alder. He's related to old John Hill.'

'John Hill with the cottage along the shore?' she asked, showing a mild surprise.

'The same,' agreed Sam Lawson. 'Alder lives there now. Old John had to be shipped out to a nursing home on the mainland about six months ago. I don't think we'll see him back, not at his age.'

'I'm sorry. He's nice.' His daughter sighed. 'Alder – what's he like?'

'English with money,' said Lawson shortly. 'A lawyer – not the courtroom variety, one of the breed who get involved with banks and company deals. Calls it "escaping" when he gets up here.' He sucked again at the gap in his teeth and scowled. 'Friendly enough. Likes scuba diving as a hobby, spends a lot of time at it.'

'Married?'

'No.' Lawson's face reddened. 'Damn it, girl – '

Carrick cleared his throat, reminding them both that he was still there. 'He did a good job out there. But now that the body is recovered, what happens?'

'The usual, I suppose,' said Lawson vaguely. 'The body will be in Harry Gold's boat repair yard – he does undertaking as a sideline. The village doctor may look in.'

'Police?'

'Police?' Lawson hesitated. 'When this kind of thing happens, something in uniform usually drives over from Tobermory and asks a few questions. There's no hurry about that.'

'None,' agreed Carrick woodenly. He thumbed behind him. 'When we were getting ready to come ashore, one of the harbour people said it was just the old story of someone getting legless drunk then falling in.'

'It looks that way,' said Lawson with little interest. 'That seemed to be his style. He only arrived a few days ago – one of those mainland smoothies who go around the doors buying junk at junk prices for things that might be antiques. He was working the island, driving a white Ford van – living in it too, from what he said.'

'You talked?'

Lawson sucked. 'He looked in at the shop two or three times, to buy food. He paid cash – I don't give credit to a stranger. Any stranger.' He grimaced a little. 'I suppose he was likeable enough in his own way. He said his name was Cormack – Fred Cormack.'

Carrick froze, staring at him.

Lawson was puzzled. 'Something wrong, man? Could you – well, have known him?'

'No.' Mind still numbed by the scarred man's words, Carrick shook his head. But the odds were heavy that there could be only one stranger named Cormack recently arrived in Port Torquil. The first man fed into the scene by Fishery Protection. The man who had only managed to send out a brief arrival report. Moistening his lips, he tried to scrape together what he hoped was a passable lie. 'I used to know a man named Cormack who dabbled in antiques – but that was a few years ago.'

'What age?'

'Now?' Carrick shrugged. 'He must be in his sixties.'

'Not this one.' Lawson gave a reassuring gesture. 'This Cormack would be late forties, no more.' He gave his lopsided twist of a grin. 'Taller than me, not so good-looking.' Pausing, he stooped, lifted the heavy suitcase without any apparent effort, and beckoned to the girl with a bleak affection. 'Home, right? I've a business to run.'

'Home.' She looked at Carrick and smiled. 'You've an invitation to visit, Webb. Don't forget.'

'I won't.' He gave a nod of thanks, while he tried to grapple with what could have happened.

Cormack had come in to gather information on the salmon gang and their bombing.

Now a man named Cormack was dead.

Had it been an accident – or an execution?

'I'll say goodbye, Carrick.' Sam Lawson showed an edge of impatience and gestured with the suitcase. 'You'll find your boat moored near the repair yard, on the other quay.' He paused, gave his daughter an almost wary sideways glance, then went on. 'A word of advice, man. The kind that could save you grief. Most people here are split between two families – fishing families. There are Grants – Liz and I are Grants because of her late mother, rest her soul. Then – ' the scar tightened ' – then there are Stewarts. Grants and Stewarts don't mix.'

'Dad, that's dinosaur stuff,' said Liz Lawson in a blend of distaste and disbelief. 'I thought that was ending. That you all sat down and watched old Westerns on TV instead!'

'Things happen, things change again,' snapped Lawson. 'We don't like them, they don't like us – probably never have, maybe never will.' His eyes glared at Carrick. 'Friendly guidance. Nothing more.'

Then he was off, moving quickly, swinging the suitcase. His daughter sighed, shrugged at Carrick, then set off and caught up with the little man. More alike in temperament than either would probably have cared to admit, firmly separate, they headed straight along the length of the quay towards the village. Suddenly, Carrick saw they had acquired company. A tall young man wearing denims had come striding towards them. He wore a sweater and denim trousers, he had a short straggle of dark beard, and an old hat was shoved at the back of his head.

Grinning, the bearded arrival grabbed Liz Lawson, hugged her, and swung her off her feet for a moment. Then he put her down. He made to take the suitcase from her father, but Sam Lawson shook his head. Unperturbed, the tall young stranger fell in beside them and they walked on.

Whoever he was, right at that moment it didn't particularly matter. Carrick had more important things to think about. Like exactly what to do next.

For now, he had to keep up the pretence, follow it through. But maybe – yes, maybe allowing for a small variation or two. Nursing his travel bag in both arms against his chest, he looked out at the outwardly sheltered calm all around him.

He had to narrow his eyes against the bright reflection of the sun on the water as a few boats began easing their way out of harbour, catching the tide. The first was a little lobster boat with varnished yellow hull and a spluttering kerosene engine that had still to warm. A fisherman who was smoking a pipe sat nursing the tiller bar at the stern. Another tanned figure, young enough to be the man's son, was baiting the small mountain of basketwork lobster creels piled near the bow.

As a scene, it could have been painted in oils. Peace and tranquillity. In the background, the rock wall of Torquil's Shield glinted and sparkled, dwarfing everything.

In all, four more boats went out after the first. Three were small trawlers, the other was a Danish boat rigged for blue whiting fishing. Each in turn left a small, rippling wake to mark a path. As the last went past, a big fish suddenly surfaced and splashed close astern, chasing something, catching. The silver shape appeared again a moment later, just under the water this time, a large mackerel now hunting again.

Except that suddenly it was thrashing round, frightened, trying to escape, while a dark, much larger shape torpedoed up from the bottom of the harbour. A maw of a mouth closed like a trap. The mackerel vanished, the shape sank down again.

The sea's life was that way. Carrick grimaced to himself. Reality was that first *Pippin* and her crew had been bombed. Now a man named Cormack was dead.

His job was to find out why and avoid being next on the list. He began walking, the travel bag swinging in one hand again, his nostrils filled with the usual harbour-side smells of fuel oil and yesterday's fish. He could hear a radio crackling in someone's wheelhouse next to where one crew was unloading boxes of crab while their neighbours shovelled crushed ice aboard or worked at repairing nets.

A hundred and one things had to be done any time a boat got ready for sea. Few of the fishermen even glanced his way as he passed, most ignored him.

The way he'd expected, there wasn't as much as a hint of salmon netting gear anywhere.

Keeping a deliberate, unhurried pace, he reached the shore end of the north quay then crossed over towards the boat-repair yard. A fishing boat with the engine

46

hauled out for repair was sharing the slipway with an older, partly dismantled hulk that looked as though it might have started off life as a naval minesweeper. Two men were working on the fishing boat, the ex-minesweeper lay deserted. There was a wire fence round the area, and a gate which lay open was topped by a board which said Harry Gold, Marine Maintenance, and gave telephone and FAX numbers.

There was no challenge as he walked in and crossed the yard towards a flat-roofed office block. Its few windows were grimy, but there was a glimmer of light behind one and he caught a brief glimpse of moving figures. A moment later, he heard a murmur of voices from inside. He saw a harbour porter's hand-truck lying a few paces away, outside the office-block door. The floor of the hand-truck was still wet, and a trail of drying water stains led from the hand-truck to the door.

Going to the door, Carrick gently tried the handle. It turned, and he opened the door then stepped into an area which had the appearance of a carpenter's woodstore. A partition wall blocked one side and had a door marked Private. The trail of drying smears led towards it and the voices he'd heard as a murmur outside had become much louder.

Suddenly, something fell with a thud on the other side of the door. Someone gave a short laugh, then two male voices were arguing, one of them thin and complaining. As he went over to the door, the argument ended with an exasperated growl from a third voice.

'Give over, both of you. Just get him back up again, damn it!'

There was movement and rustling – then, as it ended, Carrick knocked deliberately on the door.

The result was momentary silence, then suddenly the door swung open.

'And who the hell are you?' asked the middle-aged man who glared out. The man had a thin face to match the thin, complaining voice Carrick had heard earlier. He

47

wore a crumpled grey suit with an equally crumpled shirt and the stringy remnants of a tie. 'Well?'

'I'm looking for Harry Gold,' said Carrick amiably.

Two other men were looking at him questioningly from inside the room. It was laid out like a small, temporary mortuary. Some partly completed coffin shells were propped upright against one wall. In the middle of it all, the body of a man lay on what looked like an old door placed across trestles.

'I'm Harry Gold,' snapped the thin-faced man. 'What about it?'

'Sorry to trouble you,' said Carrick. He nodded into the room. 'Him. The dead man. I'd like to see him.'

One of the men in the background snickered. He was lean and bald and dressed like a fisherman. Carrick recognized him as the man who had rowed the dinghy off the quay. The third man, plump and in his mid-thirties, looking mildly prosperous and professional in tweeds, said nothing, but allowed a mild curiosity to show on his face.

'Just like that?' The boatyard owner stared at him, then reacted with a flush of anger. 'I asked you who the hell you were, mister. How about that first?'

'Steady, Harry,' murmured the plump man in tweeds. 'Maybe he's a relative. Relatives can pay for funerals.'

Gold swallowed and nodded. His scowl moderated.

'I'm joining the research boat.' Carrick completed the basics of his name and arrival at Port Torquil. 'When I landed, people said the man who drowned was from the mainland, that his name was Cormack and that he bought and sold – '

'And maybe you know someone who might match?' Gold accepted Carrick's vague nod, and beckoned him in. 'Go ahead.'

Carrick went over then glanced questioningly at the others. Cormack's body looked as though it had been dumped down on its temporary plinth. One leg was twisted over the other, his right arm dangled down towards the floor, and what remained of his clothing was badly rumpled.

'Let me explain,' said the plump, tweedy man wryly. 'We – ah – we dropped him, just before you came in.' He frowned to himself. 'That's not strictly accurate. I'm the local doctor. I was examining him, Harry and our friend Willie were turning him over for me when it happened. A small accident. That's all.'

The bald man Willie and the thin-faced Gold exchanged what could have been a shrug. Ignoring them, Carrick looked down at the dead man. In early middle age with thinning grey hair, he had been of average build and height. A large dome of a forehead gleamed under the single overhead light and went with prominent ears, a small nose, and lifeless brown eyes.

'I'm James Kennedy,' said the plump doctor easily. 'Ah – don't worry about the froth from his mouth. It's reasonably normal.'

Carrick said nothing. A thick ribbon of white froth was gradually issuing from the dead man's mouth, something that often happened to some degree after drowning, a mix, he knew, caused by a bubbling up of air, mucus, and water from the lungs.

'Like I said, we dropped him,' said Kennedy unhappily. 'Things inside would get shaken around.' He paused then nodded at the body. 'Well?'

'No,' said Carrick. 'My Cormack was older – a lot older.'

'That's that.' Kennedy gave Harry Gold a mild grin. 'I'm finished. Body-bag time, Harry. I'll make out the usual certificate, and leave you to cope with the rest.'

Gold nodded. Then a new thought struck Kennedy.

'Found your boat yet?' he asked Carrick. 'No? Then I'll point you in the right direction. Don't thank me – today's good deeds make sure of tomorrow's patients.'

Carrick found himself swept from the room, out of the office block and through the boat repair yard gate on to the quay again.

'Straight along there. Half a dozen or so boats along.' Kennedy pointed along the start of the south quay beyond the yard then was prepared to linger. 'A pity you didn't know him – always helps the tidying up.'

Carrick nodded. But it had been another lie. The dead man was someone he had seen, had spoken with maybe once or twice at Headquarters in Edinburgh. His name had been Fred Banks, he was ex-navy, invalided out after the Falklands. Department sometimes used him on the shore end of things. The kind of man who usually made a religion of avoiding risks.

'Straightforward enough.' The village doctor gave an almost bored grimace. 'Once he has been shipped out to them, the pathology boys will still look him over and earn their corn. They'll check blood-alcohol level, that kind of thing. But he was drinking, he fell in the harbour, he drowned. Some bruising on his body, yes. But just the usual. You expect that when a body has bumped around a harbour.'

'They can come worse,' said Carrick softly.

'You've seen?' Kennedy warmed to his topic. 'The last one I had was scalped by a propeller. The one before had been nibbled by some rather large fish.' He paused, reaching under his tweed jacket to scratch an armpit. 'I work from my house – second street back in the village. Appointments not necessary.' Then, pausing again, he grinned. 'I also keep a reasonable bottle of reasonable whisky handy for occasional company.'

'Medical?' queried Carrick.

'Hell, no!' declared Kennedy. 'That's when I use the cheap stuff!'

'I'll be company,' promised Carrick, and they parted.

The marine research vessel *Dirk* was berthed on the south quay just beyond a laid-up motor cruiser and a couple of old, paid-off trawlers. It was the kind of corner that existed in most small harbours, where the unusual could be tucked away from sight.

Webb Carrick was surprised at what he saw. She was almost twice the size of a patrol launch and his guess was that at some time she had been converted over from being a small coaster. Her hull was fat, her bow was blunt, she had a stumpy single exhaust stack midships, and her stern was rounded. Painted white overall, some of the white stained brown with rust, she had some strange items on her superstructure. They ranged from extra boat davits and small cargo booms to observation platforms and some other items he couldn't identify. The result didn't give her any particular appearance of heavy-weather capability.

The lettering on her stern said the *Dirk* was Liverpool registered, which didn't tell him much. There was no one on deck as he went aboard, although a generator motor was working somewhere. He shouted twice, had no reply, then dumped his travel bag on deck, laid his borrowed jacket on top, and climbed up to the enclosed bridge. It was a conventional layout and what he saw looked well maintained, but someone had hung up a washing line across the middle and had pegged out a batch of feminine underwear to dry.

'I know,' said an unexpected voice behind him. 'It would have dried better in the open. But I thought it might rain.'

He turned. The woman who had quietly joined him was in her fifties, average height, and whipcord thin. She had straight grey hair cut haphazardly short and framing a confident, bright-eyed face. Small ears, a beak nose, and a small but pleasant mouth gave her the appearance of a watchful maiden aunt of a bird.

'Dr Steeven?'

'Correct.' Her voice was casually cool. 'We've been expecting you. Carrick, isn't it?' A slight warning frown showed for a moment. 'You've arrived at a good time. I've a visitor you should meet.'

'Fine.' Carrick hid his surprise at the sight of the man who had just arrived on the bridge behind her. It was the scuba diver from the harbour. His long fair hair was still damp but he was wearing a designer-style blue cotton sweater and tight black trousers. He had an elaborately braided leather belt around his waist.

'Michael Alder,' said the man, smiling. 'Good to meet you, Carrick.'

'I saw you at the harbour,' said Carrick. 'You were in the water, getting that body up.'

They shook hands while Margaret Steeven completed the introductions. Her manner was friendly. 'Michael does *Dirk* a lot of favours. We owe him, owe him a lot.'

'It can cut both ways,' said Alder mildly. 'Like right now.'

Carrick guessed that he and Alder were about the same age. Alder was taller, thinner, and had cool, deep-set green eyes, a narrow face, and a long thin neck. The result couldn't be called handsome. One of his front teeth had been chipped at some time and needed capping. He had the air of a man who didn't particularly waste time on pleasantries.

'Does that mean we're helping you?' asked Carrick.

'Not in any big way,' corrected Margaret Steeven firmly. 'There's nothing major about recharging a couple of air bottles, is there?'

'No. As long as it helps.' Carrick took a moment to look more closely at the *Dirk* team leader. Her feet were bare and she was dressed in a faded grey shirt-blouse and matching trousers. Her only jewellery was a wedding ring, worn thin with age. She wore a man's wristwatch on a leather strap and her only make-up was a light touch of a coral shade of lipstick. He glanced back at Alder. 'Anything else I can maybe do?'

'No.' Alder shook his head. 'You came in on the coaster?'

'Just as you were surfacing,' said Carrick. He leaned back against the compass binnacle. 'When I got ashore, I thought maybe I knew the man. But I didn't.' He shrugged. 'One thing, it looked as though it could be tricky down there.'

52

'You've done scuba work?' Alder raised a mildly interested eyebrow.

'Some.' Carrick left it at that. 'I like to learn.'

'Any time you dive off Port Torquil, be ready for currents – even where you wouldn't expect them. The same applies further out.' Alder economized on words but appeared to like the role of teacher. 'We've also some jungle stretches of wrack and oarweed down there – so don't fool about.'

'I'll remember.' Carrick nodded easily. 'How was – ' he broke off, glancing at Margaret Steeven. 'You heard about this, I suppose? A man named Cormack?'

'Part of it from Michael,' she agreed.

'So – well, how was it?' asked Carrick.

'For a start, he was dead.' Alder grinned a small apology to the woman. 'Joke over. Sorry, Margaret.' He shrugged and went back into his teacher role. 'We knew the body hadn't been more than a few hours in the water, and a lot of that time would be when the tide was dragging him out of the harbour. The trouble was where he ended up. He had a foot jamed among some broken bottom rock, then I also had to chop a lot of weed he'd tangled into.' He dismissed it with a deprecating gesture. 'They can come worse.'

'How soon do you want those air bottles?' asked Margaret Steeven deliberately.

'No hurry.' Alder smiled at her then switched back to Carrick again. 'When you dive, what kind of outfit do you use – single cylinder or twins?'

'Single.' Carrick had always preferred the big single air cylinder, with less underwater drag and less buoyancy. Twin cylinder outfits could have more endurance but were more complex.

'Mostly, I favour a twin. Though I keep a single as a spare.' Alder massaged a hand along the back of his thin neck, briefly annoyed. 'I have my own compressor, I do my own recharging – except that the damned pump on the thing has blown a gasket and I'm waiting on a spare arriving. After the harbour dive, the twin hasn't much left on the gauge.'

'But he's been using our compressor the last few days,' explained Margaret Steeven. 'Late this afternoon, Michael?'

'This evening maybe,' suggested Alder. 'Or tomorrow.' He switched his chipped-tooth smile to Carrick. 'We should talk again, Carrick. Mainly about scubas.' He paused then suddenly asked, 'What was your last ship?'

'The *Maura*, Captain Pendleton,' said Carrick calmly. He'd been expecting someone to ask, sooner or later.

'Deep-sea?' asked Alder casually.

'Deep-sea, general cargo – on the Far East run.'

'Then this is something different,' murmured Alder. 'Well, we'll certainly talk. Thank you again, Margaret.' A quick half smile went in Margaret Steeven's direction then he left the bridge, padded quickly down the narrow stairway to main deck level, and from there ignored the gangway, took the deck rail at a smooth leap, and was ashore. There were several vehicles parked near, and his was a blue Japanese four-wheel-drive Toyota pick-up festooned with whip aerials and auxiliary spotlamps.

A moment later it was roaring away in a spatter of quayside gravel.

'Is there a *Maura*?' asked Margaret Steeven as she watched the vehicle go out of sight.

'Yes.' There was a *Maura*, working a general cargo timetable mostly out of Singapore. Harry Pendleton, her captain, was a friend. 'Want to start at the beginning again, Dr Steeven?'

'Do we need to go to the trouble, Skipper Carrick?' Her manner had chilled. 'I agreed to this deception. I've already regretted it.'

'Why?'

'I head up a marine life research team.' The grey-haired woman gave a long hard sniff in a way that made the nostrils of her beaked nose flare. 'Part of that involves staying friendly with fishing skippers and their crews –

54

and that isn't easy. It gives problems enough without them finding out we're actively helping Fishery Protection run a spy in their midst. Even for your kind of reasons.'

'It won't be for long – '

'Already is too long if I'd had sense,' she said grimly. 'Already we're the kind of people the fishing skippers blame every time they are told they are over-fishing and that their quotas are being cut back.'

'Sometimes they're right,' reminded Carrick mildly.

'And sometimes they're wrong,' she snapped back. 'Sometimes it comes down to some idiot civil servant at a desk God knows where, who wouldn't recognize a fish if it grabbed him by – by what the average seaman still calls his wedding tackle!'

'I know.' Carrick managed not to grin. It was all familiar enough. Scientists and civil servants argued over quotas and reduced catches. Quotas and reduced catches helped conserve fish stocks. But reduced catches meant less money to share out among the fishing crews affected. 'But that's not why I'm here. Will you still help, Dr Steeven?'

'Yes.' She gave a slow resigned nod. 'And everyone calls me Margaret – Margaret or Dr Margaret.'

He relaxed, relieved. 'Have we anyone else aboard – right now, I mean?'

'No. Some are in the village, the others are working on a project along the shore.'

'And Michael Alder?' He hesitated, but decided to get it over with. 'Is he – well, just a friend?'

'Michael?' She blinked, puzzled, then understood and laughed. 'Good God, I'm old enough to be his mother!'

'Think of it as a compliment,' soothed Carrick.

'That's one thing I won't do.' The words came like chipped ice. She wasn't finished. 'Mister, there's something I want you to understand, starting right now. On this boat if you want to pretend to be paid crew you behave like paid crew – at least in front of the others. You rate as mate, there's an engineer and a deckhand.

55

There's a scientific team of five, including me. I'm in charge of what this boat does – in every way. I've allowed you aboard, I've agreed to help. But you ask – you don't demand.'

'Fair.' He nodded.

'Then we should get along.' She seemed satisfied.

'I need help right now.' He gave her a moment. 'The man who drowned was named Cormack. Did you know him?'

'No. Why?'

'He was Fishery Protection.'

Dr Margaret Steeven stared, then moistened her lips. 'Are you sure?'

'I saw his body.'

She stood staring at him while *Dirk*'s generator continued its soft background hum. Carrick could hear the harbour water lapping gently against their hull and, from somewhere across the water, there was a crackle of talk coming in over a wheelhouse radio – the distant end of a gossip between two skippers.

'Webb, I didn't know.' The woman made it an apology. 'I was only told your people would have someone else working in the village. But I wasn't told a name or anything else about him – and he would contact me in an emergency. Nobody did.'

Their eyes met and Carrick knew they were sharing the same thought. Maybe the emergency had happened the night before. Maybe the man had been trying to make his way around the harbour to reach *Dirk*, where he had been told he could seek help. But his fate had caught up with him before he could make it.

'You can't go ahead now.' Margaret Steeven shook her head fiercely at even the thought. 'The whole thing is too dangerous, too risky. You'd be a fool.'

'There's no real change,' Carrick told her. 'No compromise to what I'm supposed to do.' He took a few thoughtful paces around the confined area of the bridge, then asked, 'No one else aboard knows about me?'

'No one.' She read the rest of it from his face, and her attitude thawed. 'All right, go ahead if you're mad enough. But a man may have been murdered. Is that to be ignored?'

'No. But the police at Tobermory can handle this stage.'

'If you want to use *Dirk*'s radio – '

'Not now.' Any transmission from the middle of the harbour might be picked up by one of the other boats packed around. He had his own arrangements. 'And we stay with your normal routine. When is *Dirk* due out next?'

'Tomorrow, for a few hours. Then the same for the next few days. We're completing one of our study programmes.' She forestalled him. 'No, not salmon – not this time. You know our background?'

'No.'

'We're a foundation-sponsored inter-universities project, monitoring general marine life conservation – all private funding, no Government status. The Foundation bought *Dirk*, fitted her out, pays our salaries.' She was trying to be patient. It showed in her eyes, then she grimaced wryly. 'We don't have to stand here like you were on watch. Come down to the office – at least we can be comfortable.'

He followed the woman down to the main deck then along to a cabin door marked Private. Opening the door, she led the way in and beckoned him to follow, then closed the door firmly again once he was inside.

Margaret Steeven's office cabin was panelled in plain dove-grey plastic sheeting and the deck was covered in equally plain cork tiling. The furnishing began with a large desk and a separate computer work station. There were filing cabinets, there was a large drawing board, and a small library of books filled a rack of plain metal shelves. But there was room in the middle of everything for two well-worn leather armchairs.

'Sit down,' she invited.

Carrick settled in the nearest of the chairs while the grey-haired woman went over to one of the filing cabinets. Opening the top drawer, she produced a bottle of whisky and two glasses. The label on the whisky bottle said it was Laphroaig, one of the best of the island single malts. Margaret Steeven glanced round at him, her tanned, beak-nosed face considering him impassively for a moment, then she set the glasses on top of the filing cabinet and poured a generous measure into each.

There was no sign of water, she didn't offer any. Bringing the glasses over, she handed him one then settled into her chair.

'*Slainthe*.' She raised her glass.

'*Slainthe*.' Carrick returned the Gaelic toast, sipped, and let a first ritual trickle of the fiery, peat-flavoured malt descend like clean fire down his throat.

'There's a West Highland saying that neither whisky nor a woman should ever be rushed,' said Margaret Steeven unexpectedly. She took a similar sip of whisky then stayed silent for a moment.

It gave Carrick the chance to take a second glance around the big cabin. He could see only one definite personal touch among its furnishings, a framed colour photograph mounted on a bulkhead, secured by wire to a protruding bolt. The photograph showed a man and woman, arm in arm. The woman was a much younger Margaret Steeven who had long dark hair and who had happiness in her smile. The man was big and cheerful and wore airline uniform.

'He was my husband – I'm a widow.' She spotted his interest. 'He was a captain on long-haul jets, and I used to worry about it. Two months after that picture was taken, he was killed in a road accident.' Abruptly, before Carrick could say anything, her manner hardened. 'All right, salmon. This takes time. Ready?'

'Yes.'

'I have to do this one step at a time – to be sure you understand.' She took a larger sip of whisky. 'Suppose your Fishery Protection people find a fishing boat illegally netting Atlantic salmon in UK waters. What happens to him?'

Carrick shrugged. 'Everything. It can be a jail sentence, heavy fines, and his boat forfeited.'

The law was draconian. A skipper found to have a salmon net aboard his boat could be arrested. A skipper who accidentally caught a salmon while fishing, but who then kept it aboard, could be arrested. A skipper who tried to land a caught salmon, however he got it, could be arrested.

'But there are still highly organized poaching raids.' She leaned forward from the depths of her chair. 'Major raids – worth a lot of money.'

'A great deal of money.' Carrick tasted the Laphroaig again.

Experts said that Laphroaig, which was marketed in modest quantities, had the strongest personality of all the Scottish malts.

Personality. He wouldn't argue with the choice of words.

The whipcord-thin woman wanted more. 'If you search a boat, how do you identify a salmon fishing net?'

Carrick shrugged. 'Things like size and shape. It's a curtain net, length not depth – and the mesh is large, about the size of a man's hand.'

Only a very few people were licensed to use salmon nets in tightly controlled conditions in a few river estuaries where they mostly used stake nets. That had its roots back in history, back to a time when salmon had been so plentiful in Scottish river estuaries that they'd once caused a strike of apprentices in the tenement warrens of the old city of Glasgow. They stayed on strike until they won a promise that they wouldn't be fed on salmon more than three times a week.

'You're saying the full weight of the law comes down hard on any fishing skipper who goes salmon netting.' Margaret Steeven finished her whisky and set the glass down on a scarred teak table. 'Yet the same law accepts that today we have fish farmers who breed salmon by the ton in sea-loch cages, who harvest by the ton?'

He nodded. It was true – to the extent that the salmon farming industry now had worries about over-production. There were fierce allegations by some Scottish producers that Norwegian salmon farmers were dumping over-production anywhere they could.

'Then why all the fuss about wild salmon?' asked the woman stonily.

Carrick hesitated, realizing she was deliberately bringing him to what mattered in her own way, doing it with an intensity of purpose. He heard *Dirk*'s hull creak a little around them in some small shift of tide or current.

'That can keep.' Margaret Steeven relented. But the intensity was still there. 'To marine biologists there are things about salmon that are total mysteries – some of nature's last real secrets. That's one of the reasons why the Foundation sent *Dirk* up here. That's why salmon research is one of our key projects. Where these fish travel, how they travel, how they come back again – '

'I've heard,' said Carrick warily.

'Atlantic salmon, *Salmo salar* – Pacific salmon are a different species.' She ignored his interruption. 'The Atlantic salmon uses Scotland's rivers as a principal spawning area. The smolts – the young fish – leave their home rivers each spring and head out to sea.' She paused and drew in a deep breath through her nose. 'The next we know for sure about them is that they turn up anything up to a year later, off the west coast of Greenland. Over fifteen hundred miles from where they started! Young fish that were tagged in Scottish rivers – no room for doubt!'

'Then they turn right round and come home again,' murmured Carrick. He saw her surprise, smiled, drank the last of the whisky in his glass, and set it down. 'I've worked with some of our own Fishery Research people.'

'I know them.' Margaret Steeven gave a slightly cool nod, the kind that meant some past academic clash. 'They would tell you that when these same now adult-sized salmon return from Greenland, back across the Atlantic again, they return to the exact rivers of their origin. No one knows how they do it, no one knows why.' She rose, brought over the whisky bottle, poured them each another sizeable measure then took the bottle back to the filing cabinet and stayed on her feet as she drank again. 'How and why – these fish are driven by some basic life-mystery.'

In a few short descriptive sentences she took him on from there. Research teams now tagged salmon with tiny acoustic transmitters. Research craft fitted with sensitive electronic gear were now tracking the tagged fish over a gradually widening area of sea – in the same way that wartime destroyers had tracked submarines travelling far beneath them. The acoustic tags could identify an individual fish and add to its already known history.

Some would vanish for only a couple of years. Others for longer. But always the remorseless process was the same: one strange, driving purpose that took the young fish out to Greenland, then an equally strong, driving purpose which brought them back again across an ocean.

'Electronic tagging is showing things like the way salmon travel best in daylight. They get lost after dark, they just wander around disoriented. But there's something more important.' She put down her glass, went over to the big drawing board beside her desk, picked up a charcoal stick, and attacked the board's blank, waiting paper with bold, mapping outlines. 'There's Ireland. Here's Scotland. Between us, we're running a sample census on salmon movements as the fish leave or return.'

'Recent taggings?'

'No. Some were first tagged years ago. Over here, off Ireland – ' she marked a point of the squiggle that was the Irish coast ' – about there, a Dublin University team manage this sector.' The charcoal stick moved and made a new mark. 'Over here, at the Scottish end, *Dirk* runs the next census sampling in this particular project.'

'Both teams working the same pipeline?'

'Yes.' Margaret Steeven gave him a diamond-hard glance of surprise. 'John Kennan told you?'

'A little.' The sometimes stolid-featured Fleet Support man could surprise strangers that way.

'He looked asleep most of the time.' She turned back to the drawing board, the charcoal shading a path. 'This is the pipeline route I'm talking about – we know it for certain. There are others up and down the coast, all coming more or less direct from Greenland, all either totally mapped or still being surveyed. It's the same on the other side of the Atlantic – Canada and the US are monitoring off their seacoasts. Wherever there's a pipeline, salmon seem to travel it because of definite sea temperature layers and currents. Or it looks that way.'

Carrick raised an eyebrow. 'Do you know for sure?'

'We don't,' she admitted. 'But what we do know is that the scientific world has so far managed to keep any roadmap-style details about the pipelines closely guarded. The fishing industry knows there's a theory – nothing more.' Her knuckles tightened, the charcoal stick between her fingers snapped under the pressure. 'I've seen what happens when a poacher gets lucky and drops a few miles of killer net at the right place. He can leave dead salmon carpeting the sea – the ones he had to abandon because he had loaded all he could.'

He'd seen it and it wasn't pleasant – particularly once the undersea predators arrived. Carrick brought her back to the reason why he was there. 'Tell me about the salmon route south of Lannair Island.'

She shrugged. 'We call it the Noah Pipeline. The Dublin team found the first traces of it three years ago.'

'Big?'

'Yes. One of the biggest.'

'Secret like the rest?'

'Yes.' She answered curtly. 'And yes, we know it has been raided recently, several times.'

'How can you tell?' It seemed a reasonable question.

'Apart from the time the patrol launch was bombed?' Margaret Steeven stiffened like an angry grey terrier. 'Damn it, man, I explained already. The Irish team make their census checks on the Noah Pipeline. We run the next checks. Their results and our results go through a computer programme which allows for possible natural discrepancies. We expect a certain shared picture. If there's a major discrepancy, it means an outside factor. Dublin isn't getting it, but we are – and we are getting it somewhere around Lannair. Each time it happens, the salmon moving through are being decimated. There has been another raid.' Her mouth shaped a brief, tight line. 'Is that simple enough?'

'Yes.' He could hear a fishing boat's engine rumbling somewhere across the harbour, and the scream of some attendant gulls. There was another, much nearer sound which puzzled him. Very near, it was like a soft variation of the creaking from *Dirk*'s hull, then it ended. He sighed. 'Dr Margaret, we're obviously not talking about some stray fishing skipper who has just accidentally struck it lucky. We're talking about an organized gang – '

'Making a lot of money. Apparently ready to kill people.' She nodded calmly.

'Right.' Carrick stopped being mild, stopped being attentive. 'You say they're working out of Port Torquil – or somewhere near. Have you proof?'

'Proof, no.' She met his eyes without flinching. 'Nobody talks – that's partly what's wrong. If anyone knows anything, they're frightened. But I've heard whispers, I've seen the occasional nudge, so have my team. A few people around the village suddenly seem to have a lot of money to spend. There are strange things that happen. Things people don't like you to ask about.'

'Things that Cormack could have asked too much about?'

'Your man? Maybe. I – ' She stopped short, startled, as a loud howl of rage came from somewhere on the quay outside. Next instant they heard feet racing along the

63

research boat's deck, then the same feet clattering down her gangway.

Margaret Steeven sprang across the cabin and flung open the door, Carrick right behind her as she ran out on deck. But she halted. Three small boys, all aged about ten or eleven, were running hard along the quay. They were being chased by a plump, black-haired man who was already losing.

'That's Peter Kee,' said Margaret Steeven. 'Peter is our engineer – he was taking time off ashore.' She pointed wearily. 'This time, it looks like he got back before they could finish.'

'This time?' Carrick stared at the graffiti obscenities that had been spray-painted on part of the upperworks below *Dirk*'s bridge. In their haste, the perpetrators had abandoned the aerosol can they'd used. He remembered the soft noises he'd heard. 'Has it happened before?'

'Lately, yes.' She grimaced. 'The little fiends can't even get the spelling right.'

He saw what she meant.

'Peter won't catch them. We never do – but I told you that not everybody likes us.' She led the way back into her office and closed the door again. 'We can finish this before Peter gets back. Like everyone else, I've told him you're the replacement mate – at least for now.'

Carrick nodded. How long the story would survive could be doubtful.

'Webb.' She stood beside one of the leather-upholstered chairs, one hand resting on the back. Her thin weather-beaten face was suddenly earnest. 'I'm no kind of a fanatic. But the wild Atlantic salmon is being net-killed at sea by commercial poachers at a rate that could head it for oblivion.' She paused and the nostrils of that beak nose flared. 'A wild salmon which makes it back to a Highland river can be a sixty, a seventy, even an eighty pounder – and anglers reckon it gives the finest rod-and-line sport in the world.'

He listened, still saying nothing. But he was remembering his father, who had once managed to wangle a day's fishing permit on the River Tay and who had caught a twenty-five-pound salmon with a home-tied Red Butcher fly. It had been one of the proudest moments of his father's life.

'A few miles of salmon river sold by auction went for over fifteen million pounds not long ago. Another stretch was bought for twenty million by a Japanese investment company.' She was giving him facts, nothing more. 'I heard of an American three-rod syndicate who tried to rent less than half a mile of river with a couple of good salmon pools. They offered two hundred thousand dollars – a West German beat them by just doubling it.'

'Nice money,' said Carrick woodenly.

'I don't give a damn for wealthy landowners,' she said searingly. 'I wouldn't give a damn if not another salmon was ever caught – what matters to me is that they are there.' Her hand slapped down on the armchair leather. 'But an estimated thirty thousand Scottish jobs in the tourist industry are calculated as certain to vanish overnight if the day ever comes when there are no more salmon in those rivers.

'Thirty thousand jobs, Webb Carrick. You're guarding them too.'

'I could have done without knowing.' He gave her a wry edge of a smile, but Margaret Steeven had also been starting to tell him something else when the alarm had been raised outside. 'You said things had happened off Port Torquil. What kind of things?'

'Lights at sea that come close into the harbour late at night but are gone again before dawn. Another high-speed boat I've heard come into harbour late at night then go straight out again – heard, never actually seen. Ask around the harbour, and they'll deny it ever happened.' She wasn't finished. 'There are nights when all the local boats suddenly seem to decide to stay in harbour, when no one ventures out – no real reason when you ask why. One of those nights was when a long-line boat from

Skye just vanished last month. It may have happened somewhere near Lannair.

'There were three men aboard – a father and two brothers. Their bodies weren't found, their boat wasn't found.'

He gave a small, slow nod.

Somehow, he'd almost expected it.

3

Peter Kee returned breathless and empty-handed from his chase, and Margaret Steeven transferred Carrick into the engineer's care. Her manner was cool and informal, introducing a new member of crew, nothing more, then she left them and went into her office cabin.

'They come worse than that woman,' said Kee amiably. *Dirk*'s engineer was Liverpool Chinese, with a Scouse accent to match and a shy, friendly manner. A plump, small man in his late thirties, black hair closely cut, he had a tiny moustache, and was wearing faded denim trousers, canvas shoes, and an old sweater. The sweater had leather patches at the elbows. He considered Carrick and seemed satisfied. 'Want the guided tour?'

'Sounds good.' Carrick lifted his travel bag.

'Stay close, don't get lost,' advised Kee with a wink. 'Dr Margaret wouldn't like that.'

They began with an inspection around the bridge and main deck. The extra superstructure and deck equipment included power booms for operating research gear, extra lighting units, stowage for sampling nets, and a couple of big temporary holding tanks for specimen fish brought aboard. A full diving platform could be rigged aft, and the *Dirk* also carried a proliferation of marker buoys and floats in steel lockers which were crammed with other gear.

Peter Kee didn't pretend to know much about a lot of it. Finished on top, he led the way down a companionway stair to the lower deck, where everything for'ard had been partitioned into well-equipped laboratory space. Other partitioning had created a midships area where a number of individual cabins were located on both sides of a narrow central messroom cabin.

'You like poker?' asked Kee hopefully.

'When I win,' said Carrick carefully.

'Good.' Peter Kee beamed in a way that made Carrick feel he had just established his place aboard. 'Sometimes we run a little game on Saturday nights. Just poor sailor-man stakes.' His plump Chinese features shaped a pious grin. 'If you'd like an invitation one time, we might have room.'

He beckoned and Carrick followed him aft, through a sparkling-fresh galley and past separate male and female washroom areas. Beyond that was some utility space including a workshop, then three more cabin doors were located like a cluster at the stern. The middle cabin door lay open.

'Yours.' Peter Kee indicated the open door.

Carrick went in, dumped his travel bag on the decking, and glanced around. What he had was more or less a sleeping cupboard with a bunk, a full-length locker, a tiny dressing chest and a miniature washbasin. It wasn't luxury, but he had known worse.

'The mattress is brand new, everything else got a total washdown. Dr Margaret insisted on it.' Kee leaned against the door and sucked an edge of his thin moustache. 'Webb – do we call you Webb – ?'

'Or worse.'

'Good.' Kee smiled. 'Webb, did you ever meet the man you're replacing?'

'No.' Carrick shook his head. 'I don't know anything about him.'

'Be glad.' Peter Kee was emphatic. 'His name is Bert Andrews. No one could accuse him of working too hard, and a lot of the time he smelled like he needed a disinfectant bath.' He paused, his dark eyes inspecting Carrick again. 'We weren't sad to see him go. Surprised, yes. It was sudden. Uh – how did you hear about the job?'

'Luck.' Carrick tried the washbasin taps. One ran rusty brown for a moment, then both were clear. 'I needed a

68

job, a friend phoned and said they wanted someone like that day.'

'True,' mused Kee. 'The dreaded Bert suddenly announced that he'd got a shore job down south, that he'd been having back trouble because he'd been working too hard. Him!'

'Strange thing, back trouble,' said Carrick woodenly. 'It flares up.'

'True.' Kee either gave up or lost interest. 'Want the rest of the tour?'

Carrick left his bag lying in the little cabin and they set off again. Leading the way with a proprietorial pride, Peter Kee took him down a narrow companionway ladder into the level shared between the engineroom and more metal laboratory tanks with windows in their sides. Several small fish were swimming in the nearest of the tanks.

'Not my scene.' Kee shook his head at them and beckoned Carrick on into the engineroom area, an oily gleam of well-maintained metal. 'This I know about, this is all I have to know about.' Then, forestalling Carrick's question, he thumbed at the sleeping machinery. 'We've two Volvo marine engines. They've a lot of sea-time behind them, but they'll still run for ever if you ask nicely. Twin screw, single rudder, and she's good for fourteen knots – except don't go over twelve unless you're desperate, right?'

'Right.' Carrick grinned his understanding. 'So what's she like outside a harbour?'

'Deck asks engineering?' The engineer was pleased and surprised. 'Anything more than a moderate swell sends her rolling like a pig. She also vibrates like she'll fall to bits if you hold her around seven knots. Take her through seven, and everything settles down.' He sucked his tiny moustache again, showed his white teeth, then gave his considered verdict. 'Treat her right, don't let our Dr Margaret expect miracles too often, and I won't have problems, you won't have problems.'

'Does the lady often ask for miracles?' asked Carrick mildly.

Peter Kee gave what was maybe meant to be an inscrutable Oriental smile. It stretched his plump face in a cat-grin. Then he lifted a bundle of oily waste and began polishing one of the already glinting lengths of engine fuel piping. Carrick understood. Back on *Tern*, Sam Pilsudski did exactly the same when he wanted to end a conversation. Maybe engineers went on a course to learn it.

He left the engineroom, went back to his cupboard-sized cabin, unpacked some of the kit from his bag, then shoved the partly-emptied bag under the bunk. Ignoring vague clanging and banging noises coming from the engineroom, Carrick explored his way out and up to the open main deck near the stern.

There was more cloud and the wind had freshened. A change of weather seemed on the way, and scores of seabirds had begun soaring and planing on the strengthening thermals around and above Torquil's Shield. A small fire was burning somewhere behind the rim of the great rise of green-veined rock, a thin thread of dark smoke located somewhere behind a stump of old lighthouse tower which stood like a silhouette on the rise. He noticed two ant-like figures toiling up from the village in that direction, watched them for a moment, then also noticed that the fire must have burned out as the smoke had ended. He switched his attention back to the scene across the harbour.

There were more gaps around the harbour, and a small procession of wooden-hulled long-liners was making out to sea. The coaster *Duchess May* had long since gone, to overnight at one of the outer islands before working her way back towards Oban. Carrick sighed and frowned down at his long, strong hands, deliberately tightening his grip on the deck-rail until the knuckles showed white.

The things Dr Margaret Steeven had told him, the things Department had not told him, only stoked his own doubts about how much he could achieve from *Dirk*.

The illegal netters had already shown they were highly organized. Were they expected to come out of the shadows just because he had arrived?

For no particular reason he thought of the date. In exactly a week it would be his father's birthday – the 'big sixty' this time. He smiled. Between them, his parents ran a small dairy farm in the middle of Ayrshire. How they'd managed to produce a son who wanted a life at sea remained the biggest mystery in their lives.

His mother had written him, had reminded him about the all-important birthday. She had threatened him with violence if he didn't send some kind of card. He had bought the damned thing. It was lying in a drawer in his cabin aboard *Tern*, unposted. There was also a bottle of single-malt whisky, the special kind with no label to stupidly tell Customs where that kind of magic was created. It had still to be wrapped –

'You're standing there like you need someone to wind up your clockwork,' said a man's voice. 'Are you our trusty new sailorman?'

'He can't be any worse than the last one,' said a second tolerant voice, equally near. 'Or can he?'

Startled, he spun round. The two men who had come aboard grinned and came nearer.

'Welcome, fellow slave,' said the first, a tall beanpole of a man.

Both were dressed in open-necked sports shirts and well-laundered, well-ironed khaki lightweight trousers. They were wearing rubber-soled jogging shoes, which explained why he hadn't heard their approach.

'You're Carrick?' asked the second man.

They made their own introductions. Both were on *Dirk*'s research team. The tall beanpole was Tom Barratt, a Londoner and an electronics technician. His companion, younger, smaller and average build, had a curly brown thicket of a beard. His name was Paul Wilson, he was Canadian, a graduate researcher, and he was carrying a large brown paper bag filled with groceries.

71

'I also double as cook most of the time,' said Wilson, clutching the grocery sack closer. His eyes widened as he noticed the graffiti on the superstructure. 'Not again?'

'And like our Dr Margaret says, the little swine still can't spell,' sighed Barratt. 'Don't worry, I'll clean it off. We have a magic removal fluid – if there's any left from last time.'

Still chattering about the graffiti, Barratt and Wilson went below and Carrick ventured into the research boat's modest chartroom. He tracked down an unpleasant smell to one of the chart cupboard drawers, where there was an old, long-forgotten meat sandwich, leathery with age and growing green mould. He tossed the sandwich overboard and a gull which swooped and snatched promptly dropped it and flew off again.

Tom Barratt reappeared and cleaned away the graffiti. Peter Kee emerged to work on one of the powered derrick booms located midships, and Margaret Steeven was next. She talked to Kee, and gave Carrick a remote nod she might have kept as a polite greeting for strangers.

The message was clear. When anyone else was around, Carrick was hired help.

The rest of *Dirk*'s crew returned aboard at six p.m., when general activity around the harbour had begun to quieten down for the evening. A small boat powered by a noisy outboard engine came threading its way in from the harbour entrance, passed the lines of fishing craft, then slowed and eased towards *Dirk*. There were three people aboard, two of them women, and the moment the dinghy's hull bumped the research boat a youth, still in his teens, scrambled up with a bow line which he secured to *Dirk*'s rail.

Carrick helped as the youth and both women brought aboard several marked bottles of seawater and bottom ooze samples. Then they got round to names.

The women were Martha Edwards and Rose Cullar, the youth was John Torrance, *Dirk*'s deckhand. All three were barefoot and wearing shorts and cotton shirt-tops, both women had broad-brimmed sunhats and had been using sunglasses still slung around their necks on cords.

Martha Edwards was in her forties, fat-faced, built like a small barrel and with a damp straggle of mousy hair. She was a marine biologist and she had been using green sun-block cream around her already blistered nose and lips with alarming results. Rose Cullar, starting to ferry some of the sample bottles away, was younger, with curly dark hair, a freckled, pleasant face, and average build. She had a modest little two-stone diamond engagement ring hung on a thin chain around her neck. She was the research team's laboratory assistant.

That left Torrance. Once the two women had gone below with their collection of samples, Carrick helped the young deckhand swing the dinghy aboard and lash it down in its cradle.

'Thanks, pal.' Torrance had pimples, a bristle of short, fair hair, a thin build, and a single gold earring. He hauled a battered pack of cigarettes and a book of matches from his shirt pocket and offered them. 'Smoke?'

Carrick shook his head.

'Bert Andrews – the last man in your job – smoked a pipe. Hell of a big tar-boiler thing.' Casually, Torrance took one of the cigarettes, lit it, then tossed the spent match away. 'Well, pal – '

'You.' Carrick cut him short in a voice like stone. 'Pick that up.'

'Uh?' Torrance blinked.

'That.' Carrick pointed to the spent match lying on the deck. 'Do it.'

Startled, John Torrance swallowed, bent quickly, and obeyed.

'Now listen,' said Carrick softly. 'I am not your pal, I don't want to be your pal – so don't call me that ever again. I've seen around this boat, she's in reasonable shape. We'll keep on that way – and whatever other ideas you had in mind, forget them. Understand me, boy?'

'I – I – ' Torrance's pimpled face showed shock, then

unhappy confusion. Then he swallowed, nodded, remembered the cigarette burning between his fingers, and quickly flicked it away over the side into the oily water. 'Sorry, Mr Carrick.'

'You've got the general idea, John,' said Carrick gently. 'So now we work happily together. Unless you want to feel my boot on your backside!'

Watching the young deckhand retreat, Carrick knew he hadn't gained a friend. But it had been necessary, right at the start.

Interesting smells began drifting from the stub of a galley chimney, then the evening meal was ready at seven p.m. Research team and crew ate together in the mess-room area, helping themselves buffet style from the food laid on a shelf outside the galley kitchen. Paul Wilson presided over it all, a blue and white striped apron around his middle, a beam on his bearded face.

'Enjoy,' encouraged the Canadian researcher as Carrick filled a plate. He pased over an extra chunk of fresh-baked bread and a pat of creamy butter. 'Stoke up! You need stamina to face our Blessed Margaret.'

Dr Margaret Steeven was already having her meal at the head of the mess table. Others were drifting in, and Carrick took a place next to Peter Kee. They were across from Martha Edwards, who was picking at a salad. The bulky woman's sun-blistered face was empty of expression, her thoughts obviously far away from her surroundings.

Dirk's crew ate well. Wilson had prepared a partan bree starter – an island dish made from boiled crabs, rice, and milk. Meat from the crab claws was kept separate, the rest was strained and liquidized. Then the thick, rich liquid that resulted had the claw meat added, along with anchovy essence and cream. It was easy to prepare, just as easy to get wrong. For a main course, the Canadian had cooked braised oxtails where the secret was in the marinating. Wilson's choice was a blend of oranges and herbs with red wine, and he made mildly apologetic noises about the wine not being a Burgundy.

'The man is a damned sadist,' said Martha Edwards, grimly helping herself to a thin sliver of cheese while Wilson produced a chocolate cake dessert. She scowled at Rose Cullar, who had joined them. 'I diet hard, I look like a horse's end. She eats all she likes, and where does it go?'

The younger woman had the sense not to answer. Carrick escaped, brought himself back a cup of coffee, and was seated again when Margaret Steeven came over.

'My office, in half an hour,' she ordered, then swept out.

Carrick lingered over his coffee, saw Tom Barratt was eating at the other end of the table, and looked around for the one absent figure.

'If you're looking for young Torrance, he's sulking in his cabin,' volunteered Peter Kee. 'Sulking or hiding.' He switched to a mock Chinese accent. 'Wise teenager should always hide in hole when trouble threatens.'

'Trouble?' asked Carrick innocently. 'What trouble?'

He exchanged a grin with Kee, finished his coffee, shoved the cup aside, then left and went up the companionway stairs and out on deck. The sun was setting, and had already almost vanished behind the rise of Torquil's Shield. But the clouds that had threatened had gone – at least for the moment. The fishing boats still heading out would have a clear night for work. Glancing at his wristwatch, he headed towards Margaret Steeven's office. Carrick had good reasons of his own to be punctual.

Then he slowed, hearing voices from the cabin. There was a pause, he heard a woman laugh, then the cabin door clicked open and the owner of the laugh came out into the softening gold light of the approaching dusk.

He stared.

She was tall, in her early thirties. She had shoulder-length copper-red hair tied back tightly at the neck and she had the build of a slim-hipped Amazon. An Amazon in a blue-and-white striped shirt worn loose over tight and faded denim trousers. Her bare feet were in thonged sandals. Pausing in the cabin doorway, she beckoned to someone still inside.

'We'll do it, Margaret,' she promised. 'The way you ask. We'll be there – and ignore my brother. He shouldn't be allowed out without a full-time keeper!'

Muttering, a man followed her out into the open – and Carrick stared again.

They were twins – had to be. They shared the same height and the same copper-red hair, the same broad-boned build and features. But the man badly needed to lose weight. His face was fleshy and he had the start of a beer belly, partly held in by a broad leather belt around his sagging middle. He wore a broad-hooped maroon and white football shirt and black trousers, the trouser cuffs tucked into the usual cutaway seaboots.

'You know your real trouble, Margaret Steeven?' he yelled back into the cabin. 'You're like my damned sister – you think you know it all. Except you're worse! The day someone gave you your first white coat, you thought that made you God!'

Then he turned angrily, striding fast along the deck, halting abruptly as he almost collided with Carrick. He glared with eyes of blue steel.

'So who the hell are you?' he demanded. 'The new man, right?' He didn't wait for an answer. 'Well, get out of the way – let me ashore before I hit someone!'

Shoving past, the angry giant clattered down the gangway. Behind him, unhurried and unperturbed, the copper-haired woman followed at her own pace. She looked at Carrick with eyes that were the same pure blue, gave a grimace which was a mix of mild interest and faint apology, then followed down the gangway. As Carrick watched, the man stopped and waited for her. She said something, laughed, elbowed him in those fleshy ribs, and they walked off along the quay together.

Webb Carrick crossed over and tapped on the open

cabin door. Margaret Steeven was at her desk. Swinging round in her swivel chair, she nodded.

'Come in, and close the door.' She waited, then waved him into one of the other chairs. 'I've had guests.'

'I saw.'

'You already met Sam Lawson, boss of the Grants,' she said dryly, a hint of amusement on her slightly tired face. 'That large bluster who just left is Charlie Stewart, who makes similar noises for the Stewarts.'

'And his sister?'

'Keren, his twin sister – Keren, not Karen.' Margaret Steeven allowed herself a slight chuckle. 'You noticed her?'

'I noticed. What was the noise about?'

'That almost amounts to Charlie Stewart being friendly.' She shrugged. 'I need some help – fishing boat help. Last time, I hired a Grant boat. This time, the Stewarts get their turn. As usual, Charlie came along to bluster while Keren agreed the deal. He's the brawn, she's the brains – ' She paused, then added slyly, 'Did you get to noticing that too?'

'No.' He grinned.

'Charlie's latest trouble is a new tax demand from the Inland Revenue. He thinks I've been spying on how much fish he's been landing – which I haven't. He also isn't happy that west coast mackerel quotas are being cut back.' Abruptly, she changed the subject. 'Meeting any problems with my people?'

'None that matter.' Carrick shook his head. 'Not yet.'

'Good. Charlie Stewart had heard about you, so I told the obligatory lies.' Margaret Steeven grimaced, then her thoughts moved on. '*Dirk* still has to maintain a work schedule. We sail tomorrow at seven a.m., we'll be back in harbour by late afternoon.' An edge of sarcasm entered her voice. 'Can I ask if you'll be aboard?'

'I'll be aboard,' agreed Carrick dryly. 'But I'll be ashore for this evening, looking around the village.'

77

She frowned. 'Doing something stupid, like using yourself as bait?'

'Not particularly – not tonight.'

They stopped at the sound of a brisk double knock on the cabin door. Carrick raised an eyebrow, the woman silently shrugged, and he went over and opened the door.

'Only me,' said Michael Alder, standing outside. He nodded to Carrick then looked in past him. Seeing Margaret Steeven, the yellow-haired diver gave one of his chipped-tooth grins. 'It's about those air cylinders, Margaret. Any chance they're ready for me?'

'They should be.' She gave a middle-aged wince as she rose from her chair. 'I told Peter Kee about them.'

'If you told Peter, they'll be ready,' said Alder firmly. He had changed his clothes and now sported a designer-knit fawn cardigan over a white shirt and fawn trousers. They were matched with dark-brown custom-made suede shoes. Coming into the cabin, he leaned aginst a bulkhead wall and invested a smile in Carrick's direction. 'Started finding your way around yet?'

'I'm trying,' said Carrick politely.

'That's the way – try.' Briskly, Alder switched his attention back to Margaret Steeven. 'I looked in at Harry Gold's yard before I came here. He says the police have collected his dead body – knowing Harry, he probably gave them his bill before they left. But he also said you'd had those little spray-paint vandals back.'

'And saw them.' She nodded. 'But they got away.'

'Think you'd recognize them again?' asked Alder carefully.

She shook her head. 'I doubt it.'

'They could be into something more than graffiti,' mused Alder. 'Cormack drove an old Ford van, lived in it. The van was set on fire – or it looks that way. It was found burned out this afternoon, and Harry says there's talk that people saw children playing up there earlier.' He shrugged. 'But it doesn't help much. They were only seen from a distance.'

'Children?' Margaret Steeven stared at the man in startled doubt.

'It can happen,' shrugged Alder.

'It might.' Carrick nodded, although he didn't feel that way. The news roused a new, raw anger inside him. But he saw Alder was watching him and hid behind a grimace. 'Kids – I'll believe anything. But where did it happen?'

'Where Cormack was camping – on the open moorland behind Torquil's Shield. He walked to the village when he came drinking.'

'Don't drink and drive.' Carrick nodded at the irony of it. For Fred Cormack, the option had meant walk and drown. 'Is there any real proof the van was torched?'

'None – but it looks that way.' Alder put his hands into the pockets of his designer cardigan. He seemed more relaxed again. 'Not that there's any chance of witnesses up there, Carrick – except for a few sheep. By the time people who had seen the smoke wondered enough about it to go and look, it was a waste of time. Everybody had forgotten about his damned van!'

Everybody. Carrick remembered the thin curl of smoke he'd seen himself, the smoke he'd ignored as probably being from a bonfire.

'I don't always like this world,' said Margaret Steeven sadly. Then she beckoned. 'Air tanks, Michael.'

They followed her out on deck. Then Carrick stayed there while she led Alder out of sight down a companion-way. For a few moments, he leaned on a rail and looked out at the harbour, cursing whatever was going on around Port Torquil.

Then he went ashore.

Very suddenly, the world had become dusky grey with a cream three-quarter moon overhead. There were work-lights aboard some of the berthed fishing boats and at the repair yard, and more lights – even a few neon signs – were beginning to show from the village itself.

Sam Lawson's chandlery store, immediately opposite,

was the first place to catch Carrick's eye as he walked out through the harbour gateway. Its big shop windows had brightly lit displays of marine equipment and as he passed them there was also a glimpse of Lawson himself, a squat figure stacking cartons of tinned goods behind a counter. There was no sign of Liz Lawson, but he could hear women's voices coming from the living quarters above the store.

A woman sitting in a chair at a cottage doorway wished him a polite good evening as he passed. A large German Shepherd dog was lying sleepily at her feet, and there were children playing a skipping game further along. A girl went by pushing a baby in a pram and singing to herself.

Port Torquil was ending its day quietly. Any real activity left seemed centred around the two bars located within easy sight of each other on the sea-front road across from the harbour. Several cars and trucks were parked in front of their pools of light and the sounds of cheerful voices and the occasional laugh.

The Stewart faction's den, the Stewart Arms, was nearest to Carrick. It was a long, narrow, stone-fronted building and he went into a bar busy with customers. He ordered a beer at the scarred mahogany counter, paid, took a first swallow, and wiped foam from his lips.

'Does that Steeven woman know you're out on your own, friend?' piped a spiteful voice.

Elbowing his way past some other drinkers, a malicious grin on his thin face, Harry Gold came towards Carrick. The repair-yard owner was still dressed like a tramp but he was drinking brandy from a large balloon glass.

'If I stay out after midnight, I turn into a frog,' said Carrick woodenly.

Gold gave a squeal of amusement. Willie, the bald-headed boatman who had helped recover Cormack's body, had come over with Harry Gold. Carrick nodded to the man then turned to Gold again.

'I heard about Cormack's vehicle being burned out –

you told Michael Alder it could have been children.' He saw the immediate, wary flicker in Gold's eyes, but kept on. 'Who saw them up there?'

'I – uh – ' Gold hesitated. 'A couple of the Grant boys looked in at the yard. They'd seen or they'd heard – Willie, can you remember their names?'

The boatman shook his head.

'Doesn't matter,' said Carrick easily. 'Something else I wondered about. Did you find much in Cormack's pockets?'

'Eh?' Gold was startled, then indignant. 'There was nothing – except the price of a few drinks, like I told the police. Anything else must have been lost in the harbour.'

'Even the keys for his Ford, I suppose,' said Carrick sadly.

Gold paled and forced a nod. But Carrick stopped it there, looking beyond the man, across the busy bar. Charlie Stewart was holding court at one of the tables, the two men seated with him listening intently while the big, copper-haired Stewart leader talked. Suddenly, the fleshy-faced giant paused, turned, and looked round. He considered Carrick with apparent minimal interest for a moment, then turned back to his companions.

A woman laughed at another table, and Carrick glanced over that way. She was one of several women at a table on their own, and there was a sprinkling of other women in the bar. But Keren Stewart wasn't among them.

Harry Gold had vanished when Carrick looked round for him again. The other drinkers around were talking about fish prices and football.

He quietly finished his drink and left.

On the way out, he saw Gold again. The repair-yard owner had joined Charlie Stewart at his table. But the other two men had gone.

There was bright moonlight outside as he deliberately loitered his way along the village's sea-front street. He passed a few modest shops and a village hall which had a corrugated iron roof and a sign which said that a lending library opened on Tuesday and Thursday afternoons. He could hear the steady murmur of the sea and the constant piping chorus from terns and pipits nightfeeding along the shoreline.

But it was time to visit the Grant stronghold, the village's other bar. He walked back to the Pride of Mull, a two-storey brick building with a flat roof where there was a flagpole with a tattered Union Jack hanging more or less limp.

He went into another busy bar-room. In one corner, but ignored, a TV set was showing a sports programme with the sound turned down. A young barmaid in a Grant tartan dress smiled at him.

'Give the man a whisky, Annie,' boomed Dr James Kennedy, who was leaning further along. 'A large one, girl – put it on my tab. He's a poor sailorman!'

'Whatever you say, doctor.' She grinned and turned away.

Kennedy beckoned and Carrick joined him. The plump, tweedy village doctor already had company, the young man with the wispy beard who had met Liz Lawson so enthusiastically after she'd disembarked from the coaster.

'Meet Tom Grant,' introduced Kennedy. 'Tom runs a line of lobster creels part time, plumbs in kitchen appliances too – not much good with lobsters, magic with dishwashers.' He indicated Carrick. 'Tom, this is the new man on *Dirk*, the man we talked about.'

'I'd already heard about you.' Tom Grant gave him a wary smile and a handshake. 'Liz said you came in on the boat with her.'

'Tom has been carrying a torch for Liz since school days,' winked Kennedy. 'There's one small problem. It's called Sam Lawson, who doesn't approve.'

'True,' admitted Grant sadly.

The barmaid arrived with Carrick's whisky. He nodded his thanks to Kennedy and took a first taste.

'Exploring, Carrick?' asked Kennedy. 'Or escaping?'

'Both.' Carrick looked around. Someone had tried to modernize the bar's decor with drapes of old fishing net and large, crudely carved wooden fish. It hadn't worked out. 'You drink here, doctor?'

'I drink anywhere,' said Kennedy solemnly. 'I've a golden rule. Stewart or Grant, never offend tomorrow's patient. Most days I look in here and I look in at the Stewart Arms – one social drink at most, catch up with the day's gossip, dispense medical wisdom, be generally available.'

'How's today's gossip?' asked Carrick.

'Mostly sad, mostly true.' The plump face grimaced. 'This man Cormack who wasn't your friend – did you know he was drinking here, in the Pride of Mull, last night?'

Carrick nodded.

'Anyone who remembers him leaving says he was well lubricated.' Kennedy shrugged. 'Alive or dead, some people have no luck. He had a van – '

'Some kids set it on fire,' said Tom Grant angrily.

'I heard,' said Carrick. 'Michael Alder came visiting *Dirk* and told us.'

'Kids.' Tom Grant tugged at his wisp of beard and scowled. 'Damn them.'

'Someone saw them?' asked Carrick with apparently minimal interest.

Grant nodded.

'Who?'

'Two Stewart crewmen. They were driving into the village, using the old road up there. They remember seeing children playing around an old van.'

'They told you?' Carrick raised an eyebrow.

'No.' Tom Grant frowned. 'I talked to Harry Gold at his repair yard and he'd heard about it from someone else.' He shook his head. 'Kids!'

'Their elders and betters once burned down a police station,' mused Kennedy.

Carrick nodded, keeping his face empty of interest. Harry Gold had claimed the children had been seen by two of the Grant faction. Now they had become Stewarts with equally vague identities. It was a tailor-made way to spread a story.

'I'd stake money that we'll never know much more,' murmured Kennedy. 'Not here.' Then he straightened. 'Duty calls, Carrick – outpatient time! But remember my invitation to look in.'

He left them, and began talking to a young fisherman and an obviously pregnant young wife.

'He's a damned good doctor,' Grant confided to Carrick. He gave a slightly awkward grin. 'Don't swallow all that Grant against Stewart crap, Carrick. Not all of us feel that way – I don't.'

'And Liz's father knows?' guessed Carrick.

'That's the problem,' admitted Tom Grant wryly. He brightened. 'Liz should be looking in here later. Are you – uh – staying?'

'Another time.' Carrick finished his drink and laid down the glass. 'Say hello for me. I've got to get back.'

But not straight away.

He left the Pride of Mull as an unlikely twosome from the *Dirk* came in. But he merely nodded to Martha Edwards and Tom Barratt and kept moving.

Outside, he looked around in the moonlight. The little street seemed empty, then he thought he caught a flicker of movement in a doorway further along.

It might have been there, it could have been his imagination. He deliberately waited until an old farm truck had rattled past in a glare of headlights, then he started off.

When Carrick found the vehicle lane which led up towards the top of Torquil's Shield it was a ribbon of narrow farm-like track that accomplished the route in vicious hairpin loops. He left it for a fast footpath shortcut climb for the final stretch, arrived breathless at the top, and paused to look back down. Seen from the top of Torquil's Shield, the fishing village looked like a child's toytown – a toytown of twinkling lights. The long, clean outlines of the harbour were clear in every detail, and the moon glinted on the sea from there to the horizon.

The view was long silver miles out towards the great sweep of the Passage of Tiree. He could see tiny, distant tips of land that might be as far away as Staffa and the Treshnish Isles.

He hadn't come for the view.

The top of Torquil's Shield was a long valley of scrub and heather which sloped inland. He heard noises, then saw sheep moving, disturbed by his arrival. The stub of the old lighthouse tower made a good landmark, and he used it to place where that thread of smoke had been located.

A few more disturbed sheep later and he had found the burned-out remains of Fred Cormack's van. A patch of scrub and heather had been left as blackened ash and scorched root-stumps, with the fire-gutted remains of the old Ford in the middle. It had been reduced to a heat-buckled shell, and a harsh smell of burning still clung over the area.

Carrick took a small pen-torch from a jacket pocket and looked through some of the charred, wind-teased debris. It was a waste of time. It made no difference now whether Fred Cormack had prepared a report. Anything left in the van had been totally destroyed.

He put the pen-torch back in his pocket. That same north-west wind, magnified by the height of Torquil's Shield above sea level, suddenly gusted around him and sent more of the black ash flying off into the night.

'Bloody useless,' he told the world loudly.

There was a noise like a hoarse, agreeing bleat some-where out in the darkness, then a night bird exploded skyward. Nothing else.

He left the blackened wreck and set off down the dirt road towards the lights of the village. At last, he had reached paved streets again and was close to the shore when a car appeared and stopped not far ahead. Lights and engine were switched off and two people got out. Carrick immediately recognized them both. The driver had been Keren Stewart, who had a short leather jacket draped loosely over her striped shirt. Her passenger had been Dr James Kennedy.

He didn't particularly want to be seen and there was a patch of black shadow almost beside him. Carrick stopped in its cover and watched while the couple walked the few paces through a small garden to the front door of a darkened house. Kennedy fumbled with a key, used it to open the house door, then switched on an inside hallway light.

He was near enough to hear their voices.

'Want to come in for a moment?' asked Kennedy.

'No. I've things to do.' She shook her head. 'And you've your own problems.'

'I know.' Kennedy made it a snap.

Keren Stewart waited on the doorstep while Kennedy went into the house alone. Another light went on deeper in the house, then he returned and handed the tall, handsome woman a shoebox-sized package. She nodded a silent thanks, turned, and went back to her car. As soon as she was behind the wheel she had it started and moving. A light-coloured BMW coupé, it drove past Carrick's patch of shadow a moment later and the glare of the headlight beams narrowly missed him.

Kennedy went in and his door closed. Staying where he was, Carrick watched the BMW's lights and was puzzled then surprised. First the coupé made a turn further along the street, then he lost it for a moment. When it reappeared, it was heading up the narrow direct road that led up to the top of Torquil's Shield. It was a route that Keren Stewart obviously knew well, and she didn't waste time. In about another minute, he saw a last red wink of the car's tail lights. Then it had disappeared over the rim of rock, still heading inland.

Carrick left his patch of shadow. Kennedy had said he lived in the second street back from the harbour, and there was a metal plate 'James Kennedy MD, Medical Practitioner' attached to the front gate.

Kennedy, who had been in surprise company. But why Keren Stewart had been with him, what was in the package, and where she was now going – even if it was beyond Torquil's Shield – were probably things that Carrick knew could be none of his business

He certainly didn't need complications, even the kind that involved Keren Stewart. Quietly, Carrick started walking away – then stopped again. Something had caught his eye, high up on the wall of that house. He stared, took a step back, stared again, and knew he was right.

Kennedy's home was a small, neat, Victorian villa, located just far enough away from the sea-winds to shelter an old gnarled climbing rose bush clinging like ivy all the way up one wall. Even in daylight what mattered would have probably been invisible. But a trick of that cool, bright moonlight caught a straight black line of thin wire running from one of the unlit upstairs windows. It was partly hidden by the profusion of climbing rose but it ended in the short, upright stub of a radio antenna.

There could be explanations. For anything. But for the moment it was something else to put on 'hold'. Carrick considered the unlit window and the aerial wire for a moment longer then quietly walked back to Port Torquil's main street. When he got there, he stopped hugging shadows and went on openly under the moonlight. The Stewart Arms and the Pride of Mull were both still busy, with more vehicles parked outside. A young couple went hand in hand along the street ahead of him then he heard them giggling in a shop doorway as he went past.

The attack came as he entered the harbour area. There were sudden, running footsteps from behind. He turned, had time to see two figures, then they were on him.

Their first rush almost knocked him down. A wild kick

from one man grazed his side, an even wilder punch from the other caught him just below his left cheekbone and stung. They were young, they were strong, there was a lot of liquor on their breath, they were swinging more punches, but they weren't very good at it.

'You! You hear me, right?' The taller of the twosome made it a spittle-spray snarl as he grabbed at Carrick's throat but missed. 'We don't like any o' you stinking mainlanders.' He swung a new punch, which slammed into Carrick's chest, then he got in the way of the other man as he stormed in. He yelled again. 'Not in Port Torquil. An' stay away from our women – understand me?'

'Leave him to me,' bellowed his companion, almost dancing with rage, trying to get closer. 'For God's sake, Petey – get the hell out o' it! Give me a chance at him!'

Petey hesitated, his grip loosened, and Carrick took the chance. Tearing away, he drove an elbow into the tall fisherman's stomach in a way that brought a whoop of pain. Sidestepping a new rush from the second attacker, he stumbled over a small pile of short, thick spars of wood lying on the quay and grabbed at Petey's jacket to save himself from falling. Carrick regained his balance to the sound of ripping cloth.

'Bastard!' yelled Petey. 'Fix him, Joe, fix him good!'

The other man rushed to oblige, a whirlwind of arms and legs, and Carrick retreated. It was no time for civilized brawling. Stooping, he grabbed the nearest of the thick spars and swung it up like a club in a curve which began at quay level and terminated in a thudding impact in the fisherman's middle.

The whirlwind that had been Joe staggered back, then sank down on his knees. Turning, Carrick raised the thick spar again.

'Jesus,' yelped Petey. 'No, mister – no! Forget it, right?'

Then he was running for the village, his companion lurching along after him. Drawing a deep breath, Carrick let the spar drop back beside the others in the heap.

88

'Nice swing you've got, skipper.' The bulky, unmistakable figure of Chief Petty Officer William 'Clapper' Bell ambled out into the moonlight from where he'd been concealed behind a stacked mound of empty fish boxes. The Glasgow-Irishman grinned broadly at Carrick's expression. 'Play golf like that, an' you'd win prizes!'

'You didn't think of giving me some help, did you?' asked Carrick sarcastically.

'Help?' Bell blinked. 'Hell, skipper, there were only two of them.' His grin widened. 'But make it last longer next time, and I'll sell tickets!'

'Fine, I'll try to oblige,' said Carrick grimly. The punch which had taken him below the left cheekbone had cut enough to draw blood. His left leg throbbed where a boot had gone home. He sighed. 'They don't matter – they're local friendship league, nothing organized.'

'So we let them go?' asked Clapper Bell, watching the two figures still retreating. He shrugged. 'I had that feeling, skipper. No sense in sticking my nose in.'

'True.' Two local drunks out to teach a stranger some manners were a minor irrelevance. 'When did they start following me?'

'They didn't,' said Bell simply. 'They were waiting near the repair yard, like a reception committee.' He saw the other question coming and shook his head. 'I was outside the Pride of Mull when you left, the way we'd arranged. I tailed you to the top of the rock an' back – you'd no other company. Guaranteed.'

'Good.' It was the way they'd agreed things, before Carrick had left the patrol launch. 'How are things on *Tern*?'

'No problems. Or not as many as you're having, skipper.' Clapper Bell rasped a thumbnail along his bristled chin. 'Department radioed about Cormack as soon as they heard. He was married.'

Carrick sighed, then glanced at his wristwatch.

'How long have you got?' asked Bell.

'Call it a couple of hours,' said Carrick.

The fight hadn't attracted any apparent interest from the moored boats around. Scuffles were common enough around any fishing harbour, particularly when crews were heading back to their bunks after a few drinks ashore.

He let Clapper Bell lead, and they walked away from the harbour, north along the shore road. Clear of the village, *Tern*'s bo'sun suddenly left the road, crunched his way over a short length of shingle towards the water's edge, then stopped where he'd hidden a small rubber boat. They carried the little inflatable down to the water's edge, launched it, and scrambled aboard. The outboard motor started with hardly a murmur and stayed a murmur as they headed out. Five minutes later, Clapper Bell gave a quick single flash from a hand-torch and a light winked back twice from ahead.

Another minute, and they were bumping alongside *Tern*. The patrol launch wasn't showing lights, she was riding the swell with her outer diesels barely whispering, and Second Officer Andy Grey's face offered a welcoming grin.

'How goes it, skipper?' he asked as Carrick clambered aboard.

'So far, it can only get better,' admitted Carrick.

Glad to be back aboard, he stepped into the comforting familiarity of the patrol launch's broad enclosed bridge. Gogi MacDonnell was at the wheel, his thin face softly outlined in the low glow of red night-vision lighting coming from the main instruments. Elsewhere, other tiny lights glowed and a narrow crack of green light was escaping from under the hood of the radar screen.

'We've had nothing happen that matters, skipper,' said Grey, who had followed him in. The dark-haired young Second Officer thumbed towards the radio handset hooked beside the empty command chair. 'But *Puffin* has been almost non-stop on the air, all-singing, all-dancing, telling the world she's well south of Lannair Island.'

'He's your brother-in-law, not mine,' reminded Carrick.

'And that's the way it was meant to be,' admitted Grey. 'But he loves it.'

Carrick took the small bundle of radio messages that were waiting weighed down by someone's jack-knife, and read them under the red glow from the instrument dials.

They told him little. Some were a record of *Tern*'s sentry-duty role, spending the hours until dawn on patrol off Port Torquil, then hiding in the secret inlet at Sanna Head where she could still monitor local fishing-band chatter and listen to Johnny Walker's diversionary radio shouting south of the Lannair line where *Pippin* had been bombed. There was the first signal from Fleet Support when they'd been advised by the police of Cormack's death, then a couple of confirming follow-up signals.

But beyond that, nothing.

Someone was missing. He looked around for their engineer. 'Where's Sam?'

'Getting some sleep. He needs it.' Andy Grey answered almost aggressively. 'I made it an order, skipper. He was almost out on his feet.'

'You were left in command,' agreed Carrick mildly, and tried not to smile. Andy Grey being ready to growl was something to be encouraged. He turned away, looking through the bridge glass towards the shore. They were close in, only about a mile north of Torquil's Shield and close enough in for him to see the white line of surf along the shore. 'Anything on radar since you left Sanna Head?'

Grey shook his head. 'Only what looked like fishing traffic – the usual.'

Clapper Bell had gone aft. He returned from the galley with two large mugs of coffee, one for himself and the other for Carrick.

'Thanks.' Carrick sipped the hot coffee. The cut on his cheek was stinging again, thanks to the fine drenching of spray from the little rubber boat on the way out to the patrol launch. He touched the cut gently, saw Clapper Bell grin, and scowled a reply.

Then he got to work, using *Tern*'s low-band radio on

the dedicated Fleet Support frequency, switching to scrambler straight away. Inside a few seconds he had John Kennan on the other end. The Fleet Support chief stayed very quiet while Carrick gave a short, factual outline of how things stood.

'You're not happy,' summarized Kennan at the end.

'I'm not happy,' agreed Carrick stonily. He saw that Andy Grey had decided to vanish, but Clapper was standing behind him, blatantly listening, and Gogi MacDonnell was eavesdropping at the helm. He didn't care. 'I'm not happy about several things – like the things you didn't tell me about. Like three men missing in a fishing boat last month. Margaret Steeven had to tell me about them.'

'That was deliberate. If it was wrong, I'm sorry.' Kennan's voice faded under a low mush of static for a moment then returned. 'The boat's name was the *Iris*. There was a storm, she vanished. There was a normal, full search without success. You know it happens. But – ' Kennan punched the next few words hard ' – we had no reason to link her disappearance with anything. Dr Steeven may think the *Iris* was near Lannair, we've no reason to agree. The woman means well, but that doesn't always help.'

'Agreed.' Carrick moved on. 'Cormack – he was on your personal team, wasn't he?'

'Yes.' The Fleet Support chief's voice became flat and angry. 'He was no drunk – that was an act. He was a good man, Carrick. I saw his widow this evening. She's still in shock.'

'Another casualty.' Carrick nursed the handset, guessing how Kennan was feeling. 'When will you have the autopsy report?'

'The police say some time tomorrow. They took the body to Tobermory, then helicoptered it out to Oban.' Kennan paused. 'Unless or until we're told otherwise, I'm viewing it that Cormack was murdered then his vehicle later burned by the same people.' There was a sound like a sigh. 'How are you getting on with Margaret Steeven?'

'I'm surviving,' said Carrick.

'Stay that way,' said Kennan. 'And the moment your cover for being on *Dirk* gets threadbare, drop it and get out – that's an order. For now, do you need any help?'

'Some background checks.'

'You'll get them,' promised Kennan. 'Send a list.'

They ended the call. Replacing the handset, Carrick went down to his cabin. There was the birthday card for his father, and the special bottle of no-name malt whisky – he grimaced, knowing they'd have to wait. He found a sheet of signal pad and wrote the list he'd promised Kennan. He wanted more detail on that strange, anonymous Mayday call after *Pippin* was bombed. He wanted anything known about Dr James Kennedy, or about the scuba-diving Michael Alder. He wanted a few other things, including any Fishery Protection intelligence on unusual foreign fishing boat sightings anywhere around the Passage of Tiree.

A little later, he gave the list to Andy Grey to radio on. Clapper Bell ferried him back to the shore in the little rubber boat.

They were almost there when they first heard it – the high-pitched howl of a powerful engine. Suddenly, Clapper Bell stiffened and pointed at a tiny shape racing out under the moonlight, banging across waves, leaving a white wake astern.

It had the profile of a small raider boat and the speed to match. Heading out to sea, it had come from somewhere south of Torquil's Shield. It was travelling so quickly that inside another minute it had gone and the engine noise had faded. Something so small could easily flit unnoticed across any radar screen.

But they hadn't imagined it. Margaret Steeven had been right again.

Carrick landed, saw Clapper Bell start back again, then walked in towards the harbour. He boarded *Dirk*, and when he went below found Martha Edwards and Rose Cullar watching TV in the main cabin.

'Well, look at this!' Martha Edwards laughed and shifted in her chair as she eyed the cut on Carrick's face. 'What happened to you? Did you meet a friend?'

'Something like that,' agreed Carrick neutrally.

'So I can mind my own business?' The heavily built woman grinned maliciously. 'All right, I will.' She changed the subject. 'Have you heard the weather forecast? We could find it rough out there tomorrow!'

A sad noise came from Rose Cullar.

Martha Edwards chuckled. 'And guess who'll be seasick again?'

Rose Cullar glared, but didn't answer.

It was one a.m. when Carrick reached his cabin, undressed, got into his bunk, and waited for sleep.

It came quickly. But with it came a strange blend of dream and nightmare, of being hunted without knowing why. A face kept recurring, a face that changed – a face that one moment was a dead man named Cormack with froth coming from his mouth, then the next moment became that of a beautiful, copper-haired woman. But the blend of dream and nightmare kept on. He was trapped and drowning somewhere deep under the sea, the copper-haired woman had vanished. Her twin brother was there, and so was an angry scar-faced Viking dwarf.

He woke in the darkness, sweating, and decided to blame Paul Wilson's cooking – probably that partan bree starter.

After that, he just slept.

4

Yet another low swell of sullen, dragon-green sea broke hard against the rust-stained white of *Dirk*'s fat little hull and, the way she had been doing for hours, the research vessel seemed to shudder down to her last rivet and weld. There were more of those low, lumping swells waiting all the way to the horizon.

'A little rough, but nothing more,' declared Dr Margaret Steeven above the steady throb of the big twin Volvo engines. She had returned to the bridge after a spell in her office cabin, and had once again jammed herself in at a bulkhead corner with long-practised ease. Cheerfully, she watched a fine curtain of new spray drench down the outside of the bridge windows. 'A little rough – fair description, Mr Carrick?'

'Fair.' Webb Carrick smiled and made another check along the bridge repeater dials. The readings all sat steady. Torrance was at the helm, but the pimpled teenager was in a sullen mood.

'Rough – but we've a sturdy little ship,' mused the woman.

'Sturdy.' Carrick nodded.

The truth was that *Dirk* sailed the way he'd been warned. At around seven knots she rolled like a pig. Under seven knots, she handled like a brick. Around twelve knots, she rattled in addition to the shudder. Yet, yes, she was probably sturdy – or she wouldn't have survived.

'John.' Margaret Steeven glanced over at the teenager. 'What's our heading, please?'

'Steering 250 magnetic, doctor,' said Torrance dourly.

'Thank you.' She shaped a wince towards Carrick. 'And our position now, Mr Carrick?'

'One mile north of the Sula Rocks.' Carrick guessed she knew at least as well as he did. The rocks were to port, for anyone to see, a low line of smooth, sea-worn black reef. It was covered at anything more than half tide. At the moment, it was edged with a heavy white lacing of surf. 'On course as you ordered.'

'Good.'

A moment or two passed, then he heard a strange new sound added to the background noises of the little ship and the sea. Puzzled, he glanced at Torrance, who simply shrugged then jerked his head towards Margaret Steeven. The small, grey-haired woman was singing to herself. A new, quivering shudder as *Dirk* took punishment from another of those low, monotonous swells didn't cause her to miss a single note.

Happiness came in all sizes.

Carrick thanked Torrance with a nod, then used the bridge glasses again. There was a fishing boat a couple of miles or so ahead of them, bow-on and sailing very slowly towards the research vessel – there would be plenty of time before he had to think about her.

He brought the bridge glasses round in a slow sweep. The boat was the only other craft in sight. They were about thirty miles due west of Port Torquil, it was afternoon, and the fat little research vessel was out beyond the southern edge of the Passage of Tiree. One of those tiny blobs of island to the north was Lannair, where *Pippin* had been bombed. Another, larger and behind it, was the south tip of Tiree. There were others, a thin, widely spaced scatter. Each with a name, most of them once proudly inhabited, but very few still that way. The rest had only gradually vanishing ruins to remind of their people, long since gone to the mainland.

Even their lighthouses were now automatic.

Suddenly, Margaret Steeven stopped her singing.

'There's a fishing boat on ahead,' she declared.

'On the starboard bow.' Carrick nodded.

'We're here to meet her,' said Margaret Steeven. She

glanced at the man's watch she wore on her wrist. 'They're on time.'

Then, eyes half closed, she lapsed back into her singing again.

'You heard, John,' said Carrick resignedly. 'I'm maintaining engine speed. Bring us round two points to starboard.'

'Starboard. Two points.' Wearily, Torrance fed the wheel through his hands. The rhythmic thud of the swell breaking against their hull altered fractionally, and then *Dirk* obeyed her rudder.

'She's *Stargirl*, one of the Stewart boats,' said Margaret Steeven as *Dirk*'s bow came round. 'That's why the Stewart twins were aboard last night. I chartered *Stargirl* for a half day.'

'Half a day?' Carrick raised an eyebrow.

'We're on a budget,' said the project director grimly.

Carrick nodded. He was rapidly becoming accustomed to Margaret Steeven's frequent 'do what you're told then keep out of my way' approach to things, which just as suddenly could be followed by someone being thrown a small compliment as a rewarding bone.

Outside the bridge, a brief squall of rain joined the spray flecking across everything. The weather forecast had been justified. Overnight, the wind had swung round to the south-west, coming in moist and steady from the Irish Sea. With the clouds, the colour of the sea had changed to green and the water's mood had changed to white-flecked, broken waves which held no welcome.

Dirk's crew had been awake soon after dawn. Breakfast had been coffee and rolls, and it had been Martha Edwards' turn for galley rota. On schedule, they sailed from Port Torquil at seven a.m. – and once five miles out from Mull the day's research work had begun, and had kept on. At one location they loitered while Paul Wilson took bottom mud samples. Later, they spent a full hour charting salinity and water temperature readings then lowered small, muslin-fine nets to collect plankton samples. Further out, they used slightly larger nets to capture samples of slightly larger marine life – all carefully stowed into one of the live specimen tanks.

Lunch was more coffee and mounds of thick-cut cheese sandwiches while they sailed to a new location. Then, on Margaret Steeven's orders, *Dirk* anchored and stopped her engines.

The research team took over again. A remote-control underwater TV camera was produced from one of the deckhouse compartments. Mounted on a little power sledge, linked by an armoured umbilical cord to a control area below the bridge, it was also capable of taking colour still photographs – and it was totally Tom Barratt's baby.

Carrick was just another spectator as the tall, thin Londoner disappeared into the control area, a windowless space where his only effective outside view would be what was captured by the TV camera's lights and lens. As the control area door closed, Rose Cullar had taken charge on deck. Still visibly going one shade greener each time the research vessel rolled but doggedly keeping on, the dark-haired girl supervised until the power sledge and its load had been lowered into the swell on a hydraulic davit.

Submerged, released, its electric motor-driven propellor churning, the power sledge began travelling down with the line of umbilical cable following. Then it was gone from sight somewhere below them, Margaret Steeven appeared, joined Barratt in the control area, and the door closed again.

Dirk had pitched and jerked at anchor for another half hour before an invitation arrived for Carrick to come to the control area. He went, Barratt let him in, then the cabin door closed behind them. Once again the daylight was shut out, leaving only the strange greenish glow from the identical pictures on three TV monitor screens above the control panel and the faint gleam of tiny worklights.

'Something for you to see.' Margaret Steeven had beckoned without looking round from the monitors. 'Tom – '

The picture on the monitors changed and shifted as Barratt moved two of the little joystick levers on the control panel, then a large fish swam placidly into the camera's lights. The lens zoomed in, the fish grew in size, the shape familiar, the head unmistakable.

Salmo salar, the Atlantic salmon, had come visiting.

'He's just a stray on his own,' had been Barratt's verdict while the big fish continued to fill the camera lens. 'I'd say a forty pounder, around five years old – give or take. But still a stray. Hell, you heard of that salmon poaching rumpus around Lannair? Go there, and sometimes it's like dropping the camera into the middle of a herd of salmon, all queuing to look at you!'

'A stray,' Margaret Steeven had agreed. 'But I thought you might be interested.'

Barratt had been more enthusiastic about something they'd seen a few minutes earlier, a rare parrotfish which belonged to warmer waters. *Dirk* was at a regular anchorage where some thin vein of the Gulf Stream often brought unusual visitors.

Then, a little later, the camera was brought aboard again. *Dirk* had sailed again and had continued her sampling schedule. Until Margaret Steeven had ordered this change of course, out past the Sula Rocks. To rendezvous with the slowly approaching Stewart boat.

The *Stargirl* was slightly smaller than *Dirk*, a coastal trawler with a dark hull and a broad, distinctive white flash at her funnel. She still flew a warning 'fishing' cone at her masthead, and now she was nearer the reason was clear.

A small purse-seine net which she had used was being dragged along beside her in the water and contained a silvery boil of struggling fish. Two of the *Stargirl*'s crew were on deck, their oilskins glistening with spray. But they were making no move to bring their catch aboard. They were watching the approaching research boat.

'It looks a good catch,' said Margaret Steeven. She sounded pleased. 'They were fishing for herring.'

'To order – your order?' Carrick tried not to sound too puzzled.

'Correct. Charlie Stewart wouldn't win any charm contests, but he's a damned good fishing skipper.' She gave a satisfied nod. 'Bring us alongside them with that net between us – but don't use it as a fender, please! I don't want that catch damaged. Any problem?'

'No.' Sea conditions weren't bad enough to pose any difficulties – not yet, at any rate.

'They've done this before, we've done this before,' declared the grey-haired, nut-brown woman. 'I want five hundred herring from that net, I want them individually tagged – then that's today over. *Dirk* has a total target of six thousand taggings to meet, spread over the season. So far we're on schedule, and we can stay that way.'

Carrick brought *Dirk*'s white, rust-stained hull round in a curve which first placed her astern of the slow-moving trawler, then took the helm himself for the final approach. When that was completed, the two boats were riding close together, almost stationary, just holding steerage way, both heavily fendered against any chance of collision.

'John.' Margaret Steeven glanced at Torrance. 'I'll have the loud-hailer please.'

The teenager scurried to bring her the battery-powered megaphone. Taking it, Margaret Steeven opened the starboard bridge door and stepped out on to the open wing. For a moment, she looked down at the narrow gap of broken water below them, and the fish seething in the net between the two vessels, then she used the loud-hailer.

'Good afternoon, Charlie.' Her amplified voice barked across at the trawler. 'You're on schedule. Ready to start?'

'Ready when you are.' Charlie Stewart's bulky figure had emerged from the *Stargirl*'s wheelhouse. He bellowed back through cupped hands. 'Let's get on with it, woman. Start brailing. I'm in a hurry.'

Margaret Steeven stayed on the bridge and sent both Carrick and Torrance to help the rest of *Dirk*'s team on deck. Within a couple of minutes, the process was under way.

The brailing net was a small, basket-shaped scoop which swung out on the end of one of the research vessel's slim, telescopic midship boom arms. A guide line had been heaved across to the two oilskin-clad figures on the trawler's foredeck, and they used it to help steady the brailing net as it swung out for the first time. It plunged down into the middle of the watery chaos of struggling fish in the trawler's net, then rose again, filled.

The boom swung and retracted back to where another of *Dirk*'s pieces of special equipment was waiting. Basically, it was like a large, rounded metal bath with a steady flow of seawater running through it, controlled by canvas chutes and drains. Paul Wilson and Martha Edwards were poised beside it, each with a small, electronically controlled tagging gun on a mounting.

'Now,' yelled the bearded Canadian as the brailer arrived.

'Now,' yelled back Rose Cullar, who was at the boom.

The brailer tilted. Some fifty or so fish rained down and began sliding along the canvas chute. Quickly, so quickly it was hard even to follow their movements, Wilson and the plump Martha Edwards scooped up individual silvery-scaled herring and began feeding them one by one to the tagging guns. Each time a fish touched the metal 'muzzle' there was a short clicking noise.

'They're fast – and that isn't as easy as it looks.' Tom Barratt had appeared at Carrick's elbow and gestured to where Wilson and Martha Edwards were still totally concentrating on their task. 'These tags are stainless steel, each just over a millimetre long – you inject the tag into the musculature area of the fish, immediately behind the head. The fish doesn't know.'

'If you get it right,' said Carrick dryly.

The emptied brailer basket had swung out again and was being guided back down into the *Stargirl*'s seething net. Carrick knew the rest of the story, though it was the first time he'd seen tagging in process. Each tiny needle was a coded microwire that the fish would carry for the rest of its life. Underlining the importance of fish stock monitoring, more and more fish processing plants throughout the Western world were being equipped with magnetic detector units. As each newly arrived landing of fish passed through the processing plants, the detectors would record the presence of any tags and their codings. Computers could take the results, juggle with calculations, and decide the health of herring stock.

There had already been temporary prohibitions on herring fishing in some waters, as a conservation measure. It was going to happen more often in the future, no matter how much fishermen howled.

Barratt had moved on. Carrick watched the tagging process again, seeing how the tagged herring continued on their way down into the metal bath along with discarded fish of any other species. John Torrance was there, using a hand-net, sweeping them all into another canvas slide where another cascade of water along another canvas chute returned them all to the sea and freedom.

'Webb, I could use some help,' called Rose Cullar and Carrick crossed the pitching deck to help her operate the brailer and its boom-arm. Another load of fish swung in, and they sent it cascading down into the canvas chutes. She seemed to have recovered from her earlier seasickness – or to have fought it down.

Between them, they sent the brailer net out and back again and again while the tagging machines clicked and Wilson and Martha Edwards worked on, ignoring spray and the way *Dirk* was rolling. Margaret Steeven had wanted five hundred fish tagged, five hundred she would get.

The brailer was going out yet again when Carrick saw that a new figure in an oilskin jacket had taken over at the guide line on *Stargirl*'s deck.

'Hey, Keren,' shouted Rose Cullar, and waved. 'How goes it?'

'Hello, Rose.' Keren Stewart waved back. Her copper-red hair was plaited back in a pigtail and she was wearing a sweater and denim trousers with the oilskin jacket and short sea-boots. She called back, 'Is your new help any good?'

'Too early to tell.' Rose Cullar spluttered as a wave broke spray down *Dirk*'s length. 'Webb, meet Keren. She's not as bad as her brother.'

Carrick grinned a greeting across the swaying gap. Then there was more spray, the brailer was bringing in another load, and Charlie Stewart was shouting to his sister from *Stargirl*'s wheelhouse. Whatever he wanted, she went on her way to help.

It kept on. Margaret Steeven had wanted five hundred herring tagged. To that, she added another thirty to be retained in one of the tanks aboard to monitor general condition.

But when that was done, the task was finished.

The little ships parted. Charlie Stewart was in *Stargirl*'s wheelhouse and his crewmen could be seen hurriedly hauling the trawler's net aboard. Then her big single screw began thrashing the water while the heavy, rough-sounding beat of her four-cylinder engine increased.

The waves breaking steadily over her bow, the blue trawler with that white funnel flash swung away and built up speed. She was on a direct course for Port Torquil. In minutes, she had left the *Dirk* far behind.

Margaret Steeven had been working with her team in the lower deck laboratory area, checking their recordings, and when she returned there was a satisfied expression on her beak-nosed face. But she winced when she saw how the *Stargirl* was pulling away.

'The way Charlie Stewart flogs that boat of his along, he should be charged with cruelty,' she said frostily. 'One day, she'll collapse and die on him. No warning!' Looking around, she gave a sudden suspicious sniff. 'Where's young John?'

'Off watch.' Carrick had been glad to see the pimpled deckhand sulk his way below. But Torrance had certainly earned his keep when they were fish-tagging. On ahead, Stewart's trawler was still increasing her lead and had almost gone from sight. 'Margaret, a favour. Any problem if we ease nearer to Lannair Island on the way back to Port Torquil?'

She shrugged but nodded.

'While there's the chance, I also need some help.' He fed the steering wheel through his hands and watched Dirk's bow come round. 'About people.'

Margaret Steeven raised an eyebrow and waited.

'The Stewart twins,' said Carrick. 'Tell me about them.'

'Why?' she asked bluntly.

'They interest me.' He forestalled any comment from her. 'Both of them. Family background, anything else you know.'

'Basic gossip?' Margaret Steeven considered with some distaste. 'Eighteen months or so ago, mother and father Stewart decided they were going to retire and took themselves off to live in the Florida sunshine. They'd managed to invest enough over the years, so they could do it without selling up the family empire. That was passed on to the twins to manage – '

'Any other brothers or sisters?'

'I'd call Charlie and Keren enough family for anyone.' She shook her head. 'But they were handed a reasonable responsibility. You're talking fishing boats, you're talking property – including a half-share in Harry Gold's repair yard. There are houses, there are a couple of farms, Charlie owns the diesel fuel concession in the harbour, Keren has her own marine insurance agency – '

'They don't starve,' mused Carrick. He nursed the wheel, steadying the research boat on her new course, spray breaking along her port quarter. 'Where do they live?'

'Torquil House.' She almost grinned. 'It's a vast old

104

derelict of a place, with no heating and a roof that leaks. You can see it south of the village, almost on the shore – over on the other side of Torquil's Shield.'

'At the far end of the dirt road?' Where Cormack's vehicle had burned.

Margaret Steeven nodded. 'Or take a boat round – they've a private jetty. That's almost as quick.'

Carrick nodded. 'Have they friends?'

'Everyone has friends. Even I have friends,' said the grey-haired woman tartly.

'Suppose I say Michael Alder – '

'My alleged toy-boy?' The sarcasm was heavy. 'Michael, yes. Why not? He also happens to act as their lawyer, just the way James Kennedy is their doctor.' Then she stopped, her mouth tightening. She pointed to starboard. 'Salmon net – not a lot, probably torn loose. Got it?'

'Got it.' But she had seen it first. Carrick watched the tossing, heaving line of small floats that danced on the wavecrests. The fine monofilament mesh between them had trapped some of the inevitable garbage of the sea – weed and a dead seabird, a white plastic bag, what looked like a splinter of old fishbox. Then more weed, a few small and decayed fish, and something dark and bloated. It was only a short length by salmon-net standards, maybe five hundred metres, but he steered *Dirk* well clear. Lost or abandoned, it could be awkward news round the research boat's propellor shafts. 'It looks old.'

'Probably drifting for a few weeks.' Margaret Steeven considered the net and its sad harvest. Eventually, it would either sink or wash ashore somewhere. 'I'll warn the local boats.' She sighed and looked again at the net, already drifting astern. 'Damn them – whoever they are. And damn the Noah Pipeline for causing all this.'

The anonymous net was a memory somewhere far behind by the time *Dirk* came in close and slow to Lannair Island. Lannair was high and it was rugged, it was sur-rounded by fanged reefs and guarded by strange islets where the sea swirled around or broke white, and it had the shape of a giant wedge. Along its sheltered eastern side, rock cliffs rose straight and raw with traces of that same green-veined rock which formed Torquil's Shield back on Mull. On the exposed west side, wind and weather had broken that rock down into a long, grass-covered slope.

A few families of grey seals were basking along the beach. Some hastily slipped back into the water as the sound of *Dirk*'s diesels echoed back from the awesome, towering cliffs.

Lannair was uninhabited. But it hadn't always been that way. Margaret Steeven had taken the wheel and Carrick used the bridge glasses, focusing on where the ruined remains of a cluster of tiny cottages clung together under a sheltered overhang. A larger ruin which might have been a church still existed not far away, with a thin, worn tracery of collapsed dry-stone wall which might have been a churchyard.

Paul Wilson had joined them on the bridge. Out on deck, Martha Edwards had appeared and was clinging to a rail as she stared.

'It would be one hell of a life over there,' said Wilson softly. He borrowed the bridge glasses, looked at the ruins then at the way the sea was beating in along the shore, and shook his head. 'Now I know why someone invented Canada.'

Carrick grinned. Then he took over the wheel from Margaret Steeven and the research boat swung away, weaving a careful path out past the rocks, homeward bound.

But he had seen something that mattered. Someone had been careless, Lannair had had visitors. One of the ruined cottages showed a flapping length of canvas used to block a hole that had once been a window. A definite path had been trampled through the grass and scrub by feet going back and forward to the shore and a landing place.

The visitors appeared to have left again. The surest sign of that was the way a number of seals were basking on the rocks beside the landing place.

Carrick took another glance over his shoulder. Lannair's highest point would make a perfect lookout post. Stick someone up there with a radio, and any boat that came within miles would be spotted.

Even at night. Unless a boat chose to sail without lights.

Maybe the same someone would be back. Maybe the same someone even knew something about the high-speed raider boat that only appeared at night.

The trick would be knowing when – and why. It was something worth thinking about. Carrick suddenly felt better about life in general. He hummed a tune under his breath.

'You look happy,' accused Margaret Steeven.

'It happens sometimes,' he admitted.

She took over the helm again and he went below. He wanted a mug of coffee, he felt he'd earned it.

Travelling at twelve knots, the sea conditions unchanged, it was another couple of hours before the plodding *Dirk* reached the Mull coast. Margaret Steeven had brought the white research boat in towards Port Torquil from the south, the way she had promised.

Carrick was on deck near the bow. He had borrowed a spare pair of bridge glasses and had persuaded Rose Cullar to join him.

'You want to see Torquil House?' She stood beside him, now totally at ease with the steady roll of the little ship, and chuckled. 'The real trick would be to miss it.' Using a hand to brush back some of her dark, curly hair, she cursed mildly as the wind immediately blew it into another tangle, then gestured at a wooded point of land ahead. 'As soon as we round that, you'll see it – and if Dr Margaret takes us in any closer, we'll use their front door!'

Dirk was sailing close enough to the shore for her wash to be rippling in along a sandy beach. Carrick could see cattle grazing in a field and could hear one of them bellowing. Smoke was coming from a wood fire beside a tent pitched near the sea, and a woman camper waved at them. She had a large brown dog beside her.

'Dr Margaret likes to cut it fine,' said Rose Cullar mildly. 'Like she's in a game against herself.'

But Margaret Steeven seemed to be equally sure of what she was doing, decided Carrick. There was still plenty of sea under the research boat's hull, and it was water which had lost some of the menacing dragon-green colour of the morning. Schools of tiny darting fish were everywhere, clearly visible as they fled from *Dirk*'s path or dived to hide in the dark forest of kelp weed waving down below them.

A mile or so ahead, the bulk of Torquil's Shield – a different shape, viewed from a different angle – rose high as a skyline. But the wooded point ahead was very near. *Dirk* was already easing out to gain more clearance, and her engines had slowed a little.

'Any moment now,' promised Rose Cullar again. 'As soon as we've rounded.'

'How well do you know them?' asked Carrick, remembering the way the young research assistant had joked with Keren Stewart while they worked the brailing net between the two boats.

'The Stewarts?' Rose Cullar thought about it. 'Keren, reasonably well I suppose – we were in the same university year at Aberdeen, taking an arts degree, sharing the occasional boyfriend.' She brightened more than he'd ever seen her before, fingering the engagement ring on its thong round her neck. 'Not this one, though. He's private property, in off-shore oil. I'm in this job for the money for another three months, then we get married – and hi-ho, we've jobs waiting in Australia.' She remembered his question. 'We've always stayed in touch as get-along friends. That's why I've got this job. Keren heard Dr

108

Margaret needed someone to be a well-paid dogsbody on *Dirk* for this season, and wrote me.'

'That's Keren.' Carrick hesitated for a moment, dubiously watching the point of land ahead. Unless *Dirk* did something more and soon, she'd ram it. But then he saw the angle on the bow increase once more and relaxed. 'What about her brother?'

'He may be her twin, but he isn't my kind of person.' Rose Cullar wrinkled her nose at the thought. 'I went out with him once, when he visited Keren for a few days at Aberdeen. But he was all hands and hot breath, and once was enough. Still – ' she shrugged ' – he's not always quite as tough as he makes out.'

They had rounded the point with a couple of overhanging tree branches brushing *Dirk*'s deck-rails. Carrick saw a compact bay, a secluded little beach of silvery sand, a thick background curtain of more trees – and a house at the water's edge. A big three-storey house that was as plain and ugly as a barracks block.

'Torquil House,' said Rose Cullar dryly. 'In all its glory – or whatever. I'd demolish it and build a log cabin with central heating and double glazing.'

Carrick grinned. The big house had its own stone-built private jetty, with enough depth of water there for the trawler *Stargirl* to be alongside. Another trawler was anchored further out, and some smaller craft lay off the jetty.

The Stewarts seemed to have their own private navy. He raised the glasses to his eyes, adjusted the lenses, and Torquil House came into tight focus. He sucked his teeth in a blend of surprise and dismay. The sprawling old mansion had been constructed of a grey granite stone, the kind that the original builder must have shipped in from the mainland. The cost would have been horrendous, even in Victorian days of cheap labour. The roof was tiled with heavy black slates.

But the slates were almost covered in patches of green moss. More streaks of moss clung to a damaged chimney, the stonework below was badly cracked in places, and the

109

windows needed a full painter squad. On the upper floor, he saw a couple of panes of glass were missing and another window had simply been boarded up.

'It would cost a fortune to put to rights,' said Rose Cullar sadly. 'Blame their father – he bought it as a bargain, for buttons, after it had been lying empty for a generation or so. He always thought he'd live in it for a spell then sell it at a profit. Except his wife took him off to Florida instead.'

Still using the glasses, Carrick could understand why. Part of Torquil House's grim air was due to its rows of windows. They were small and cell-like, except for one great curved area of glass shaped like a conservatory. It was located at ground-floor level and looked out towards the sea.

Margaret Steeven was making a courtesy of now staying out a reasonable distance from the shore while following the curve of the bay. *Dirk*'s siren gave a brief, cheerful blast of greeting towards the house and the other boats and Carrick brought the glasses round in a sweep. He saw no particular reaction on any of the boats. One man was working on *Stargirl*, hosing down her deck, but barely looked up. The stone jetty was deserted. A small speed-boat was tied to it, bobbing on the end of a line. It was the kind of little craft that would be useful to use as a taxi to and from Port Torquil –

Then he stiffened. There was a boathouse located immediately behind the jetty. Large, old-fashioned, but with closed metal doors that were modern in style and recently painted.

There were two men standing outside it. Carrick tightened his focus on the glasses a fraction more, then stared in surprise.

What in hell's name was First Officer Johnny Walker, skipper of Her Majesty's fishery patrol launch *Puffin*, doing over there in uniform, even a shirt and tie, and talking with Charlie Stewart?

Dirk's siren yelped again then echoed back across the

110

water. Over at the jetty, a scowling Charlie Stewart raised a hand in a half salute. Johnny Walker did nothing.

'Something wrong?' asked Rose Cullar, puzzled.

'No.' Carrick told the lie blandly.

But he had checked back along the jetty again with the glasses. Something he had missed earlier was tied behind the little speedboat. It was *Puffin*'s grey Zodiac boat.

Clapper Bell had warned him that *Puffin* would visit Port Torquil for the first time that day. But what was going on?

'Can I have a look?' asked Rose Cullar, still curious.

He passed her the glasses. She used them briefly, then gave them back.

'Who's the man in the sailor suit?' she asked with minimal interest. 'Someone you know?'

'No.' The lie came easily this time. He gave her a lopsided grin. 'Must be some visiting bum-boat admiral – definitely not my type.'

'Uh-huh.' Rose Cullar gave him one of those calculating, earth-mother wise inspections all women he knew seemed able to produce when they decided it was needed. 'Would you say the same about Keren Stewart? That she wasn't your type?'

Carrick laughed and turned away. *Dirk* had almost completed the curve of the bay while they talked and was starting to head out to sea again. He took another glance back at Torquil House and saw Keren Stewart's BMW coupé and a couple of other vehicles parked on what looked like the remains of an old tennis court.

Somebody long years ago had planned a grand mansion. Like so many other things, it hadn't worked out.

But still what the hell was Johnny Walker playing at?

The research boat's hull gave a sudden kick and twitch as she felt the swell outside the little bay. A fine wet spray cascaded along her length, then another. He accepted the swaying roll, going with it, listened to the engine speed, and grimaced.

Dirk had come down to seven knots, and was back to

being a pig again. What was worse, he had a sudden, almost unbelievable premonition about why *Puffin*'s skipper might have come visiting the head of the local Stewart tribe.

Twenty minutes later, the research boat was back at her berth again on Port Torquil's south quay, under the shadow of Torquil's Shield. He had seen *Puffin* on the way in. The grey patrol launch had squeezed her way into a berth on the north quay, where she had tied up between a couple of long-line boats. Her blue Fishery Protection ensign was flapping loosely aft, and he had even had a glimpse of Bill Martin, her diminutive Second Officer, ambling around on deck. Martin didn't look happy.

Very soon, Webb Carrick knew why. So did everyone else on *Dirk*. Peter Kee had gone ashore almost the moment the research boat had berthed. He had an urgent errand, which amounted to bringing back a spare roll of heavy black insulating tape from Sam Lawson's chandlery store and a six-pack of beer from the off-sales counter at the Pride of Mull.

When he came back, he was chortling. He was still chortling when he thumped a fist on Carrick's cabin door then walked in without any further ceremony.

'Hey – ' he peeled one of the cans from the six-pack and tossed it to Carrick, who caught it in mid-air ' – this, you'll have to believe. You saw that patrol boat across the way, the Blue Ensign job?'

'I saw.' Carrick had been putting on a clean shirt. He laid the can on his bunk, stuffed the shirt tails inside his trousers, and zipped up his flies. 'What about her?'

'The last time that patrol launch was here was three years ago!' The last of Kee's Oriental inscrutability vanished behind another heaving giggle. He clutched the cabin door-frame for support. 'Three years ago – when it rams and sinks one of the Grant boats on its way into

112

harbour! So what does it do this time? It rams a Stewart boat!'

'No favouritism,' said Carrick woodenly. 'Did the Stewart boat sink?'

'Her crew managed to run her ashore.' Still chortling to himself, Peter Kee produced another can of beer, opened it, and took a first gulp. 'But she's going to cost to put together again – the thump almost chopped the Stewart boat in half. So now the patrol boat skipper has gone off to tell Charlie Stewart he's very sorry – poor sod!'

'Something to remember,' agreed Carrick solemnly. His can of beer opened with a satisfying hiss, there was the sheer luxury of letting some of the liquid trickle past his lips and down his throat, and he allowed himself a happy moment thinking about Johnny Walker's predicament. But it mattered in another way. 'How about *Puffin*?'

'*Puffin*?' The Liverpool-Chinese engineer blinked.

'That's her name. I noticed as we came in.' Carrick covered his mistake quickly.

'Only a crumpled nose, like she was dropped on it from a height.' Kee was suddenly doing the inscrutable Oriental again. 'They're tough little beasts, so I've heard. When you see a boat's name, do you always remember it?'

Carrick shrugged. 'I thought it was a good name for a boat. I like puffins.'

Kee seemed satisfied. Raising his can of beer in salute, he left and Carrick heard him clattering down one of the companionway ladders towards his sleeping engines.

'Bloody hell,' said Carrick to the world at large.

Then he sat on his bunk, thought of Johnny Walker's new moment of glory, and shook with silent laughter until it hurt.

It was Margaret Steeven's turn on galley cook duty for the evening meal, and she was using a small, sharp knife to prepare a roast of beef when Carrick came through.

'Eating aboard?' she asked.

He shook his head. 'I had a sandwich.'

'So you'll be ashore, having your head punched in again like last night?' She was sarcastic. 'Can't you be more careful?'

'I'll try, Mother,' he promised mildly.

She threw the small sharp knife, and it bounced off the galley bulkhead just behind his ear. Stooping, he lifted the knife and placed it on the tray beside her.

'Try,' she said, in a way that meant it.

Carrick nodded and left. Once ashore, he joined the steady trickle of fishermen and villagers who were strolling down the south quay to inspect *Puffin*'s dented nose. Her Zodiac boat had returned and was back on her stern davit, and as Carrick made a suitably casual study of the damaged bow Johnny Walker emerged from the patrol launch's cockpit bridge.

Their eyes met. Walker flushed but said nothing, then turned away.

'Fishery snoops aren't popular with their bosses when they break their toys,' mused a voice Carrick knew. 'Will they hang him, do you think?'

He turned. James Kennedy had come along behind him and was also looking down at the damage. The village doctor had his medical bag in one hand and was wearing his usual tweed suit, but with a tiny rose in his buttonhole.

'Working?' asked Carrick.

'Working,' nodded Kennedy. He gestured further along the quay. 'A sick deckie who thinks he's dying. When they think that way, they don't.' Pausing, he returned a greeting from a passing fisherman then glanced at his wristwatch. 'Must move, or I'll be into drinking time.'

'I hoped I'd see you,' said Carrick. 'I could use some help.'

'Half an hour, and I'll be in the Pride of Mull,' said Kennedy. 'No, better make it the Stewart Arms this time.'

'I meant a private word.'

Kennedy shrugged. 'All right. My house in an hour –

two streets back, my plate on the gate.' He considered Carrick through hooded eyes for a moment. 'Not medical?'

Carrick shook his head.

'Fine.' Kennedy strode off down the quay, his medical bag swinging.

Johnny Walker was still on *Puffin*'s deck. He looked up at Carrick again, his face still expressionless.

'Bugger off,' he said coarsely. 'We don't need spectators.'

Carrick smiled politely and turned away. Several of the fishing boats nearby had just returned and their boxed, iced catches were being swung ashore. Most of them seemed to have hit a good seam of mackerel, and he carefully looked away when he caught a glimpse of a couple of middle-sized salmon just visible in one box, under a thin layer of haddock. Fishermen had always taken one or two for the pot, always would as a natural right.

Why challenge it?

He walked the rest of the way through the harbour then crossed the road outside the gates and went into Sam Lawson's chandlery store. The door was fitted with a bell that chimed as he entered, and Sam Lawson bustled out from behind a counter. For the moment, the front of the store had no other customers.

'Evening – ' the friendly shopkeeper smile faded on the small, thick-set man's scarred face as he recognized his visitor ' – hello, Carrick. What do you want?'

'Some help,' said Carrick. He gave a mildly interested glance around the shop area, with its piled cartons of stores, its filled shelves, and its displays of canned goods. Then he took a step nearer to the chandler, his manner cool and quiet. 'Pass the word to your personal mafia, Sam. The next time any of them try to jump me at the harbour or anywhere else, I'll break their legs.' He saw the flicker of surprise that showed on Lawson's scarred

115

face, and decided it was genuine. 'You mean you didn't know?'

'I heard about a brawl.' Sam Lawson said it slowly. 'You say you were attacked by Grants?'

'That was the suggestion.' Wryly, Carrick touched the cut on his face. 'I didn't ask for anything in writing.'

'Then ask next time,' snapped Sam Lawson. 'But I'll check.'

They both glanced round as a door clicked and opened behind the shop counter and Liz Lawson appeared. The chandler's daughter grinned when she saw Carrick.

'I heard the shop-bell – '

'And thought it was someone else,' said her father grimly. 'Like Tom Grant.'

'Yes.' She gave Lawson an affectionate challenge of a frown, then grinned at Carrick again. She was wearing a figure-hugging short black dress, which had a white belt with broad silver buckle. Her long chestnut hair gleamed under the store's lights, and the perfume she was wearing was French and expensive. 'I'm glad you came, Webb.'

'He's here on – ' her father hesitated ' – on a business matter.'

'Then it can wait.' Liz Lawson seemed to have rewritten a few of the house rules in the very short time she'd been back home. 'Webb, I've a couple of people sitting upstairs you've already met. Come on through.'

Carrick glanced at Sam Lawson.

'All right,' scowled Lawson. 'I'll – I'll check on that matter.'

'And send Tom up if he comes,' instructed Liz Lawson.

Lawson nodded. Reluctantly.

'Don't be a total bear, Dad,' sighed Liz Lawson.

Lawson grunted and turned away, going over to a telephone on the shop counter, while his daughter beckoned Carrick. He followed her through the doorway behind the counter, into a big rear warehouse area, then up a flight of steps. There was another doorway with a heavy plastic curtain at the top. Behind the curtain there was carpeting, then a brown velvet curtain, and beyond the velvet they were into the living quarters above the chandlery store.

'What have you been doing here?' asked Carrick dryly, thumbing down towards the store and her father. 'Having a palace revolution?'

'Fighting a battle.' She was serious. 'I might be winning. So far, my father agrees I'm old enough to vote.' They had walked down a small corridor which smelled of teak polish. There were small pink roses in a silver bowl on a wall table, and a room door lay open. Liz Lawson gestured an invitation. 'In here.'

Carrick went into a large living room where the furniture was heavy oak or thickly padded brown leather. There was more silverware and delicate Royal Albert porcelain in a glass-fronted sideboard, a near-antique of a TV set, and framed family photographs. It was the kind of room he knew. It matched one in his own parents' home. But Keren Stewart and Michael Alder were seated in chairs on either side of the fireplace, each holding a drink and looking up at him.

'Carrick.' Alder gave a lazy nod of recognition and his usual chipped-tooth grin, but didn't stir. He was in jeans and another of his designer sweaters. 'You know Keren?'

'We've met over a few fish,' said Keren Stewart dryly. 'Dr Margaret had him working at the time.' She rose sinuously from her chair, and even though she was wearing flat-heeled sandals she was taller than Carrick. Her handshake was pleasantly firm. 'Webb as in Webster?'

'Yes.' Carrick realized he was still holding her hand, grinned, and released her. Keren Stewart was wearing a simple white shirt-blouse and tailored cream-coloured linen trousers. Her jewellery was a single, chunky gold neckchain and a slim gold wristwatch, and her copper-red hair was still in that thick single plait, but now woven through with a thin ribbon of white lace. 'Before today, we almost met on *Dirk* last night.'

'When my dear brother Charlie went past you like a

117

mad bull.' She had an impish touch of humour in her slightly husky voice. 'He usually behaves that way.'

'Like he should have a ring through his nose,' said Alder flatly.

'Have a seat – and a drink,' invited Liz Lawson.

'Another time.' Carrick shook his head, glancing at Alder and Keren Stewart. 'I'm gatecrashing.'

'You're not,' declared Liz Lawson. 'You know Keren and Michael, and you met Tom Grant – '

'Last night,' agreed Carrick. 'Don't tempt me, Liz. I've a list of things to do.'

'I tried.' She accepted it.

'Our loss,' said Michael Alder dryly. 'Another time.' He paused, then glanced at Keren Stewart. 'He scuba dives.'

'Does he?' Keren Stewart's blue eyes glinted with immediate interest. 'Did you bring your gear with you, Webb?'

'Doesn't matter whether he did or not,' shrugged Alder. 'There's plenty of scuba gear he could borrow on the *Dirk*.'

'Dr Margaret's people don't work Saturdays,' murmured Keren Stewart. 'So – it's fixed.' She raised her drink in a mock toast. 'This is Wednesday. That gives you two days to get it organized. Come to Torquil House, early afternoon.'

'I'll be there.' He glanced a question at Liz Lawson.

'Not me!' She shook her head firmly. 'Unless I just come and watch.'

Carrick was puzzled and showed it. 'You two don't have any troubles with the Grant versus Stewart thing?'

'That's an exclusive male-ego preserve,' said Keren Stewart sardonically. 'Women are allowed to be neutral, don't count. Liz and I have always got along. I'm a few years older, but we were at school together.' She shrugged. 'It can be a small world. I was at university with Rose Cullar.'

'I heard,' agreed Carrick.

118

'Can I yawn?' asked Alder rudely. He sat back in his chair. 'Carrick, I'll hope you're good. We might have some interesting diving for you. Any problems before Saturday, let me know – I'm a two-minute walk south from here on the shore road, at Gull View cottage.'

They talked for a moment or two more. Once Tom Grant arrived, they were driving across the island to a tiny restaurant that a couple Grant knew had opened near a tourist bay on the south shore.

Carrick said he could find his own way out, left them, and made his way back down to the front counter of the chandler's store. Sam Lawson was dealing with a fisherman customer but saw Carrick, gestured for him to wait, and came over as soon as the fisherman had gone.

'That problem of yours,' said Lawson curtly. 'I checked with people. Whatever you were told, they weren't Grants.' He paused, laid both powerful hands on the store counter, scowled, and admitted, 'Maybe not Stewarts – not the way I hear it.'

'Who does that leave?' asked Carrick dryly.

'Troublemakers off one of the mainland boats. Now an' again they like stirring it up.'

'Mainlanders as in salmon raiders?' Carrick saw the small Viking's scarred face twitch then harden, the way his eyes widened for a moment in surprise. 'Fair question?'

'What the hell do you know about salmon raiders?' demanded Lawson hoarsely.

'Only gossip since I got here – and I heard what happened to that Fishery Protection boat.' Carrick gave an easy shrug but watched Lawson closely. He was worried. Maybe more than worried. 'Whoever they are, they sound like they stir things up.'

'Take advice,' said Lawson grimly. 'Go around talking like that, and you'll walk into something a lot worse than a harbour scuffle. You hear me, Carrick?' He didn't wait for a reaction. 'We've had police, we've had fishery people – and I don't mean that damned fool down in the harbour now – and they've found nothing!' He slammed one of his hands down flat and hard on the counter. 'Not a thing to say anyone in Port Torquil was involved! Understand?'

'I hear you,' murmured Carrick.

Scowling, Sam Lawson stomped away.

Carrick left, the shop door clanging again as it opened and closed. This time he noticed that Michael Alder's blue Toyota pick-up was one of the row of vehicles, mostly light trucks or four-wheel drives, parked along the street. The scuba-diving lawyer won hands down in terms of extra aerials and lights. But there was no sign of the BMW coupé he'd seen Keren Stewart using the previous night.

He glanced at his watch and saw he had a few minutes before he was due to visit Kennedy. It was time enough to make an apparently casual tour south along the shore road for a couple of minutes and locate Alder's home. Gull View cottage was single storey with white stone walls, very narrow window slits, outlined in green paint, and an old-fashioned thatch roof. The thatch was held down by fishing nets weighted at the ends with blocks of stone, but Alder didn't seem devoted to traditional values. He had a large satellite TV antenna dish mounted on one gable end.

There was no one else in sight. Carrick walked the small sea-pebbled path across the narrow strip of front garden and pretended to knock on the heavy oak-faced front door. It gave him a chance to peep in at the nearest of those narrow-slit windows, and he saw a word-processor flanked by its printer on one side and by what looked like a FAX machine on the other.

He looked around again. Gull View was one of a small row of cottages. Some had the look of being used as holiday homes, closed and shuttered, probably empty most of the year. He walked round the outside of Alder's cottage, staying casually out in the open in case anyone noticed him, checking the roof line in a less obvious way, satisfying himself there was no trace of a radio aerial. In fact, the only thing of real interest was a large and separate outhouse at the rear, obviously older than the cottage. It had been given a corrugated iron roof and the windows were guarded by wire mesh. Their glass had been obscured from inside with whitewash.

'Hello – ' It was a woman's voice, and he looked round. She was middle-aged, and she had appeared in the garden of a cottage two along from Gull View. 'If you're looking for Michael, I saw him go out.'

'Doesn't matter. It wasn't important,' he called back. 'Lives alone, does he?'

'Mostly,' she called back. 'There's a woman comes mornings to clean house.' She paused. 'Can I give him any kind of message?'

'No thanks. I'll try another time,' Carrick told her.

She nodded and went back into her cottage. As she did, Carrick started walking back in towards the village. Then he turned off the shore road, heading along the next street back, making for Dr James Kennedy's house and surgery. When he reached it and went in past the brass medical plate at the garden gate, he took a deliberate outwardly admiring glance up at the glory of that climbing rose bush.

He had been lucky, very lucky, spotting that thin moonlit shadow of wire. In sunlight, even knowing it was there, it was almost invisible behind the high foliage.

A moment later, he was glad he hadn't done more than look. The village doctor was back from the harbour, and must have been waiting for his visitor. The house door opened while Carrick was still heading towards it.

'Whatever else, you're prompt,' said Kennedy, giving a welcoming nod from the open doorway. He beckoned Carrick in, then closed the door again once his guest had entered. 'You did say this wasn't medical?'

'Personal,' agreed Carrick. The Victorian house might appear drab from the outside, but some work had been done to brighten the interior. The hall had been repapered

121

and painted, there was fitted carpeting. 'It won't take long.'

'I'm in no rush.' Kennedy led the way past a waiting-room door and another marked Surgery. Then he ushered Carrick into a surprise of a living room where the furniture was a blend of pale leather, chrome and bleached wood. A few books lay on a shelf. An alcove cupboard had been converted into a small bar. 'Sit down.'

'Thank you.' Carrick settled into one of the leather and chrome armchairs. It was more comfortable than it looked. 'Nice room.'

'I picked most of it from a catalogue. Now, what will we drink?' Kennedy spent a moment contemplating the bottles on the bar, a frown on his plump face. 'Ever tried Aultmore whisky?'

'Not often,' said Carrick.

'Never a drop is bottled until it is twelve years old.' Taking the bottle, Kennedy half filled two tumblers as he spoke. 'It comes from one of the magic circle of north-east mainland distilleries. What's wrong is that most of it is exported abroad.'

He brought one glass over to Carrick, returned for his own drink, raised his glass in a token toast, then carefully sniffed the aroma of the whisky before he sipped. He watched closely as Carrick took a first, matching taste.

'All right?' he asked.

Carrick nodded. The malt had a delicate tang and maturity that was all its own.

'So.' Kennedy sipped again, then his moon-like face took on a more serious expression. 'This personal matter – what's it about, how can I help?'

'I'm getting caught up in the hassle between the Grants and the Stewarts – and I don't want it.'

'I see.' Kennedy nodded pensively, came over, and lowered himself into another of the chrome and leather chairs. 'You want me to spread the word for you?'

'They know you stay on your own fence. They'd trust you.' Carrick waited. He had originally had another approach in mind, but this one seemed better – more likely to be believed.

'l could talk to some of them,' agreed Kennedy, frowning. 'Have you done anything in particular to upset anyone?'

Carrick shook his head.

'You've met people – '

'From both tribes.'

Kennedy took a swallow of whisky. 'Women?'

'I've spoken with Liz Lawson, I've spoken with Keren Stewart.' Carrick shrugged. 'I'm going scuba-diving with them and with Michael Alder – at least Liz said she'd come along and spectate.'

'But not to go and swim,' said Kennedy. He grimaced. 'That doesn't surprise me. Fishing families around here almost never learn how – it's like religion with some of them.'

Carrick understood, although he had nearly forgotten. It still happened. It came down to a harsh acceptance of the risk of drowning at sea. In the chill waters off the Hebrides, the grim outlook was that to be able to swim only lengthened the ordeal. Drown sooner was better than drown later.

'Will you do it – help me?' he asked.

'Yes. It shouldn't be too difficult.' Kennedy smiled. 'You can't be in deep. If anybody in Port Torquil wanted to fix you, they'd do it for real.' He swirled the whisky in his glass, considering it as he spoke. 'What you've got to remember is that people around here are particularly sensitive to strangers just now. You heard about the salmon gang that bombed a Fishery Protection boat off Lannair?'

Carrick nodded, his face carefully neutral.

'That brought in more Fishery Protection people, then police – ' Kennedy grimaced ' – and the police were back again today, more questions about our body from the harbour and trying to locate the kids who set his van on fire.'

'If it was kids,' murmured Carrick.

'Who else?' Kennedy looked at his glass, drank what was left of his whisky in a single massive gulp, and frowned at Carrick's glass. 'You'll take the other half.'

It was a decision, not a question. But exactly as the portly, tweed figure got to his feet the house doorbell rang, then rang again with an urgency. Kennedy groaned, then walked over to the living-room window and looked out.

'Damn,' he said dispassionately. 'Business.'

Carrick came over and joined him. The window was at the front of the house, giving a view of the door. Harry Gold was standing on the doorstep, and the thin-faced repair-yard owner had a badly bloodstained towel wrapped around his left hand. He rang the doorbell again then looked along, saw them at the window, and mouthed his relief.

'To work,' said Kennedy sourly. He hesitated, then thumbed towards the bar. 'Help yourself. I'll be right back.'

He left Carrick. The front door opened and Gold was ushered in. Then Carrick heard noises and voices along the corridor. After another couple of moments, he heard a yelp and then Kennedy reappeared.

'Harry was playing with a wood chisel,' he said briefly. 'It slipped and went into his hand like it was a tin-opener.'

'Bad?' queried Carrick.

'No, a couple of stiches will fix things.' Kennedy gestured again towards the whisky bottle. 'Stay on, and we'll talk – I've parked him in the surgery.'

Kennedy left again, going back down the hallway. Carrick heard the surgery door open and close, then Gold's piping voice protesting about something.

The aerial wire on that outside wall came from an upstairs window. A window almost directly above where he was standing. It was a chance – a chance he decided to take. Going out into the hallway, Carrick quickly mounted the carpeted stairway to the upper floor. There

124

were four doors. Two were open, one a bathroom and the other a bedroom. He went to the two closed doors.

The first he opened was an ordinary storage cupboard filled with boxes. He closed it again, tried the other handle, winced as it turned with a squeak, then eased the door open a fraction. He opened it wider, staring at a compact, high-powered radio transmitter which sat mounted on a table.

The voices from the surgery were still a background murmur. Carrick slipped into the room and gave the transmitter a quick visual inspection. It was a Ferranti – GEC make, an apparent twin of a set he'd seen fitted aboard naval minesweepers. If it was a total twin, then it had enough range and power to match any patrol-launch equipment.

He corrected himself. It had enough range and power to reach out beyond the Hebridean islands.

But why did Kennedy need it?

Dry-lipped, he took another look around the room. It was scrupulously clean and sparsely furnished, which didn't help. There was an extension telephone plugged into a jack on the wall. There was a blank signal pad in front of the radio transmitter's microphone and control panel, but with no indentations left over from any previous use. He checked the transmitter's frequency dial and swore under his breath.

The set had been left tuned to the standard fishing wavelength.

Somebody was very, very careful.

But had overlooked one thing. It was there, pencilled above the tuning dial for a small auxiliary set that sat to one side. He read the letters DL and 048.

DL 048. Meaning what?

It would have to do. The voices below had stopped. Slipping back out on to the landing, he gently closed the door behind him, heard the surgery door downstairs open again, and both men talking.

Carrick entered the bathroom, silently closed the door,

flushed the toilet, ran the washbasin taps, then noisily opened the door again and went downstairs.

James Kennedy stood at the foot of the stairs.

'I found your bathroom,' said Carrick.

Kennedy looked at him, sucked his lips as if calculating, then relaxed and nodded.

'Patient survive?' asked Carrick.

'Give or take a yelp,' said Kennedy ascerbically. 'He's going to have to pay to send me to embroidery classes if this happens much more.'

They went back into the living room. They had the 'other half' of the Aultmore malt. When Carrick mentioned salmon, James Kennedy first looked totally blank and then made vague, totally uninterested noises. Carrick tried again, even more directly.

'Where *Dirk* was working today, we were near where that Fishery Protection launch was bombed,' he said pensively. 'I've heard the gossip about what happened, and the people in this salmon gang must be out of their minds. It sounds like a miracle that no one was killed.' Pausing, he shook his head and said it again. 'A miracle – but they had their nets at the right place.'

'Oh?' Kennedy raised polite eyebrows.

'Dr Margaret says there's always a heavy run of salmon off Lannair right about now. Same time each year – ' Carrick paused, trying for a response ' – like they were coming in through a gate!'

'I think inside my own patch,' said James Kennedy wearily. 'I've got enough to worry about here in Port Torquil.' He brightened. 'I had an eleven-year-old boy brought in the other day, concussed. He'd been tormenting his ten-year-old sister, and she hit him with her rag doll – she'd loaded it with sand. That's enterprise!'

Then Kennedy had somehow swung the conversation back to what appeared his favourite topic – whiskies and their legends, like the west coast harbour where skippers could always find their way into port, even in thick fog, by the bouquet from the stills ashore. Then on to some of the equally legendary stories of illicit distilling around the islands, from whisky smuggled past excisemen with kegs hidden inside coffins to the still that operated successfully underground until a straying cow fell through the roof.

They were old stories, and Carrick had heard all of them before. But James Kennedy told them well. When they'd finished their drinks, Carrick made his excuses. He was leaving, standing on the front doorstep of the house, the evening a grey dusk, when he heard his host make a sudden and strange mistake.

'Look in again soon,' said James Kennedy. He beamed. 'Next time – yes, next time you can help me make a small reduction in a bottle of Glenmorangie. That's a reasonable proposition, eh?'

'Very reasonable.' Carrick nodded with suitable respect.

'One of the greatest,' declared Kennedy affably. 'Not many candidates could top it – can you think of any?'

Carrick shrugged, trying to appear suitably interested, his mind more on the radio hidden in that upper room – a radio he couldn't ask about.

'Maybe Bladnoch?' he suggested.

'Bladnoch – ' Kennedy seemed to hesitate, then wagged an admonishing finger ' – tricky, but yes, I know it. Distilled up in Kirkwall, in the Orkneys – a good choice, but not one you're likely to find around here.'

'I'll look around for you,' promised Carrick. Then he said goodbye and left.

Dr James Kennedy, so fond of talking about whisky, so affably confident in his role as the astute village doctor, had just fallen into a trap of his own making.

There were Orcadian whiskies, including the great Highland Park. But Bladnoch wasn't one of them.

Bladnoch was one of those strange exceptions – a Lowland whisky, distilled in the far south of Scotland, far away from the magic mists of the Scottish Highlands. Carrick hadn't named it as any kind of trick, just as a name which stuck in his mind because there was a River Bladnoch, where the distillery was located, a river that ran down from the Carrick hills of South Ayrshire.

He had chosen it because it was a superb malt. As a choice, it had worked in the most unexpected way.

Nobody like Dr James Kennedy could have made that kind of mistake in quite that kind of way.

Dr James Kennedy, who had a secret radio and some interesting friends.

How much of a key was the plump, tweedy medical man to the truth about the various kinds of hell that were being distilled around Port Torquil?

5

'You can't just condemn a man out of hand because he pretends to be a whisky expert – not even in the islands.' John Kennan's voice emerged with a metallic calm from *Tern*'s scrambler radio. The Fleet Support deskman back those miles away in Edinburgh paused, there was the brief hum of a carrier wave, then he added dryly, 'But when the same poser has a navy-strength transmitter parked in his spare bedroom, then I'm not happy. Sod's law – things will get worse. Be ready.'

'I'll try.' Webb Carrick grimaced at the mouthpiece of the radio handset he was holding. He was in *Tern*'s command chair, and that felt good. The patrol launch had crept two and more miles out to sea from Port Torquil and was now gathering speed. The thick rubber deck matting vibrated under his feet as the mid diesel joined in song with her two other sisters – that felt good. 'We may have an edge on them. I'm making a run out to Lannair.'

'You're what?' The radio voice lost its calm and almost yelped. Then Kennan tried again. 'Confirm that.'

'We're heading for Lannair.'

'Dear God,' said Kennan feebly. 'There are times when you and that fool Walker on *Puffin* could make a good double act. What about your cover on *Dirk*?'

'So I'm a sailor who finds a friendly bed ashore,' said Carrick dryly. He winked across the bridge area at Clapper Bell, who was in the helmsman's chair. 'Or I found a poker game – I can do the round trip and be aboard *Dirk* again before dawn.'

Clapper Bell grinned, nursing *Tern*'s slim, quivering steering wheel while he took another routine glance along the red glow of the instrument panel in front of them.

Behind them, Second Officer Andy Grey sat as if someone had welded him to the green of the radar screen. They were running without navigation lights, they were breaking most of the rules in the Fishery Protection book.

Not the first time.

'Damn you, Carrick! Lannair is exactly where you were ordered not to go – ' Kennan's voice became a resigned, static-laced growl, then he gave up ' – all right, try this your way. But if it goes wrong, if we lose the little we've got – '

'My neck,' accepted Carrick. *Tern* was still gathering pace, the three diesels yammering, her triple screws carving a broad white wake astern, spray patterning the bridge windows. It was the kind of night he needed, with cloud and little moon, with broken seas that were rough enough to give cover, yet still easy enough to cope with. Over to starboard, he noticed a sudden boil of phosphorescence in the dark, heaving water. A great shoal of mackerel were fleeing from the strange menace rushing their way. He shifted his grip on the handset and asked, 'What are the police saying now?'

'Not a lot, but some of it matters.' Kennan had listened to Carrick's report without interruption, now it was his turn. 'The post mortem on Cormack confirms drowning in seawater, with a thirty per cent elevation in blood chloride content. No possible doubt.'

Fresh-water drownings had blood chloride readings down by fifty per cent, seawater drownings went the other way. It was standard, Carrick knew, with water entering the lungs passing to the left side of the heart.

'There's more.' Kennan's voice crackled on. 'Some plankton identified in air passages and stomach, naturally. He'd taken a very small amount of drink – beer. They found two small ante-mortem bruises to the head. That's medic-speak for the poor devil having had one, maybe two beers at most, having been clubbed down when he left to go back to his van, then being heaved into the harbour to drown. Forget the people who thought they heard shouts from the water, unless someone else was shouting for him.' There was a moment's pause, then the radio crackled again. 'The police also say that Cormack's van was a definite torch job.'

'No witnesses?' cut in Carrick.

'No witnesses to anything and they don't expect to improve on that. They're probably right. At least they've agreed a deal with us about keeping their official mouths shut for a spell.'

'Do we tell Cormack's wife?' asked Carrick.

'Later. Let the poor damned woman get used to being a widow first,' came Kennan's rasp of a reply. 'You've seen the signals sent to you earlier?'

'Yes.' There were three of them, waiting when he'd come aboard *Tern* as she lay off-shore south of Port Torquil, after he'd again been collected by Clapper Bell and the same little inflatable. 'Your people have been busy.'

'My people have been calling in favours,' replied Kennan. His voice sounded sour, but pleased. 'Not everybody is happy – our chief political master is going around with a face like a robber's dog because we won't tell him what's happening. Not that I bloody well know, anyway!' There was a noise that could have been something tapping the Fleet Support man's microphone, or a grim chuckle. 'Maybe I'll tell him about Walker trying to sink another fishing boat, give him something else to worry about while we do more work.'

'I'll radio in as soon as we've checked Lannair,' promised Carrick.

'Not to me,' declared Kennan, his voice briefly a wavering echo, then steadying again. 'I'm going home to my wife and my bed, Carrick. I'll hear soon enough, one way or another. Go in carefully – if you need them, there are two big sisters ready to help. But they'd need time to get to you. Understood?'

'Understood,' said Carrick. 'Out.'

'Out,' agreed Kennan, there was a click, and the radio sank back to a low hiss.

Carrick put down his handset, drew a deep breath, and looked at the night ahead. Two big sisters meant two of the large Fishery Protection cruisers, each the size of a small destroyer. If they were loafing around somewhere not too far distant then it was just one more pointer to the way in which Department were determined to track down the bombers who had almost sunk *Puffin*.

Lannair might help – had to help, one way or another.

He signalled Andy Grey to take over, levered his way out of the padded command chair and made his way aft to the chartroom space while the patrol launch thudded and bounced her way on through the swell. *Tern* had reached the optimum speed which brought her bow down again into the flat, planing ride which made her class of patrol launch so distinctive. He switched on the chartroom's tiny light in its flexible tube, sat on the bolted-down navigation stool and spread out the message forms that had been waiting for him.

First was *Tern*'s own report for the previous night, after he'd gone ashore again. They had heard the roar of the raider boat's engines, and Andy Grey had even managed to get a brief speck of a radar sighting. Where it had come from, they couldn't say. It had been heading north-west when the thin trace faded from the radar tube.

Tern had spent most of the rest of the night prowling off Port Torquil. If the raider boat had come back, it hadn't been seen and hadn't been heard. What she had spotted were some unusual small-ship movements south of Port Torquil, heading in at around one a.m. towards the bay where Torquil House was located. Three apparent trawlers had come in, nearly together. One had left almost immediately, heading round to Port Torquil. Another had left about an hour later, and the third had still been lying somewhere in the bay when dawn began to threaten and the patrol launch had been forced to sneak off again to her day-time hiding place.

'Skipper.' Gogi MacDonnell appeared, doing one of his balancing acts, bringing a mug of tea and a thick, hot, bacon sandwich which still dripped grease and tomato sauce. He produced a scrap of kitchen paper from his hip pocket as a tablecloth. 'Something to keep you going.'

'Gogi – ' Carrick stopped the ex-fisherman as he turned to go ' – you know about last night's radar sightings?'

MacDonnell nodded, his face impassive. 'I saw them, skipper.'

'And?'

'That rock at Torquil's Shield is like the stuff out at Lannair,' said MacDonnell carefully. 'Does sick things to a magnetic compass, and produces ghosting, some blind spots on radar.' He used a forefinger to scratch the bald head under his tight-fitting wool cap, hesitated, then nodded for'ard to where Andy Grey sat with his back to them. 'The boy did well, skipper – the way things were. But – uh – '

'Don't tell him you said it.' Carrick nodded. 'Anything else, Gogi?'

'The boats had local skippers – or skippers who knew this patch of coast like the backs of their hands,' said MacDonnell simply. 'They came in at a lick, they left the same way again.' Just outside the tiny pool of light thrown by the flexible tube, his gaunt face was a shadowed outline. 'Local, or they'd had a lot of practice.'

Carrick let him go, gulped some of the scalding coffee, bit into the bacon sandwich, and wiped the grease from his hands with a waste rag before he turned to the radio messages. They had come in on *Tern*'s radio-linked telex, a burst of compressed signal which the patrol launch's electronics then sorted out.

There were three. The top sheet answered his plea to Kennan for more details about the strange, anonymous Mayday message after *Pippin* was bombed.

The Mayday, picked up by Oban coastguard thirty minutes after the satchel charge had blasted the patrol launch, had been brief, immediately repeated once, and then there had been no further call. The signal had been low to medium strength, had come in on the always

133

monitored fishing distress frequency, and there had been no reply to return calls from the coastguard radio operator. Mayday calls were taped. The voice didn't have a West Highland accent, seemed agitated, and the coastguards' best guess was that some badly frightened yachtsman had made the call. The location given had been accurate, and a MacBrayne passenger ferry on an overnight from Stornoway and the Outer Isles had been the nearest ship to respond.

The MacBrayne ferry had stood by the stricken *Puffin*, which took cool nerve anywhere around Lannair's rocks. A Royal Navy rescue helicopter had brought in medical help and lifted the worst of the injured off to hospital at about the same time as the Fishery Protection cruiser *Barracuda* had hammered out of the night after racing down from off Hawes Bank fishing grounds, on the west side of Coll.

Pippin had been patched, towed like a hulk to Oban, then later towed down to the Firth of Clyde for repairs. The radio Mayday had been too brief for any directional bearing to be accurately established. From start to finish of the rescue operation, Port Torquil had played no part. No help had been asked – or offered.

Carrick took another bite of bacon sandwich, chewed, and washed it down with a mouthful of MacDonnell's tar-like notion of tea. He went for'ard, drew a nod from Andy Grey which meant all was well, then completed what amounted to a regular ritual by clattering down the narrow companionway ladder that led into the cramped, roaring heat that was *Tern*'s engineroom.

'Skipper.' Sam Pilsudski saw him and gave a bellow and a gold-toothed grin. The engineer was wearing protective earmuffs, but lifted one clear of his head. 'You taking us to where we'll have some action for a change?'

'Maybe,' yelled Carrick. He pointed at the three pounding diesels. 'Any problems?'

'We're fine,' declared the hairy, white-overalled figure

134

expansively. 'How you liking my sports jacket? Looking after it okay?'

Carrick gave him a thumbs-up and clambered back up the ladder. A happy Sam Pilsudski was best left alone with his three air-gobbling children.

Back in the chartspace area, he picked up the other telex messages that had been waiting. He'd read them before, this time he studied them, word by word.

There was a negative. There had been no reported out-of-pattern foreign shipping or fishing movements in the Lannair-Passage of Tiree sector any time within a week before *Pippin*'s bombing and a week after.

There was a positive. Some startling tonnages of wild, fresh, sea-caught salmon had recently been finding their way on to European markets, making top prices. The selling was layered, no one even seemed to know where the fish were being landed. But some people somewhere were making a great deal of money.

Then came two puzzles, telex slips he placed side by side under the quivering little flexible chartlight.

First came Michael Alder. He was thirty-three years of age, English, and a lawyer. He had lived in the United States for some years, he had an ex-wife living in Boston, and for some three years he had based himself in London where he served a minor stable of European and North American commercial clients with United Kingdom interests.

His office was a rented room and a half share of a secretary with a small merchant-banking law firm located in the up-market London Dockland merchant redevelopment area, a yuppie strip where the address was exclusive, where costs were high, and where staff could come to work by waterbus along the Thames. His landlords knew little about him, except that he always paid his rent in advance. They didn't see him very often. His half-share secretary only knew she sometimes had to type a letter or take a telephone message.

Sometimes there would be mail to be sent on to Port

Torquil. Michael Alder had first begun that arrangement about a year earlier at the same time as he'd mentioned he had found a distant elderly relative. It was about six months since she had handled some letters which said the old man needed nursing-home care.

The half-share secretary had had no idea she was being interviewed – John Kenna's police contacts were the kind who carried briefcases in place of batons.

But there was a final sentence in the telex, a direct quote from the anonymous briefcase cop.

'Subject Alder has no criminal record. But he has been noted twice as a name on the fringe of separate marine insurance frauds. No involvement was proved, but he remains potentially interesting.'

Dr James Kennedy had a separate telex page. In some ways, the details were more positive, in other ways they were less. Basic fact was that he was 'Scottish by birth, an undistinguished medical graduate of Edinburgh University'.

His first post had been three years in the casualty department of a London hospital. He had left that for an oil company job in the Middle East, then had moved on again after eighteen months. Next he had been two years with the medical sales section of a Swiss pharmaceutical company before he moved on again.

Then James Kennedy had vanished from the known medical scene for more than five years. When he had surfaced again, it was back in Scotland with vague descriptions of 'work with medical agencies in the Lebanon and Spain'.

It was less than a year since he had arrived in Port Torquil, saying he wanted to put down roots. Younger medical practitioners were scarce around the islands, and there had been a general welcome when he set up practice in the fishing village. He was liked, he was respected, he worked hard.

But James Kennedy had appeared in Port Torquil at approximately the same time as Michael Alder had arrived. James Kennedy who had a radio hidden in an upstairs bedroom and lied about whiskies.

There was one thing more.

Old John Hill, the distant relative discovered by Michael Alder then eventually shipped out to a private nursing home on the mainland, 'is still listed on National Health Service central computer records as being one of Dr James Kennedy's patients in Port Torquil'.

Six months on – that could happen. But also six months on, Social Security's central pensions computer still continued to list the old man as living in Port Torquil, where his pension was being paid to a duly authorized agent and relative, Mr Michael Alder. The authorization, on the grounds of John Hill's frailty and ill health, had been countersigned by the old man's general practitioner – James Kennedy.

There were other fragments, scooped together by the industrious John Kennan, some without being asked. Harry Gold, boatyard owner, had served an eighteen-month term for trading in stolen boats. Even the crew of the *Dirk* hadn't escaped scrutiny. Tom Barratt, the bean-pole electronics technician, had a medal for bravery that went back to the Falklands. The plump, plain Martha Edwards had twice been fined, once been jailed as an Animal Rights activist . . .

He swept the telex messages aside. The two that mattered most, the two about Alder and Kennedy, posed their own stark, bleak, questions. Maybe some of the others mattered too.

Maybe that depended on what might be waiting ahead.

Half an hour later, Lannair Island was a growing bulk on *Tern*'s radar screen. In another twenty minutes, the patrol launch had come back to half speed using the outer diesels. What had been an air-gobbling roar had become a purr, the tell-tale white of her wash had vanished.

If Lannair had any fresh visitors, *Tern* had become a mere shadow of an outline in a grey, broken sea under a dark night sky. Andy Grey had the radar watch, Gogi MacDonnell had taken over the helm, and Sam Pilsudski had emerged like a maritime mole to sniff the air and help on deck.

'No good, skipper,' said Andy Grey for the third time in as many minutes. 'Ghosting – a lot of ghosting. The same we get around Torquil's Shield.' He glanced uneasily towards Gogi MacDonnell. 'Same with the compass.'

'Gogi?' asked Carrick.

'Aye, fine, skipper,' said MacDonnell placidly.

'Jesus,' said Sam Pilsudski piously. 'He's happy!' The engineer officer stared out at the night, at the black rise of island, and at the foaming patches of sea ahead. 'You happy, Clapper?'

'No,' said Clapper Bell solemnly, shaking his head.

Andy Grey looked round, staring at them, then swore when he saw their grins under the soft red night-vision lighting of the bridge.

'Stop clowning,' ordered Carrick with a faint irritation. Even in the darkness he could now pick up individual outlines of rock along Lannair's shore. 'Gogi, bring her down – slow ahead both.'

'Slow ahead both,' repeated MacDonnell. He eased back on both outer throttles, and immediately *Tern* slowed to a whispering crawl.

Carrick was satisfied. They were closing on the high east cliff of the island. If Lannair was half a mile long, then the patrol launch was less than that distance out. He could even see the black beginning of the downward slope to the low rocks of the western shore. The west –

'Skipper!' Clapper Bell spoke urgently, pointing. 'On the slope. A light!'

Andy Grey opened his mouth to protest at an old joke worn thin. Then he saw the way Bell was staring towards the island and changed his mind.

'Skipper?' This time, Bell made it a question.

'Got it,' confirmed Carrick. 'Mark it.'

While *Tern* muttered on at the same slow, rolling pace,

occasional spray pattering along her length, the same brief will-o'-the-wisp light danced for a few moments more on Lannair in the way a carelessly used torch might shine. Then it had gone. By then, Carrick had the bridge glasses ready. The light suddenly showed again, more a reflection this time, further along the slope. Climbing.

It vanished again. This time the light didn't reappear.

'We're in business,' murmured Sam Pilsudski. He hauled one of his thin cheroots out of his top overall pocket, stuck it in his mouth, leaving it dangling unlit, and grinned. 'Front door or back door, Webb?'

It had to be back door. With any luck, *Tern* was still invisible in the night, and someone was on Lannair. Carrick knew their immediate task was to find out why.

A hogback outcrop of islet was visible to starboard. It was big enough to give cover, safe enough for *Tern* to loiter behind.

Five minutes later, the patrol launch was snug in the shadow of the hogback islet, lying maybe two lengths off the foaming sea around its base. By then, Andy Grey had his orders, Carrick and Clapper Bell were in the scuba compartment changing into their black neoprene rubber wet-suits, and the will-o'-the-wisp light still hadn't been seen again.

Clapper Bell had two breathing sets neatly laid out. As Carrick and the big Glasgow-Irishman fastened final zips, pulled on harness, and went into a routine check of each other's breathing apparatus, Andy Grey joined them from the bridge.

'Ready, skipper?' His thin face was slightly strained.

'Ready,' agreed Carrick. 'Just remember one thing, Andy. If we flush any boat out from Lannair, don't go mad. Track it on radar. Nothing more.'

'Except come back for us,' suggested Clapper Bell easily.

They went out on deck. Together the two black-clad figures each in turn spat into his face-mask glass then rinsed the mask in the pitching sea alongside – still the

139

best way to keep the glass from misting underwater – then exchanged a final glance.

'Go,' said Carrick.

Biting on their mouthpieces, pulling down their face masks, they splashed down into the water, surfaced again, then immediately duck-dived under. The night chill of the sea hit for a moment, then receded.

The sea was black as ink, two plumes of bubbles were rising from the scuba sets, air-regulator valves were clicking in a total, disciplined rhythm. They didn't have to go deep. Using his wrist compass, checking his depth gauge, conscious of Clapper Bell swimming almost within touching distance, Carrick settled into a steady, kicking crawl beat with only the occasional snatch of a current or eddy to divert his attention until they hit a brief band of tall, thick kelp weed. The kelp clawed at their suits and scuba gear, but was only a fragile barrier.

Then they were through, their feet were touching seabed shingle and in another moment they were wading ashore on Lannair.

Where they had landed, the ground was a wilderness mix of flat slabs of rock and thick banks of small, smooth pebbles. They could hear the wind – and with it, maybe something else, something coming from the other side of the island. Bell mimed a question, Carrick shook his head in reply, and they spent a couple of minutes stripping off their aqualung harnesses then leaving the aqualungs, their fins and other equipment in the shadow of one slab of rock.

The faint, distant noise was still there. It was like the low moan and whine of a small ship's electrical generator. For another moment, they crouched and took their bearings. To their left, the slope rose steadily and smoothly to the crest of rock. But ahead, beyond the shore rock, there was only a moderate hillock rise separating them from whatever was whining on the other side.

'Let's do it,' said Carrick softly, and started to move.

Seawater was still coming in small damping trickles from his wet-suit as he began to rise.

'No,' hissed Clapper Bell, grabbing his wrist and hauling him back down.

A man was walking along the crest of the hillock, relaxed enough to be whistling under his breath, in no hurry. He had a hand-torch, and when he shone it briefly to be sure of his route then there was enough reflected glow from the little pool of light to show that he was wearing an old peaked cap and overalls and that he had a rifle slung over one shoulder.

The torchlight swung again as the man used two slabs of rock like stepping stones. Clapper Bell muttered a grunt, nudging Carrick. Carrick nodded, watching the man continue to follow a path he seemed to know until he vanished over the hillock.

'He's one o' the pair from the harbour last night,' said Bell hoarsely. 'Remember him?'

Tight-lipped, Carrick nodded. He had plenty of reason to remember Joe and Petey. The man had been Joe, who had stopped enjoying his evening when Carrick had hit him in the middle with that swinging spar of quayside wood.

It was something else he'd miscalculated, and Clapper Bell had made the same mistake at the time. The harbour attack had been planned, not the casual whim of two wandering drunks. The two had been sent off on a deliberate task, probably told to rough up the newly arrived stranger a little so that he was less likely to keep sticking his nose in where it wasn't wanted.

But now one of them was here. Carrick glanced back to where they'd first spotted him coming. That way led down from the top of Lannair's east-facing sea-cliff. Any kind of path in that direction gave a new significance to the moving light they'd seen from *Tern*. There must be some kind of trip-wire style lookout post up there at the top of the cliff.

'How about now?' muttered Clapper Bell, still crouched

low beside him. In his black rubber wet-suit, the Glasgow-Irishman looked like a large, damp seal.

'This time.' An edge of moonlight had broken through the clouds, and that helped. 'But we stay clear of trouble.'

Clapper Bell grinned, then they got to their feet. Walking under the faint, cloud-filtered moonlight, they crossed through ankle-length grass and stunted heather and headed in the same direction the fisherman with the rifle had taken. Almost immediately, they found they were on a faint but traceable path of sorts and they could go faster. Once Bell stumbled on a heather root and swore as he almost fell. Something that was either a rabbit or an island rat scurried away from them, a bare ripple in the coarse grass.

Then something that was small and fast and had wings swooped in a dive, found its prey, they heard a short death-scream, and an owl was flapping up again clutching its prey.

Bell still cursing softly, they went more carefully. The little sealed torches among the items in their wet-suit pouches were the last things either wanted to risk using.

All the time that low, moaning whine kept on and seemed to become gradually louder.

Then, seconds later, the moonlight still gradually strengthening, they topped the hillock ridge. They were looking straight down the slope towards the island's other shore – and as Carrick heard Bell's surprised grunt he felt the same momentary disbelief.

A tombstone-shaped slab of rock lay a few short strides in front of them. They reached it, hugged the cover, and stared down again.

There were the little ruined cottages Carrick had seen as the research boat sailed past the island. There were the flat slabs of shore rock where the seals had lulled him into thinking Lannair was deserted. But figures were moving beside the cottages, figures who were working hard and using shaded lights. Lower down, at the water's edge, two dinghies lay beached. Least expected sight of

142

all, two fishing trawlers lay anchored side by side a short stone's throw off shore.

He knew one of them by her silhouette and by the white flash like a painted cockade which marked her dark funnel. The Stewart trawler *Stargirl* was out again. The second, anonymous trawler was about the same size and tonnage.

'Were we invited to this party, boss?' asked Clapper Bell with a hoarse sarcasm. The big, rugged-faced man sat back on his heels and sucked his teeth hard. 'What goes on? If this is the gang who bombed *Pippin* – '

'If they are, we don't amble down and announce they're under arrest.' Carrick laid a hand palm down against the cold night rock beside them. The harsh, hard stone with that strange effect on both radar and compass needles had got them into this. 'The trawler with the white flash is *Stargirl*. She's a Stewart boat.' He saw Clapper Bell's eyes narrow at that, then he looked down again. Two long, bulky bundles were being dragged from one of the cottages. Despite their size, the bundles seemed reasonably easy to handle – and Carrick had a good idea what they were. He drew breath. 'You take a left curve, I'll do the other side. We meet down there or behind this rock again. Don't clump about!'

'When other people play wi' bombs, I'm careful,' promised Clapper Bell. 'Damned careful, skipper.'

Tern's bo'sun went crawling off. Within seconds, his black rubber wet-suit had blended into the night and he had vanished.

It was Carrick's turn, and he suddenly felt very much alone. Easing out from the shelter of the rock, he began to work a cautious, crouching way down the slope while the voices of the men below blended with the low, faulty wail of one of the trawler generators. Only an occasional pebble rattled under his feet, and he fetched up in new shelter – the remains of a low dry-stone wall in what might have once been an animal pen. It was close to the ruined cottage where the men from the trawlers were working. The cottage still had a fragment of roof, and was the same ruin with the flapping rag of makeshift curtain which had first caught his eye from the *Dirk*.

He arrived exactly as three men came out through the doorway gap carrying another of the bundles. They handled it with the same ease he'd noticed when the others were moved. It was a net – and with that lack of weight it could only be one kind, a big monofilament mesh.

One of the drowning nets, a salmon killer.

The fishermen marched down towards the shore and the bundle was dumped aboard one of the dinghies. One man gave a grunt of laugh, another paused to light a cigarette.

Suddenly, they didn't matter. Two other men, one very short and the other very tall, both thick-set, were emerging from the cottage. The tall man carried a hand lamp and was talking in a low, intent voice. The short man beside him visibly stiffened and Carrick heard a snarl of a reply. It seemed to sting. The hand lamp was raised angrily. The beam played directly into the face of Sam Lawson then Port Torquil's scar-faced chandler pushed it away.

The tall man was the flabby-faced, copper-haired Charlie Stewart.

They stood for a moment, the low-voiced argument continuing, then it ended abruptly as the three men returned from the shore. Lawson and Stewart stood where they were until another figure joined them from another of the ruins. The fisherman with the peaked cap and shoulder-slung rifle spoke to Stewart, raised an arm in a farewell to them both, and began striding back along the path that led to the east sea-cliff.

By then, Stewart and Lawson seemed to have patched their quarrel. In another few minutes they were helping as another bundle of nets was brought out.

As it emerged, as it was carried down like the others, yet another figure emerged from the cottage. He was thin and Carrick couldn't see his face. But he could hear the man's shrill, piping voice. Harry Gold, the repair-yard owner, was making a late, not totally unexpected entrance.

The group of men went down towards the shore again. One of the dinghies was launched and ferried a load of nets out past Stewart's *Stargirl* and came in alongside the other trawler. Two men on her deck swung out a boom, and the nets began going aboard.

Carrick made one try at getting nearer and was almost caught as Lawson and Charlie Stewart made an unexpected return. He pressed hard back into the shadow of a tumbledown corner of wall, turning his face away, relying on the black of the wet-suit, while the ill-matched pair went past. They disappeared into the same cottage and were there only briefly. There was a grating of stone, then they re-emerged. They walked together back to the shore, the atmosphere of antagonism between them apparently as strong as ever.

People were tidying up.

The last of the nets were ferried out, the last of the fishermen departed from the shore. Stewart and Lawson had already gone back aboard their separate trawlers. Their diesels began thumping, there was a clatter of winches as their anchors were raised, then both began heading out. As soon as they were well clear of Lannair, both darkened trawlers suddenly switched on their fishing lights. Why not, when as far as they were concerned the only Fishery Protection vessel operating anywhere on the west side of Mull was lying in harbour at Port Torquil, nursing the nautical equivalent of a bloodied nose?

Another minute passed, then he heard a soft whistle from the shadows and Clapper Bell came over to join him.

'Salmon nets,' said Bell briefly and hoarsely. 'I got near enough to be sure, skipper. What about people – know any of them?'

145

Carrick told him, and the big Glasgow-Irishman gave a speculative grunt.

'Hug and make friends style?' He was sardonic. 'But it figures. Like that other trawler, the one you didn't know, is named *Coral* – and that's one of the Grant boats, according to Gogi MacDonnell.' He scowled around at the darkness. 'Now what? Grants or Stewarts, or whoever the hell they are, they left a little friend behind.'

'And little friend may also have a friend. We'll have to find out,' said Carrick quietly. 'Once I check on something, Clapper.'

He led the way into the ruined cottage. It had probably been searched before, in the hunt that scorched through the islands after the *Pippin* bombing. But this time was different – he had a good idea where to look. While a puzzled Clapper Bell watched, he took the powerful little pen-torch from its wet-suit pouch, shielded the beam with one hand, and used it to check around the cottage's uneven, stone-slabbed old floor.

The slab that mattered was in front of where the cottage's fireplace had been. It was big, it was square, it had gaps along the edges where others had dirt, and one of the gaps was big enough to let a man's hand feel down and grip. Carrick stepped to one side, used the hand-hold, and heaved. The slab grated and shifted, he put more muscle behind the lift, and then suddenly the whole slab was swinging up.

'Hell!' Startled, Clapper Bell came over and helped hold the slab on its edge while Carrick shone the penlight down into the blackness of the hole.

They had found themselves the original cellar of the cottage, with much of the walls and floor hacked out of solid rock and the rest built with boulders and dirt. It was dank, it was cold – it was empty, apart from a mocking scrap of torn net which clung to one projection of rock.

Carrick sat back on his heels and sighed. When the handful of cottages on Lannair had sheltered the few

146

islanders who managed some kind of a precarious living from it, a cellar would probably have been a must as a protection for stores – maybe people too – during the worst of the winter storms. How many of the ruined cottages still had a useable cellar was almost incidental. To know about them, to know about this one, was more likely to mean local knowledge than luck.

'Everything gone,' said Bell gloomily. 'Well, we know who took them.'

'And maybe we'll know where.' That depended on Andy Grey, and on *Tern*'s radar. Carrick could imagine the consternation aboard the patrol launch when the two trawlers cleared the magnetic, porridge-like jumble of Lannair and popped up like rabbits on the radar screen. Carrick began to ease the stone slab back into its grooves. They had brought a personal radio ashore with them, in a plastic bag, but it was stowed with the spare scuba gear down at the other beach. And by then –

'Skipper,' said Clapper Bell very slowly, his manner almost casual. 'You were right about something else.' His eyes held their own steady warning. 'Behind you – little friend, with a big gun. I – uh – I think he'd appreciate it if you don't rush anything.'

Carrick heard a nervous snicker of a laugh behind him. Slowly, he lowered the stone slab the last couple of inches and let it grate down, released it, then looked round. The taller of the two men who had jumped him back at Port Torquil was standing just inside the cottage's doorway gap. He was slight-faced, he was wearing a duffel coat, he had a wool skull-cap like the kind Gogi MacDonnell wore, and the double-barrelled shotgun he was holding shifted from Carrick to Bell then back again to Carrick.

'Up on your feet,' said the man, his voice tense and his manner nervous. 'But like the big fellow says, pal. Slow.'

Carrick shrugged a little and obeyed.

'I know you, pal.' The shotgun barrel twitched a little. 'Let's have that torch on your face – then on his. Now.'

Slowly, Carrick obeyed again. He heard the man's sharp intake of breath.

'Carrick – '

'Hello, Pete,' said Carrick mildly. 'It looks like I should have been more positive last time.'

'No chance now, eh?' The tall fisherman forced a mocking grin then nodded at Clapper Bell, who hadn't spoken, hadn't moved. 'Him?'

'Just someone who came with me.' Carrick tried not to watch the twin barrels of the shotgun. They could hypnotize. At such close range, inside the tumbledown walls of the ruin, they represented certain, vicious death.

'Hard luck, big fellow,' said Pete sardonically. He gave that nervous, snickering giggle again. 'Almost funny, right?'

'I'm laughing my bloody head off,' agreed Bell solemnly. 'Where's your friend Joe?'

'He's why I came down,' said the fisherman, a man still beginning to realize what he'd managed to do. He shifted a little in the doorway, and a haversack slung over his back bumped one of the stone pillars. 'Left our fresh food and drink for the night down here, didn't he?' He moistened his lips. 'Frog suits – you're still off a boat. Parked somewhere near, is she?'

'Not too far,' agreed Carrick woodenly.

'Fishery Protection, right? Joe reckoned he'd seen you somewhere, some time.' The man eased himself back towards the night, carefully. 'All right, let's go. Some people are going to love hearing about this.' The shotgun summoned them with another jerk. There was another snicker. 'Walked into the wrong scene this time, didn't you?'

They came out. Hands clasped behind their heads, they were made to walk side by side away from the beach and up the sloping way that led to the ridge, then from there on towards the east sea-cliff. The fisherman behind them grunted a lot as he came close behind. Twice, Carrick sensed Clapper Bell stiffen, ready to take a chance. Each

148

time he gave a slight headshake, telling the Glasgow-Irishman to wait.

There was more wind as they reached the top of the sea-cliff slope. There was the sound of waves crashing somewhere in the dark down below. Another of those rivers of moonlight between cloud was reflected in a glint of sea further out.

'Joe!' yelled their guard. 'See what I found, man!'

Only yards in front of them, something shapeless stirred. A canvas cover over a narrow, trench-like hole was reluctantly opened. There was a glow of light behind the other fisherman as he appeared. Still on his knees, he stared open-mouthed, not totally certain of anything.

'Pete, what the hell?' He goggled.

'Found them,' began the tall man eagerly. 'It's Carrick. They've a boat an' – '

For just a second, his attention was on his companion. It was enough. Webb Carrick threw his whole weight sideways and back, falling towards the shotgun barrel, grabbing it with both hands, using his weight to force the weapon down. At the same moment both barrels fired, so close to his head that he was deafened.

But he had brought the man down. He saw the other fisherman slithering back into the shelter and Clapper Bell diving in pursuit. His own opponent was trying to pull the shotgun free, wrenching and cursing. They rolled on the pebbled grass, then the fisherman bodily pinned him down, abandoned the shotgun and grabbed Carrick's throat in a two-handed stranglehold.

'Damn you!' The man's eyes were wild and his spittle hit Carrick's face. In the background, Carrick saw Clapper Bell and the other man struggling, still on their feet. That pressure on his throat was tightening, the sky was starting to swim –

He did it the way he'd been taught. Grab your opponent's left elbow with both hands, get your right foot on the ground, raise your right knee up underneath your opponent's body. He gave a double-handed shove on the

149

man's elbow, he slammed up with his knee into the man's body.

Leverage, surprise. Overbalanced, yelping, the tall figure toppled and fell sideways. Losing his grip on Carrick's throat, he rolled clear. Then the man had scrambled to his feet. First, a heavy boot crashed into Carrick's side, knocking the wind from him. Then, through a daze, Carrick saw that his opponent had recovered the shotgun, was gripping it by the barrels, was raising it two-handed as a club –

Clapper Bell was a large man, yet large men can move fast when required. Wherever he appeared from, suddenly he was there. A bulky, avenging surge in that black wet-suit, he dived in under the downward flail of the shotgun. His shoulder took the tall fisherman hard on the chest, knocking him back. Desperately, the man retreated, starting to swing the shotgun again – then that was forgotten, because he was on the edge of the sea-cliff, losing his balance, arms starting to claw at the air, a scream half-forming. He had gone. The shotgun lay on the cliff edge, there had been the start of a thin wail. There might have been a faint thud somewhere below. But he had gone.

'Jesus,' said Clapper Bell softly, and made it no profanity. He came back to Carrick. 'Skipper?'

'I'm fine.' Still winded, Carrick got up. They were close together. He saw the long slice of a cut high on the chest of Clapper's wet-suit. He touched the cut and felt a warm stickiness on his hand. 'You're hurt.'

'Not a lot.' Bell scowled. 'An' it was my own damned fool fault.'

Carrick looked around in the night. Nothing else moved along the edge of the sea-cliff. The canvas flap of the hide was still thrown back. The inside was lit by a battery lamp. He could see two sleeping bags, some scattered personal gear, a small, modern telescope and, sheltered at the back, cocooned in plastic, a man-portable radio transmitter about the size of a large shoebox.

150

Then two other things caught his eye – a discarded rifle and, lying beside it, a peaked cap.

'That one tried to run,' said Clapper Bell. He looked directly at Carrick, his rugged face totally empty of anything. 'He ran the wrong way.' His mouth closed briefly. 'Sorry, skipper.'

'He ran the wrong way.' Carrick gave a slow, accepting nod. 'Where did he go over?'

Bell pointed. Silently, Carrick picked up the peaked cap, went to the cliff edge, and threw the cap over. The moon was back again. Far down, maybe two hundred feet below, he could make out a sack-like shape stuck on an outcrop of rock with the white of breaking waves not far below.

Then he saw the second man. He had died impaled on a spur of rock about halfway down. Some disturbed gulls were still hovering around the spur.

'So.' From the high sea-cliff, looking out across the chopping sea of the Passage of Tiree, they could see for miles. But the lights of the two trawlers had gone. He turned to Clapper Bell, who hadn't moved, who still hadn't spoken again. 'We leave their friends to find them. When their friends look for the story, maybe we can help them find it.'

Something flickered deep in Clapper Bell's eyes. He shaped a slight twitch of a grin, and nodded.

It took time, and they were careful.

First, there was Clapper Bell's wound to be tended. Under the scuba top, it proved to be a long but shallow cut about a hand's-breadth long. The flow of blood had almost stopped, and Bell padded it with some cliff-top grass held in place by two strips of white electrical tape he produced from one of his inevitable suit-pouch plastic bags.

They policed the whole cliff-top area by torchlight. They found spare shells for the rifle and shotgun in a cardboard box. They reloaded the shotgun, cleaned grit from it and from the rifle, and placed them neatly side by side between the sleeping bags in the hide. Carrick took the telescope from the hide to the edge of the cliff. Very carefully, he climbed down a few feet and jammed the telescope in a crack between two rocks, the way it might have fallen.

He climbed up to safety again, glad of Clapper Bell's massive bear-like paw dragging him back over the ledge.

'Well?' he asked Bell.

'I'd buy it.' Bell nodded. 'One o' them is making a routine scan around wi' the telescope, falls – an' the other tries to be a hero.' He frowned. 'Which was which?'

'They can toss for it,' said Carrick laconically.

He went back into the hide, where they were leaving the battery lamp still burning. He stared again at the radio transmitter.

It was ordinary enough. Even on the Lannair sea-cliff, it would have only a modest transmission range. It was tuned to the regular fishing-band frequency, where half the skippers used their own codes anyway – as obscure as Gaelic nicknames or prearranged trigger words. A brief signal among the many on the fishing band, and the lookouts could have reported any sighting that worried them.

There was nothing else; even when he used the tip of his diving knife to unscrew the backplate from the shoebox transmitter. This one told him even less than the transmitter he'd found in James Kennedy's upstairs bedroom.

He replaced the backplate. Everything else in the hide had already been checked and double-checked. Carrick went over to where Clapper Bell was patiently waiting. He nodded, and they started off, down the slope and towards the shore.

There was no urgent reason to go back to the ruined cottages. They trudged away from them, sweating and sticky in the rubber folds of the scuba suits, reached the edge of the sea on the other shore, and found where they'd hidden their breathing apparatus when they swam in. They rested.

'Skipper – ' said Clapper Bell suddenly.

Carrick had also heard it, a hardly discernible murmur. They stared out at the black outline of the hogback rock, and saw something moving in towards it from the sea. A shape they knew. Carrick used the pen-torch, gave three short blinks of light out towards it, and a light blinked back in the same sequence. It was *Tern*.

Five minutes later, brought off by Gogi MacDonnell in the patrol launch's Zodiac boat, they were back aboard. Clapper Bell went to help MacDonnell secure the Zodiac boat, and Carrick found himself faced with a very relieved Andy Grey.

'You went after them?' he asked Grey.

'Two blips, trawler-size, skipper.' Grey nodded. 'The way you wanted, doing a radar shadow job. Except – '

'You lost them?' Carrick read Grey's expression.

Grey nodded. 'West of the Sula Rocks. Sorry, Webb.' In the red glow of the bridge lights, his face was contrite. 'We had a total steering failure, hydraulics and manual – '

'Then he dived under on a line and unhitched us from a tangle of someone's old lost trawl warp,' said Sam Pilsudski, ambling out of the darkness. 'Not funny – not at night.'

'Not funny,' said Carrick wryly. He could imagine every frightening moment of it. 'The trawlers, Andy – what was their last heading?'

'Running straight-line for Port Torquil.' Grey was positive. 'I decided I might as well head back here.' His curiosity was too much. 'What happened with you, skipper? All we knew was that these blips popped up on the screen. They mattered?'

'They mattered.' Carrick wanted to change out of the scuba rubbers, wanted somewhere to think, wanted something to drink. 'We're operational?'

'Good as new,' confirmed Sam Pilsudski.

'Nice one, Andy.' Carrick saw Grey's relief. 'All right, head home. Half speed. I'll take ten minutes below.'

'Uh – something wrong with Clapper?' queried Pilsud-ski. 'He passed me heading for'ard. He didn't look too happy.'

'Ten minutes,' said Carrick again.

He looked across at the night bulk of Lannair and its sea-cliff, where two more men had died because of the strange secrets of the Noah Pipeline. His mind was numb. But that numbness would have to end, and quickly.

'Move,' he said shortly. He meant himself.

But Andy Grey jumped to obey.

Tern was under way again when Carrick reached his cabin. He peeled out of the sweat-sticky wet-suit, dumped it on the decking, then dressed once more in the clothes he'd worn when he'd gone ashore from the *Dirk*. Then, while the patrol launch bounced and banged through the swell, he hand-held his way through to the galley. There was the inevitable pot of coffee hot and waiting – except that this one, when he poured himself a mug, had been heavily laced with whisky.

Some of it slopped out of the mug as he carried it through to the wardroom. He jammed himself into a corner with a stub of pencil and a signal pad, wrote about what had happened on Lannair, then cut down almost by half on what he'd written. It was dryly factual, and nothing more. The two men who had died were allocated one paragraph. They had both 'received fatal accidental injuries' after falling during the struggle.

It wasn't much of an obituary. But it was enough for the moment.

He finished his coffee, left the empty mug shuddering on the wardroom table, and went through to the bridge. Clapper Bell was still for'ard, in the petty officers' quarters, with MacDonnell at the helm and Andy Grey sitting as proud as a king in the command chair. Carrick waved Grey down when he started to rise, took the stool at the chart table just behind his Second Officer, then made a radio call on the dedicated Fishery Protection frequency.

The moment Headquarters answered from their snug dry-land base in Edinburgh, Carrick switched on the scrambler. The way he had threatened, John Kennan had gone home. But the night-duty man at the Fleet Support desk was unemotionally efficient.

'Go, *Tern*,' he instructed. 'Taping.'

Grey and MacDonnell listening, *Tern*'s engines competing in the background, Carrick gave his report to the distant tapedeck. When he finished, the night-duty man came back on the air.

'Stand by, *Tern*.' The nightman went off the air for a full three minutes, then he was with them again, his voice as dispassionate as ever. 'Your message received and understood, *Tern*. Timed 0255. Out.'

Static roared in, and Carrick switched off. Andy Grey had twisted round in the command chair and was staring at him. He shrugged at Grey. It was the way he had expected. The waiting time had been enough for John Kennan or someone even higher up to be contacted at home. Fleet Support were maintaining their low-profile position. When some civil service offices opened for another day, then suitable noises would be made in suitable places.

'Log it, Andy,' he told Grey. 'Their time, 0255.'

'That's all we'll get?' Grey was indignant.

'For now.' Carrick said it almost absently. Time – he was staring at the softly lit digital clock set into the top of the chart table. 'Andy, what was the time when Clapper and I left for the shore?'

'Logged at 0100 hours, skipper. Maybe give or take a minute,' said Grey cautiously.

'Just a thought.' Carrick left it at that.

But he might have half of the answer to that pencilled 'DL 048' he had noticed on James Kennedy's radio. It didn't make sense as a radio frequency, he'd already discarded it as any kind of radio bearing. But suppose it was something much more simple. 'DL' might still be a mystery, but 048 might be Kennedy's shorthand for 48 minutes after midnight.

If it meant a fixed-time radio transmission, if that transmission somehow linked with the radio they'd found at the top of the Lannair sea-cliff, it explained why, a little later, the fisherman with the peaked cap had walked down to talk with the men working at the cottages – and had almost walked into Carrick and Bell.

The more he thought about it, the more likely it became. At sea level, close in under the magnetic anomalies of Lannair, the trawlers would find radio reception hopeless. They would have had to rely on the sea-cliff lookouts' set.

It wove one more little piece into the pattern. People were fitting, some of them unexpected people. Places were fitting. What it needed was still patience – and Webb Carrick knew that patience wasn't a particular asset in his make-up.

Not when so much danger and so much chance of death was still on the loose off the Passage of Tiree.

For the moment, they were into a waiting time. Carrick brought Andy Grey back to the chart table from the command chair, told his Second Officer a little more than he'd said in the signal to Fleet Support, and then went down the for'ard companionway ladder into the petty officers' accommodation.

Clapper Bell was there, sprawled out on his back on his bunk, wearing only a pair of undershorts, an opened can of beer clutched upright on his ginger-haired chest.

'It's a social call, Clapper.' He gestured Bell to relax as the Glasgow-Irishman started to rise. Then, sitting on the edge of Bell's bunk, he asked it bluntly. 'You've got a problem?'

'Yes.' The broad-shouldered bo'sun gave an unhappy grimace. 'Those two poor damned fool bandits back on Lannair.' His big, honest face grimaced. 'It was a rough way to die, skipper. They were out of their league.'

'Maybe.' Carrick waited while *Tern* bucked and gave a

156

massive groan through a heave of swell. 'That doesn't change the bottom line. It was them or us. True?'

'I suppose.' William Clapper Bell thought for a moment, then managed a small, resigned grin. 'I'll work through it.' He propped himself up on his elbow and took a swallow of beer. That made him brighten a little. 'Talk about something else, right? How about that little problem you've got, skipper – the famous Birthday Bottle for your old man. Got rid of it yet?'

'No chance,' said Carrick sadly. 'It's still in my cabin, wrapped. I've even got the damned card. Don't ask me how I get it to him.' Originally he'd been due a few days' leave and had even thought of hand delivery. Registered postal packages were another way, but any time the post office handled a package that went gurgle they seemed to drop it on something hard from a great height as part of their handling routine.

'Lie,' suggested Clapper Bell cheerfully. 'Say it must have got lost in the post.'

Carrick grinned but shook his head. It was an excuse worn thin by too many generations of sailors who forgot birthdays and anniversaries of every kind. If even a fraction of the claims were true, then there were post offices around the world jammed with stray mail.

He left Bell and went aft to his own cabin while the little patrol launch growled on through the night. At last, the engines stopped and *Tern* rolled gently with the swell. She was close inshore and a little way north of Port Torquil, near enough to see the village lights.

Carrick landed. It was four a.m. when he walked through a sleeping silent harbour and quietly boarded the research boat *Dirk*. She was in darkness as he carefully made his way below to his cabin.

He had almost made it when a torch clicked on.

'I thought I heard someone moving around,' said Tom Barratt apologetically. The thin Londoner was wrapped in a dressing gown. 'We – uh – mind our own business, of course. Dr Margaret doesn't need to know – '

Barratt retreated, his cabin door clicked shut again, and someone in another cabin chuckled.

'Goodnight,' said Carrick, and headed for his bunk.

6

Daylight that Thursday came grey and with a drizzle of soft rain. Roused with the rest of *Dirk*'s crew at seven a.m., feeling as if he'd slept for no more than thirty seconds, Webb Carrick felt distinctly red-eyed as he showered and shaved. He settled for coffee as breakfast, and most of the research boat's team seemed equally half asleep.

At eight a.m. he went out on deck and into the drizzle and began a routine inspection along *Dirk*'s deck and upper works. One of the liferafts stowed for'ard needed a lashing secured. The liferaft would soon be at its annual checkover date. He stopped to tighten the lashing.

The first shot slammed into a decklight near where his head had been, shattering glass. The second shot, while he was dropping down for cover behind the liferaft, tore a gouge in the teak deck-rail inches from where he had been standing. He heard the bullet ricochet on.

Then there was nothing more. The rain still drizzled, a fat-hulled clam dredger which was a neighbour was easing out from her berth, there were other boats getting ready to leave. No one seemed to have noticed anything. Cautiously, he got to his feet again.

'It's finished.' Dr Margaret Steeven had come out on the *Dirk*'s bridge wing and was looking down at him. Her eyes were angry, her voice sounded resigned. 'It's safe now. It was only a warning, Webb.'

Carrick stared up. Martha Edwards had appeared behind the older woman. Another flicker of movement caught the corner of his eye. Peter Kee's head had bobbed up from a companionway hatch for'ard then had vanished down again. John Torrance's pimpled face also showed briefly at a doorway. The research boat's people weren't taking too many immediate risks.

'Two shots, end,' said Martha Edwards with something close to a sardonic grin on her plump face. 'You've annoyed someone, whatever you've done.'

'Has it happened before?' asked Carrick.

'Twice – the last time was a couple of months ago,' said Margaret Steeven simply. 'I'll come down.'

She did, with Martha Edwards following her. By the time they reached Carrick, he saw Barratt and Wilson had appeared on deck at the *Dirk*'s stern. So far, only Rose Cullar hadn't showed.

'He fires from somewhere up there, we think.' Margaret Steeven pointed out across the harbour towards the weather-misted bulk of Torquil's Shield.

'Why?'

'We never did find out.' The thin, grey-haired woman shook her head. 'Each time we just stayed very quiet for a few days. We didn't go far out from Port Torquil, we didn't do anything that might upset anyone.' She shrugged. 'It seemed to work.'

'I'm glad,' said Carrick sarcastically. 'Do the police know?'

'Don't be damned stupid,' said Martha Edwards. 'Around here? Why waste time? Anyway, half the population on Mull have access to a rifle – and when they aim at something, they hit it. Dead centre.' She prowled from the shattered decklight to the gashed deck-rail, gave a pleased grunt when she found a bright new scar on a ventilator housing, then swooped and grabbed. When she stood upright, she was nursing a badly distorted bullet in one palm. 'Here's one – Margaret?'

Margaret Steeven nodded slowly. 'It looks the same as the last time. I'm no expert.'

'Carrick?' Martha Edwards raised a dark eyebrow in Carrick's direction. 'Do you know much about guns? We were told that we'd been sniped at by someone probably using a nine millimetre deer rifle – the kind of thing you use with a telescopic sight.' She tossed the metal slug in her hand for emphasis. 'Zap – goodbye! But this way, it just means go carefully.'

'Who says?' asked Carrick.

'Anyone we asked,' said Martha Edwards. She grinned. 'Who am I to argue? But whatever you've done, Carrick, watch it!'

She handed the flattened bullet to Margaret Steeven and left them. Sighing, Margaret Steeven touched the gash on the rail with her fingertips.

'You should have told me,' said Carrick.

'The last time was a couple of months ago.' She shrugged. 'I didn't say, because I didn't think there could have been any connection with this – either time.'

'When it happened before, were your team doing anything that you knew might be annoying someone?'

Margaret Steeven shook her head.

'But each time you got the same advice – stay close inshore for a few days. Did Michael Alder suggest that?'

'Yes.'

'Did he say why?'

'No. Just that it sometimes meant there was trouble brewing between the Grant and Stewart boats. We did what he suggested – it worked.' The question had annoyed her. Suddenly, she changed the subject. 'Where were you most of the night? You didn't get back until four a.m.'

'Sorry.' Carrick shook his head as his answer. He had been given enough time to think. The shots had sounded as from a distance. But they had to have been a warning to stop annoying someone – it was too early for them to be linked with Lannair. 'About when I got back. Did Tom Barratt tell you?'

'I was awake.' She looked at him again. 'Is there a problem?'

'It could be me – and soon.' Carrick scraped some of the broken glass from the decklight towards the boat's side with his foot. The glass went over and splashed into

161

the water. 'You shouldn't be involved. But I'm sorry about it.'

'Will that help?' she asked with a stony sarcasm. 'That you're sorry?'

'No. But when it happens, appear angry. Say you were fooled as well – you didn't know I was Fishery Protection.'

'You mean lie?' Her large nostrils flared at the thought, then she seemed to like it. 'All right, I will. Fiercely. Now can we talk about today? I'd scheduled a programme mainly working along the coast. That would fit in with the warning we've had – but if you want, we can still divert out towards Lannair again.'

'Stay with your schedule.' The very last thing Carrick wanted was to have *Dirk* do the unexpected. 'Your schedule, Margaret – whatever happens.'

She raised an eyebrow, but nodded.

Carrick was glad. The two dead men on the Lannair sea-cliff might still have to be discovered. But if it had happened or when it happened, the combined wrath of the Stewarts and Grants involved was certain to be unleashed.

In some direction. The next bullet aimed his way might not be a warning shot.

But he had seen Stewarts and Grants working together – that was the new strange aspect to it all. Could they bury what was still left of their old, folk-memory antagonisms so easily, even to share the riches available from the salmon pipeline discovered on their doorsteps?

Or could there be something more that people were ready to kill to win?

They sailed within the half hour. On the way out, they passed the sad-nosed *Puffin*, where, despite the drizzle, the crew were working on repairs. Further down, Carrick's mouth tightened for a moment as he saw the name *Coral* on one of a group of trawlers tied together just inside the harbour mouth. In daylight, the Grant trawler was very ordinary, very innocent with a black hull and dark-

162

red superstructure. Her wheelhouse was empty, a deck-hand was dumping a pail of garbage over her side.

Then *Dirk* was outside the breakwater's protection and her rusty hull was pitching as seas began breaking against her bow. The seven a.m. shipping forecast hadn't been good. A new deep low of a weather system was moving in from the Atlantic, bringing various forms of nastiness. Only the edges would brush along the Passage of Tiree and Mull, the main body would spend its wrath further south. But from the way the barometer was falling, the edges would be enough.

Their day stayed that way. From cloud and rain, the weather would change to bright sunshine – then change back again. The wind, from the north-west at first, rose and fell as it veered first one way and then the other. At times, it sang through the aerial wires and sent insulators rattling.

But the threatened storm never quite materialized. The deep low was holding back, refusing to behave the way it had been predicted – and the *Dirk* settled into a dull, plodding routine along the coast about a mile off shore. Her research team collected sea temperature readings and took salinity samples, checked plankton levels, and gathered other data on tide and currents for her hungry computer to digest.

There was more, including a constant monitoring of their Decca fish-finder scan and of the ever-changing view it gave of the sea-life and sea bottom beneath the hull. A sudden approaching cloud made up of hundreds of fish would be identified as a species and its movements recorded for behaviour patterns.

'It all matters, John.' Margaret Steeven tried hard to encourage any kind of enthusiasm from the teenage Torrance, whom she had summoned up to the bridge. 'Wouldn't you like to know more about all of this?'

The deckhand gave a sullen grunt which could have meant anything. Margaret Steeven sighed while a new mix of rain and spray soaked across the bridge windows, then looked at Carrick at the helm, seeking some support.

'You'd say it matters, Webb – wouldn't you?' She turned to Torrance, to try again. 'Think of the technology, John – '

Carrick hardly listened, bringing the *Dirk*'s fat bow round a shade to meet a large, incoming sea. He'd already caught Torrance dodging any semblance of work three times since they left harbour and the teenager seemed to be daydreaming most of the time in a world of his own.

He daydreamed himself for a moment while the hull lurched again. There were still a few veterans in Fishery Protection who told stories of the days before fishing skippers had acquired electronics. James Shannon, captain of *Marlin*, talked of the 'piano-wire' men as a sworn truth – fishermen who suspended a piano wire from their boats' bows with a lead weight suspended on the end. If they were passing through a school of fish, they would hear soft, pinging vibrations from the wire as the unseen fish collided with it. According to Shannon, some skippers could identify the species of fish by the vibration created . . .

'Are you totally, irredeemably stupid, boy?' A loud explosion of anger from Margaret Steeven as she gripped Torrance by one scrawny shoulder, pulling him nearer, brought Carrick back to the moment. The small, grey-haired research director's patience had cracked. 'John, have you listened to one word I've said, tried to understand anything?'

The target of her fury was the only thing that stopped Margaret Steeven losing her balance as *Dirk* took another roll. She clung briefly to the teenager, then almost threw him aside.

'Carrick, did you find anything I was explaining difficult to understand?' she demanded.

'Every word made sense, Dr Margaret,' lied Carrick, who hadn't registered any of it. Another wash of spray and drizzling rain swept the bridge windows. 'Maybe you should try again, when we're back in harbour. You'd go along with that, wouldn't you, John?'

Torrance gave him a vinegar scowl and said nothing. From somewhere down below, they heard a wail, then a door slam. It sounded like Rose Cullar was being sick again.

In all, they worked a long ten-hour day off the Mull shoreline. The barometer stayed low but the rest of the weather forecast came true, with the wind moderating and the sea moving into a quieter mood. They came back towards a Port Torquil which was framed under a vast sweep of a rainbow arch topped by a broken sky of sunshine and clouds. *Puffin*'s repairs seemed finished. The patrol launch was carrying out some sedate trial runs about a mile off shore, but ignored *Dirk* as she passed.

Inside the harbour, everything seemed totally, quietly normal. Time and tide meant that a number of boats were out, and Carrick spotted an empty space where the Grant trawler had been. Further along, the clam dredgers had had a good day and were still unloading their catches and cleaning their big sea-bottom harvester gear.

It was early dusk by the time *Dirk* had nested back in her usual berth and had been tied up for the night. Still everything seemed as usual ashore, and she had no visitors waiting. When Carrick finally went down to his cabin to change out of his work clothes, he could hear a blast of taped heavy-metal music, being played with full, thumping bass and coming from Torrance's cabin. He grinned. The young deckhand was probably trying to hit back at an unjust world.

The music stopped when Torrance went to eat. Carrick took a can of beer up on deck and leaned on a rail for a spell, just watching the harbour settling as the night greyed in. He saw *Puffin* come in, and a fast coaster head out carrying some of the day's catches over to the mainland markets. Then he went down to the mess cabin.

It had been Peter Kee's turn to be cook, and the plump Liverpool-Chinese engineer had gone for a chicken casse-

165

role with sweetcorn and a mixed stir-fry of vegetables. He had raided the freezer cabinet for a lemon-flavoured layer cake, but the cake had a sag because he'd defrosted it too quickly.

'It's different, that's all,' said Kee defensively across the serving table. 'If you don't like it, complain to the management in writing. Right?' He saw Carrick looking around the crowded cabin. 'Young Torrance?'

Carrick nodded. All of the research boat's people were in the cabin except for their deckhand.

'He ate – with two helpings of layer cake. Then he left,' said Kee. 'He's probably in his cabin, squeezing his pimples at a mirror – I did at his age.' He chuckled. 'Still giving him a rough time, are you?'

'Still trying to avoid it,' Carrick told him grimly.

Kee shrugged. Suddenly, he took a glance to make sure no one else was within earshot then leaned nearer, lowering his voice.

'Get him in a corner, no witnesses, and kick his backside raw – that's all he really needs – ' then he stopped and quickly raised his voice. 'Layer cake, Dr Margaret?'

Smiling, Dr Margaret Steeven accepted a plate.

After he'd eaten, Carrick avoided an attempt to involve him in a poker game later and went along to his cabin. There was more heavy-metal music coming across from Torrance's cabin, but the teenager's door was closed and Carrick shrugged. Picking up his jacket, he went up on deck, where he found the night was dry, with some light cloud being chased across the moon.

He went ashore. It was the kind of night when shadows seemed darker than usual, when noises, even the creak of mooring ropes or the occasional splash of a fish in the harbour water, seemed louder. Sam Grant's chandlery store was closed and in darkness. There seemed to be fewer vehicles parked along the sea-front street than the previous night, but he saw no other apparent differences.

The village's two bars were bright pools of noise and

166

light as before. He looked in at the Stewart Arms first, because it was the nearest, and found it quiet. Harry Gold was at the bar, and the repair-yard owner gave him a surly nod. But there was no sign of Charlie Stewart and the table the Stewart leader had used was empty. Tom Barratt and Martha Edwards were drinking at another table further back, but didn't look as though they needed company. The long, thin Londoner and the fat, usually aggressive woman didn't see him, and he left it that way.

He left the Stewart Arms and walked along to the Pride of Mull. It was busier, and the first people he saw were three of *Puffin*'s crew. They were out of uniform, drinking beer, and being ignored by the fishermen along the bar counter, the way Fishery Protection were often treated. The three from the patrol launch made an equal business of ignoring Carrick, the way they'd been ordered.

'Webb,' called a voice he knew. 'Over here!'

He smiled and crossed over to join Liz Lawson and the young, wisp-bearded Tom Grant at a booth by a window. She was wearing a blue linen dress, and had a small locket at her throat on a light gold chain. Tom Grant was holding her hand and his faded denim shirt and trousers looked newly pressed.

'What are you drinking?' Grant caught the attention of a barmaid, who was clearing glasses at the next table.

'It's my shout.' Carrick overruled the offer and ordered whisky for himself. Liz Lawson wanted another white wine. Grant, who had a whisky in front of him, settled for a beer. He slipped into the bench opposite the couple, then looked around as the waitress left. 'No Dr Kennedy tonight?'

'Call it a non-medical emergency,' said Liz Lawson. She chuckled and shook her head in a way that made her chestnut hair dance across her shoulders. 'He appeared at the store before lunch, then he galloped off with my father. There's a small cabin launch suddenly on offer at the south end of the island. Dr Kennedy thinks he might buy it.'

'But he wants Sam the Terrible to look it over first,' grinned Tom Grant.

'Why not Harry Gold at the boatyard?' asked Carrick.

'Sam Lawson knows boats. Knows them better than Harry Gold.' Grant glanced at Liz Lawson for agreement. 'We don't know when they'll be back – and I'm not complaining if he keeps Sam away for a spell. They talked Michael Alder into taking them over in Alder's four-wheel-drive.'

'Alder?' Carrick raised an eyebrow.

Grant nodded. 'Sam and Michael Alder may not be exactly friends, but Dr Kennedy gets on well with both of them.'

The drinks came, Carrick paid, and he sipped for a moment.

His thoughts were racing. Kennedy, Sam Lawson and Alder suddenly rushing off together – at the same time as Charlie Stewart was absent from his usual watering hole. It almost shouted the fact that the two men on Lannair had now been discovered. It also tied in Alder and Kennedy again to Lawson and Stewart.

'Your Dr Kennedy is quite an expert on whiskies.' He said it quizzically, swirling the liquor in his glass. 'Does he make it a hobby?'

'It's one of them.' Tom Grant tried his beer, then sucked froth from wet strands of his beard. 'He tells how he used to have one of the world's best jobs – he had a spell as the works doctor in a whisky warehouse!'

'Where?' asked Carrick.

'On the mainland somewhere.' Grant's attention was straying back towards the girl beside him. 'I think he told me – I can't remember. It was a few years back. Then he went off to work with some medical mission.'.

It was one attractive way of patching over some of the awkward parts of James Kennedy's professional history. Carrick took another swallow from his drink.

'These other hobbies – what are they?'

'Sailing sometimes,' said Grant vaguely. 'And he goes

deer-stalking on the hills. He's a damned good shot with a rifle.'

'I could believe that,' said Carrick softly. 'Not amateur radio, anything like that?'

Grant blinked. 'No.'

'It was just a notion.' Carrick finished his drink and pushed back his chair. He rose, then turned to Liz Lawson. 'Did last night's foursome go well?'

'With Keren and Michael Alder?' She hesitated. 'Tom and I enjoyed it. The restaurant was good, the meal was good. But – '

'But Keren Stewart and Alder aren't a good mix,' said Tom Grant flatly. 'Not that way.' He eyed Carrick speculatively. 'Another time, we could maybe vary the recipe. Different ingredients, different man.'

'Tell me about it some time,' said Carrick, and left them.

On the way out, he passed *Puffin*'s trio again. They had removed one of the big carved wood fish models from the Pride of Mull's wall decoration and were trying to pour a beer down its throat.

He grinned. They would be Johnny Walker's worry in the morning, not his. For the rest – his mouth hardened. He didn't like using Liz Lawson and Grant in the way he had, particularly when he was convinced that the girl couldn't know how her father was involved.

Webb Carrick didn't like any part of the role he was playing. But pressures were building all around him. Something very evil had to be identified and smashed – and soon – at Port Torquil before there might be even more killing around the rich, fierce beauty of the islands.

It was still dry as he walked along the shore road. Once again, Clapper Bell suddenly appeared out of a patch of shadow and joined him.

'Any problems with the locals yet, skipper?' asked Bell hoarsely.

'About Lannair?' Carrick shook his head. 'They're stirring, that's all so far.'

'We monitored some extra radio traffic – call-signs, like some people were getting worried. *Puffin* logged some radar traces heading out from here.' The burly man sucked his teeth and frowned his concern. 'I'd say they've found two bodies – and you'd better have your running shoes ready!'

'Maybe.' Carrick could only shrug. Between them, they'd done the little they could to point to another possibility, a cliff-top accident. It was a deception which might work, could at very least cause doubt and delay. 'If it starts going wrong, I'll get out.'

'Good,' said Bell fervently. Then he blocked Carrick's way, shaking his head. 'There's word in from John Kennan. He says stay home tonight, get some sleep.'

'Why?' Carrick was immediately, instinctively suspicious. 'What's going on, Clapper?'

'Something,' grunted Bell. 'But Andy Grey got his ears pinned back for his trouble when he asked – an' I'm not paid to think, right? Kennan says you've to wait, that you'll be contacted.'

Carrick sighed, then gave *Tern*'s bo'sun a quick rundown on the few extra things that could be passed on to Fleet Support.

'I'll tell them,' promised Bell. 'But running shoes, skipper – keep them handy.'

Then he had gone.

If Fleet Support wanted to play games, that was the way it would have to be. Webb Carrick walked back to the harbour through a night made darker as the moon plunged behind clouds again. A farm truck rattled past him, driving away from the Pride of Mull with no lights, apparently little in the way of brakes, and weaving from side to side. The driver gave a vague, friendly wave as he went past, and Carrick sighed, hoping the man would make it home without landing in a ditch or worse.

There was little in the way of activity along the south quay, until he neared the *Dirk*. But the white research boat was a miniature beacon of light, with some of her

170

people moving around on deck. He quickened his pace, clattered over the small gangway, and came face to face with Tom Barratt and Paul Wilson. They both looked angry.

'What's happened?' asked Carrick.

'It's John, our dear-heart deckhand,' said Barratt. 'The lousy little devil has jumped ship – done a runner, taken all his gear.'

'Among other items,' snapped Paul Wilson. The bearded Canadian graduate scowled in the glare of the decklights. 'He stole his way through some of the other cabins. By appearances, that includes yours, Carrick.'

Carrick clattered down the metal ladder to his cabin. The door was ajar. Inside, something had gouged great scratches across the veneered woodwork. His bedding had been slashed. His locker drawers had been emptied.

'I'm sorry,' said Margaret Steeven, coming in behind him. 'You suffered the brunt of it.'

'I haven't lost much,' said Carrick.

There hadn't been much to take, certainly nothing that could identify Carrick as Fishery Protection. His warrant card was hidden inside the lining of Sam Pilsudski's old jacket.

When he looked round, she had gone. But Peter Kee was leaning in the doorway.

'Messy,' said Kee mildly, looking at the cabin. 'But we've seen it coming. Nothing particularly to do with you – he's a stray that Dr Margaret found somewhere and rescued. Strays sometimes bite.' He shrugged. 'We'll find you some spare bedding. Then – uh – staying aboard, Carrick?'

'Staying aboard.' Carrick nodded.

Kee's round face brightened. 'For a small, informal game of poker? Yes? He didn't steal the cards.'

Carrick surrendered.

The way that Carrick could have forecast, Margaret Steeven went ashore to ask about John Torrance as soon as the harbour wakened next morning. She took Peter Kee with her, they were gone about an hour, and Carrick was on deck when they returned. The small, grey-haired woman came grimly over the gangway, went straight to her office cabin under the bridge, and the door slammed shut once she had gone in.

'No luck?' Carrick asked Peter Kee, as the engineer came over the gangway at a more leisurely pace.

'Total nothing.' Kee made it clear that was what he'd expected. 'He'll probably hitch a lift over to the mainland. Damn all teenagers!' He patted his stomach. 'Breakfast time – if you've left anything.'

'Anything else happening ashore?' asked Carrick.

'Not a lot. Just some talk about how a couple of crewmen walked off one of the Stewart boats yesterday.'

'No warning?' Carrick tried to show a bland, minimal interest.

'None. But they're from the mainland and it seems there had been some thieving around the harbour since they arrived. Some people had been asking awkward questions.'

'It happens,' said Carrick.

He watched Kee clatter down a companionway stair in search of whatever breakfast remained. Then he grimaced to himself. Yes, the bodies of the men left on Lannair must have been found. But they were simply going to disappear, with that smooth, quickly manufactured story of thefts slotting into place. By chance, *Dirk*'s own runaway helped, drawing away some of what little interest there was likely to be in it all.

An hour later, when the research boat finally sailed from Port Torquil, the day had shaped into grey skies and grey sea. There wasn't much in the way of wind, and there was only a moderate, chopping swell. There was an occasional light drizzle of rain. The weather forecasters still warned that a major low-pressure system was hovering off the Hebrides area, but were beginning to make vague noises about an improved outlook. Which usually meant that they didn't know and wanted to hedge their bets.

Puffin's berth was empty, whatever Walker had decided to do with the patrol launch. The trawler *Coral* was one of several other boats which had already sailed.

Margaret Steeven was with Carrick on the research boat's bridge as they cleared the harbour. For the moment, at least, she seemed to have got over the loss of their young deckhand. Paul Wilson was to stand in as a replacement when necessary.

'Mind if we take the south curve out, past Torquil House?' asked Carrick.

'If it brightens your day, why not?' The thought amused her while *Dirk* shook and quivered along. 'You're going to find the rest of it remarkably dull.'

Carrick brought their helm round and the research boat's rust-streaked white hull headed on the southern curve, past Torquil's Shield, then skirting the Stewart bay that short distance down the coast. He kept much further out from shore than Margaret Steeven had done, as a small flotilla of fishing boats now lay anchored off the sand-fringed bay with its big, ugly house. There were three trawlers, all of them with that white Stewart cockade of a flash on their funnels. There were also two large clam-fishing boats, not much smaller than trawlers, and a pair of lobster boats. A couple of motor skiffs were buzzing around the little fleet.

Dirk's wash sent the first of the clam boats tugging at her anchor. A fisherman emerged from the wheelhouse to inspect the intruder, waved, then turned away again. No one was visible over at Torquil House or along its private pier, and Carrick switched his attention to the second clam boat as they passed it.

Clam fishing was steady sea harvesting along considerable stretches of the West Highland coast, where the bottom was mostly rock. The main equipment used was the clam dredge, literally hauled along the bottom, scraping for its catch. The boat they were passing had one large dredge suspended from a derrick boom near the stern on her starboard side and another lying on deck nearby. They were simple and strong items, basic triangles of steel bars about twelve feet long, the bars as thick as a man's neck, each triangle forming the mouth of a purse-like bag constructed from thick, bracelet-sized steel rings welded together.

It was a lot of weight to haul around. But, with luck, a good clam dredge could serve generations of fishermen. Hauled along the bottom, their sheer strength tore the clams from their beds. Anything else dragged up, including rocks, was incidental.

'Do tell me when you feel like being back among us, Webb,' said Margaret Steeven in a loud voice.

'Sorry!' he grinned, knowing he'd been part daydreaming again.

'I hope it happens to be convenient,' said the small woman acidly. 'Can this boat get to work, away from here?'

'No problem, Dr Margaret,' he assured her solemnly, easing the *Dirk*'s helm to starboard and using the remote levers to coax a few more revolutions from her twin Volvo engines.

Margaret Steeven had promised him a 'remarkably dull' day, and Carrick soon discovered she meant it. The research boat began a plodding grid pattern schedule which meant first working out into the Passage of Tiree, skirting round some islands, then making her stolid way back in again on a north-west course towards Mull. At precise intervals she would drift briefly while seawater samples were collected and tide and current were measured. Then she would get under way again, her propeller shafts vibrating, her hull quivering.

Till the next time.

'Bored?' asked Paul Wilson during one of their stops. By then it was mid-afternoon and the Canadian graduate was taking a turn at the wheel. He had arrived bringing a can of beer and a doorstep-sized chicken sandwich for Carrick.

'Something like that.' Carrick chewed on the sandwich.

'But you know why we're doing it?' Wilson was trying hard to be friendly.

'Some of it.' Carrick grinned and chewed on for a moment. 'What's your version?'

'We're looking for answers.' Wilson fingered his beard, frowning down at the activity on deck. 'Take the seawater samples. Run a chemical analysis, and we get details like the silicate content. That can tell us where out in the ocean that water has come from. Margaret Steeven has come up with some early warnings of disease coming in to affect fish stocks. I've got my own hobby-horse area – environmental damage. We've taken water samples off some bays that show poison concentrates. Want to guess how they got there?'

Interested, Carrick shook his head. 'Go on.'

'From the damned brand of marine anti-foulant coatings some idiot owners were using on their boats' hulls – poison that was decimating any young fish stock anywhere near. They didn't know until we told them.'

'Did they care?'

'Some of them.' Wilson shrugged.

They were under way again, plodding in towards the high hills of Mull with the long island of Ulva to port and the shallows of Loch Na Keal ahead, when Carrick first saw a white bow-wave coming towards them from the south. It grew fast, then framed a shape he knew. Johnny Walker's *Puffin* was in a hurry, in a direct interception course towards them The patrol launch could have no other vessel as its target, for the simple reason that there was no other vessel anywhere in sight.

Puffin raced on towards them, closing the gap. Interested, some of the *Dirk*'s team appeared on deck again, watching the visitor's fast approach. Margaret Steeven arrived on the bridge, frowning.

'Another damned cowboy,' she commented caustically

as the patrol launch, Blue Ensign snapping, briskly carried out a spectacular, white-wake circle around *Dirk*'s ambling hull. 'Are we supposed to try to guess what he wants?'

Puffin slowed until she was riding almost level with the research boat, separated by a stone's throw of grey, chopping sea. Her siren suddenly brayed, sending some startled, screaming gulls winging away from the *Dirk*'s stern. Short-long-short-short . . . the letter L in Morse meant the patrol launch wanted to talk. Then Johnny Walker appeared in the open doorway at *Puffin*'s bridge. He raised a battery-powered loud-hailer to his lips.

'Good afternoon, *Dirk*.' His voice bellowed across the water. 'Dr Steeven, do you hear? Fishery Protection.'

'Damned fool. Does he think I'm deaf?' Margaret Steeven went out of the enclosed bridge into the open, and nodded.

'Dr Steeven.' Walker's voice bellowed again. 'We need your help with a problem. I'm sending a boat. Will you come aboard?' There was a suitable pause. 'Better bring your man Carrick. He might be useful.'

Margaret Steeven scowled but waved an acknowledgement. Then she stumped back inside the bridge.

'You heard him,' she told Carrick frostily. 'We're going visiting.'

He nodded. Over on *Puffin*, Walker was playing rigidly by the book. The patrol boat had raised a two-flag hoist on her stub mast, yellow over red. Skipper Come Aboard. Boat on Way. Anywhere around the fishing fleets it was an instruction, not an invitation.

Both boats had come down to a muttering steerage way, but if anything *Puffin* was letting the gap between them widen a little. Her Zodiac boat was lowered and bounced her way across with her Second Officer, Bill Martin, at the controls.

Martin gave no hint of recognition as Carrick helped Margaret Steeven down into the inflatable. As soon as they were settled, its engine rasped and it swung away in a new, bucking drench of spray. They reached *Puffin*, where Walker and another of his crew helped Margaret Steeven aboard but left Carrick to clamber up on his own.

'I presume there's a reason for this little pantomime,' said Margaret Steeven curtly, keeping her balance on the swaying deck.

'It's called protecting you,' said Johnny Walker wearily. 'Orders.'

'Just don't damage your boat on my account, skipper,' said the grey-haired woman. 'One accident should be enough in any week.'

Walker glared, but didn't answer. He gave Carrick a nod of greeting.

'What goes on, Johnny?' asked Carrick.

'Wardroom.' Walker thumbed at the aft companionway door that led directly through. 'We've other visitors.' He gestured an invitation. 'Go ahead, Dr Margaret.'

Carrick opened the companionway door, let her lead the way, then heard her surprised intake of breath. Following her, he stared while Walker pushed in behind them and closed the door again.

'Thank you for coming over, Dr Margaret.' As ever, John Kennan was in a blue civilian suit and wore his Royal Naval Reserve tie. The Fleet Support operations chief bobbed a greeting from his seat to one side of the wardroom table and gestured at the upholstered bench opposite. 'Do sit.'

Carrick hardly heard him. His eyes were on the other man in the wardroom cabin. He was the same age as Carrick, thin in build, wore Fishery Protection uniform, and had a bandaged head. But Russ Donald, skipper of the bombed patrol launch *Pippin*, otherwise seemed remarkably fit.

'Couldn't stay away.' He shook hands with Carrick while they both grinned.

'Handle with care,' warned Johnny Walker, his pudgy face showing equal pleasure. 'He's gone soft on us.'

'Hello, Dr Margaret,' said Russ Donald wryly.

'How are you, Skipper Donald?' She considered him carefully.

'Fine.' *Pippin*'s skipper gave a small shrug. 'We were lucky – all of us.'

John Kennan cleared his throat. 'The last time you met – '

'There only was that one time,' said Russ Donald grimly. 'When Dr Margaret set up that meeting at Port Torquil, then told me her theory about the salmon raids off Lannair.' He grimaced. 'I should have listened more carefully, Dr Margaret. That way, I wouldn't have taken *Pippin* blundering in – and maybe we wouldn't have got a bomb in our laps.'

Margaret Steeven had seated herself opposite Kennan. The Fleet Support man looked up at Carrick.

'Does she know anything about last night?' he asked bluntly.

Silently, Carrick shook his head.

'Then I think it is time.' John Kennan looked at all three patrol launch skippers. 'Leave us, please.'

Even Johnny Walker didn't protest. The three men left Kennan and Margaret Steeven facing each other in the wardroom and went through to *Puffin*'s bridge.

'Close your ears, Rab,' Walker told his helmsman casually.

The man, one of *Puffin*'s two CPOs, nodded easily. Around him, it was obvious that John Kennan's new visit to the patrol launch had this time found them slightly more prepared. An attempt had been made at a general clean-up.

'He radioed us about mid-day,' said Walker, and his pudgy face shaped a partial scowl. 'We had to rendezvous with his helicopter off Staffa, then he came aboard bringing Russ and some little presents for us. After that, all we had to do was find you!'

'What kind of presents?' asked Carrick grimly.

'That kind,' agreed Walker in a dry, humourless voice.

'A couple of automatic rifles for each boat. Some other minor goodies.'

'It gets my vote,' said Russ Donald simply. 'They play rough, Webb.'

Carrick nodded. 'And you?'

'I'm joining you on *Tern*.' Donald shrugged. 'You could use the help, I want to be around when this comes to the boil.' He paused then added, 'I'm here for *Pippin* – all right? I won't move in on your Second's job.'

'Wouldn't do him any harm,' grunted Walker.

'Right,' said Carrick. 'Use my cabin for now.'

Having Russ Donald aboard would be an asset. The guns made their own self-defence sense. He turned and looked out from the enclosed bridge, across the grey clutter of low, broken waves towards the fat-hulled, waiting little research boat.

'About Margaret Steeven,' he said softly. 'When you had that meeting with her, could anyone else have known what it was about?'

'No.' Russ Donald was positive. 'She set it up. It was along the beach, *Dirk* was in harbour, so was *Pippin*. We made it look like two people meeting by chance – and there was no one else around.'

It meant that *Pippin* hadn't strayed into any kind of an ambush. That the raider boat patrol was a regular part of the illegal netting gang's precautions.

Walker wanted to hear more at first hand about what had happened to *Pippin* and her crew, and because it could matter to them all, Carrick joined in. In the background, the crewman at the helm was an avid extra audience. Then suddenly the man stiffened, looking past them, noisily clearing his throat. John Kennan's bulky figure had emerged from the wardroom and was beckoning them back.

They went through. Dr Margaret Steeven was still sitting as they had left her, but her thin, lined face had lost its colour, it was hard to say whether her main emotion was shock or some remnants of disbelief.

179

'I told her everything,' said Kennan simply. He glanced at Walker. 'Don't you keep a bottle somewhere, man?'

'Yes. Of course.' Walker found glasses, produced a whisky bottle, and fussed to bring some water in a cracked milk jug. Like the others, Margaret Steeven ignored the water. Before she said anything, she took a swallow of whisky. Then she looked up at them.

'How much money is worth a life?' she asked bluntly. None of them answered and she finished her drink in a long, shuddering swallow but shook her head as an uneasily moved Johnny Walker made to fetch the bottle again. Her eyes turned to Carrick. 'You saw Grants and Stewarts – together?'

Carrick nodded. 'Loading salmon drift nets. Probably miles of them.' *Puffin*'s hull creaked and rolled. They could hear spray from a rogue swell drench along her length, then one of her diesels throbbed briefly as the helmsman brought the patrol launch's bow round a little. 'Clapper and I didn't go looking for what happened, Margaret.'

'The men on the cliff were a Joseph Branksome and a Peter Allander,' said Kennan swiftly, as if trying to avoid any further silence. 'The story around Port Torquil is that they were seen trying to break into Michael Alder's cottage and ran. I made a check. They were both known to the police – bargain basement thugs from the east coast. Convictions for armed robbery, a few other things.' He guessed the question coming. 'I've no news about your runaway teenager. John – ah – '

'John Torrance.' Margaret Steeven straightened herself, her manner firming nearer to normal again. 'He'll turn up. You've more to worry about.'

'Like why we're here.' Kennan's glass was now empty. He tried a polite glance towards Walker, then, when that didn't work, he gave a heavy throat-clearing growl and a glare. He nodded as Walker hastily obliged. 'Two main reasons. First, there's word from Michael Alder's part-share secretary in London. He called her early yesterday and told her to book him a seat on Air Europe from London Gatwick to Zurich, then an open ticket from Zurich, Pan-Am to Los Angeles.'

Carrick shaped a short, low whistle of genuine surprise. 'When?'

'Next Friday – a week from today.'

'Why?' puzzled Johnny Walker. 'Why Los Angeles?'

'How the hell should I know?' snarled Kennan. 'But Zurich is Switzerland. Switzerland is where bloody gnomes hide bloody money.' He gave another growl then swung away. 'Dr Margaret, does it make any sense beside your Noah Pipeline theories?'

'They're not theories.' It was an irritated snap, then the grey-haired woman's nostrils flared as she thought. 'The season should have peaked very soon. Any fishing boat skipper knows that much. Actual figures – ' she shrugged ' – for the last couple of days I've been asked to stay away from Lannair.'

'Thank you.' Kennan was grimly polite. He swirled the whisky left in his glass, but this time he didn't want a refill. Walker topped up his own drink, avoiding looking at Carrick or Donald. The patrol launch took another couple of lurches, then Kennan spoke again. 'The other thing is the anonymous Mayday call that yelped about *Pippin* being banjaxed.'

'God bless that voice,' said Russ Donald softly.

'It was our Dr Kennedy.' The Fleet Support management man enjoyed his moment. 'Maybe it pretty well had to be him, once Carrick found that transmitter – and our kind of evidence wouldn't stand up in a court. We had the original coastguard tape of the Mayday, right?'

Carrick glanced at Russ Donald. *Pippin*'s skipper gave a small wink, which showed he knew the story.

'We had someone phone our Dr Kennedy, making noises about special free trial offers of new lines in medical equipment for testing. We taped your Kennedy's voice,' said Kennan stonily. 'Voice comparisons, Carrick – they use a digital recording technique that translates any

damned sound into numbers and a graph. I don't understand it, I don't need to understand it. But I've a couple
of the best recording engineers in Europe who say Kennedy made that Mayday call.'

Margaret Steeven gave a sigh, but said nothing.

'That's the way of it,' said Johnny Walker with a ruth-
less, clumsy humour. 'You know the saying, Dr Margaret
– still waters run deep.'

'Damn you, be quiet,' said Margaret Steeven with a
brittle dignity. 'We're talking about people I know –
people I trusted.'

A new glare from John Kennan sent Walker retreating
out of the cabin, heading for his bridge. Grimacing,
Kennan signalled Russ Donald to follow the man out.

'Damned fool,' said Kennan softly once they'd gone. 'I
think – '

'Dr Margaret,' Carrick cut in determinedly. Just once,
without realizing it, Johnny Walker had perhaps said
something that mattered. 'You've studied the Noah Pipeline. You've studied the currents all around Lannair,
gathered endless data. Correct?'

'You've seen.' Puzzled, she nodded.

'You told me about a fishing boat that maybe vanished
off Lannair, about three fishermen who vanished with
her – '

'The *Iris*, from one of the other islands.' Quietly, without asking, Kennan had refilled her glass from Walker's
bottle. She took a sip.

'Say it was Lannair. Could you use that data to make a
computer projection of where the bodies might be washed
ashore?'

'Bodies can be trapped,' protested John Kennan. 'They
can snag rocks.'

'Most turn up. Eventually – somewhere.'

The two men waited. Among the islands, they were
talking about mile after mile of deserted, often uninhabited coastline. Beaches more often visited by seals and
seabirds than any man.

'I could try.' Margaret Steeven gave a slow nod. 'No guarantees. I should have more data.'

'You'll have to make do with what you've got,' said John Kennan heavily.

She made one more protest. 'The Noah Pipeline is more than just a current. There are other factors – '

'Make a guess right now,' said Kennan softly. 'Where?'

'North of here.' She bit her lip. 'Maybe not too far.' Pausing, the woman gave him a wry attempt at a smile. 'I'll need time – even with my user-friendly computer.'

'Tomorrow morning?' Kennan was being practical. 'No sense in starting a search if it would be dusk before you were organized.' He pointed a sudden finger at Carrick. 'Tell him – I've got to head back to a desk. Any problem for you in running this with *Tern*, Carrick?'

'No problems.' It was the way Carrick had hoped.

'Good. Talk details with Walker and Donald. Remember, we're getting near a possible boiling point – and your job doesn't include getting yourself scalded.' Kennan swore under his breath as the patrol launch took another unexpected pitch, then he switched his attention back to Margaret Steeven. He gave her what was intended as an encouraging smile. 'You'll also take damned good care of this lady.'

'That makes a change,' said Margaret Steeven with an acid humour. 'I thought I was the nursemaid.' She drew in a deep breath. 'There's one immediate problem. I've invited Sam Lawson to come aboard the *Dirk* for drinks this evening.'

'Couldn't be better.' John Kennan gave her a wolfish grin. 'Be nice to him, Dr Margaret. But have Carrick along. He can stay away from *Tern* for another evening – hell, you can even think of him as your chaperon!'

Margaret Steeven swallowed hard. Then she told the Fleet Support deskman what to do and how to do it.

Acrobatically.

Three minutes later, they were ferried back to the waiting

research boat. As soon as *Puffin*'s inflatable had returned and had been hoisted aboard, the patrol launch made a noisy departure in a boil of white wake. Very quickly, she had vanished round an island headland.

'So what was that all about?' asked Paul Wilson as Carrick took over the *Dirk*'s helm again.

'Not a lot.' Carrick used the line he'd decided on with Margaret Steeven. 'Some Spanish boats raided one of the prohibited herring nursery lochs up north. The Fishery Protection mob wanted to know where we'd been, in case we'd seen them.'

'*Y viva*,' said Wilson sarcastically. 'Why can't they do their own damned work?'

Satisfied, the Canadian winked, left Carrick, and clattered off down the companionway stair towards the main deck. Gently, Carrick eased the remote throttle levers forward, heard the big Volvo engines begin to throb in answer, and spun the steering wheel.

It was time to start back for Port Torquil. But with the same necessary testing and data-gathering as a continued apparent normality of purpose to satisfy any fishing boat that might come their way.

The wind was still blustering when they got back to Port Torquil, but at least there was no rain. The barometer had crawled back up a little, and the weather bureau forecast for fishermen broadcast at five p.m. was a classic example of how to be a meteorologist and still stay out of trouble. Every option was left open the night ahead and most of the next day. The word 'unsettled' took a lot of hard usage.

Once again, Margaret Steeven had her own priorities. The moment that the white research boat had berthed, Tom Barratt and Peter Kee were sent off around the harbour and village to seek for any trace of John Torrance. They returned in about an hour, happily smelling of whisky. The teenage deckhand had vanished. The only vague suggestion they'd gathered had been that a youth had been seen being given a lift inland on a farm

184

truck from outside the Stewart Arms some time that morning. Except maybe it hadn't been a youth. It might have been a girl, or an old woman.

'Wherever he is, he'll land on his feet,' said Kee sourly when they got back. He had lost some money, his spare wristwatch, and a couple of shirts when Torrance had thieved his way through the *Dirk* before running. He had met Carrick by accident on the lower deck. 'Hell, Webb, the watch was a cheapo. But these dam' shirts were best Hong Kong hand-tailored – they cost me a fortune. Now that little swine has them – that's sick!'

'Anything else happening ashore?' asked Carrick mildly.

'Nothing.' Kee shook his head. 'Still, it's Friday night – that's serious drinking time around the boats. Things might liven later.'

'What about the two other deckies who ran?'

'That pair?' The engineer made one of his favourite Oriental-style faces. 'Here today, gone tomorrow – they're forgotten already.'

Margaret Steeven had shut herself inside her office cabin on the main deck. Any time Carrick passed – and he contrived to do it, several times – all he heard was a faint clicking of computer keyboard keys or an occasional electronic beep. He saw Martha Edwards barge in and, seconds later, make a red-faced retreat.

'Thrown out?' asked Carrick mildly.

'Yes.' The plump woman was indignant. 'She told me to get out – just like that! What the hell's she doing that is so important?'

'Her expenses?' suggested Carrick.

Martha Edwards was not amused.

By rota, it was Rose Cullar's turn to make the evening meal. But the dark-haired girl, despite the engagement ring on the ribbon around her neck, was no kind of cook. For self-preservation, Tom Barratt was her volunteer assistant and he salvaged a partly burned meat stew. He had Martha Edwards persuade one of the clam boats

185

berthed along the quay to part with some samples from the day's catch. He scrubbed and cleaned them, opened and trimmed them, then deep-fried them, while Rose Cullar sadly located some dried-up cheese for dessert.

Margaret Steeven appeared. She collected some of the stew on a plate then went back to her computer and hadn't returned by the time they finished eating. When Carrick took a main deck tour past her cabin, the keyboard was still clicking.

Darkness brought a wind that sent ragged clouds rushing under the moonlight. Then Sam Lawson arrived aboard. The squat, scar-faced chandler was treating it as a formal visit. He had shaved, and was wearing an old-fashioned blue blazer with freshly creased dark trousers, a white shirt, a plain blue tie, and black shoes that, judging by the way he walked, were anything but comfortable.

Carrick met him as he arrived over *Dirk*'s gangway. He kept a friendly smile on his face for the man he had last seen beside the salmon nets at Lannair.

'I'm expected,' said Lawson gruffly.

'I was told.' Carrick made to lead the man along to Margaret Steeven's cabin, but Lawson halted him with a slightly hesitant growl.

'Have you had any more trouble – from anyone?'

Carrick shrugged. 'Someone took a couple of shots at the boat this morning.'

'Shots.' Lawson twitched a bushy eyebrow.

'With a rifle. To scare.'

'Aye.' For a moment, Lawson seemed almost uneasy. 'These – uh – the two who jumped you a couple nights back won't bother you again.'

'You found them?' Carrick showed suitable surprise.

'In a way.' The leader of the Grant faction avoided Carrick's eyes. 'They've gone – left Port Torquil. There had been some thieving.' He paused then added hastily, 'Nothing to do with your young deckie, Torrance. I've got my people keeping an eye open for him.'

186

'Dr Margaret would be obliged,' said Carrick politely.

He escorted Lawson along to Margaret Steeven's office cabin. She had changed her clothes for a short-sleeved beige linen dress, and she had an unopened whisky bottle and three glasses set out. As she greeted Lawson with a cool handshake and saw him settled in a chair, Carrick noticed that the computer screen and its printer had been covered by their hoods.

'So, Sam – ' Margaret Steeven waited until they all had drinks ' – let's drink to your daughter being back.'

'To Liz,' agreed Carrick mildly.

Lawson gave a small, pleased nod and they drank.

'How's she enjoying being back?' asked Margaret Steeven.

'All right, I think,' said Lawson warily.

'Bullying you?' asked the grey-haired woman. She made a good job of chuckling. 'That's what daughters are for, Sam.'

'Aye.' Lawson rubbed the side of his glass slowly over his scarred cheek. 'I suppose.' He looked at Carrick, then he looked at Margaret Steeven again. 'You – uh – have some business to talk about?'

'Yes. About hiring one of your trawlers – the usual kind of arrangement,' said Margaret Steeven. 'But there's no hurry, is there?'

'No.' The man looked at them both again, still uneasy.

'Then we can have a talk, eh?' said Margaret Steeven calmly. She glanced at Carrick then nodded deliberately towards the cabin door. 'Thank you, Webb. Once you've finished your drink – '

Carrick hadn't been given any particular choice. He swallowed the rest of his whisky, nodded at Sam Lawson, and went out on deck. But he made sure he stayed near enough to know if Margaret Steeven needed help.

She didn't. Time – over an hour of it – passed. Some of the *Dirk*'s crew went ashore, and he turned down an invitation to join them. Then, at last, the cabin door opened and Sam Lawson emerged followed by the small figure of the project director. She saw him to the gangway, then waited there until he had gone ashore and was walking back along the quay.

'Stop lurking,' she said without looking round.

'You weren't supposed to do that,' said Carrick grimly, coming out of the patch of shadow under the bridge.

'I use my own judgement.' She let him walk along the deck with her, back to her cabin.

'So what happened?' asked Carrick.

'Not a lot.' She shook her head. 'I arranged to day-charter one of his trawlers, a week from now. We talked about Liz, we talked about the *Dirk*, we talked about his business. Any time I tried to mention salmon gangs or illegal netting, he backed away from it.'

'And you hated doing it,' said Carrick quietly.

'Yes.' She stopped under a deck light, her thin, lined face tight at the memory. 'In his own thick-skulled way, Sam Lawson has always been someone I – well, I trusted a little.'

'It might be mutual,' murmured Carrick.

'You think that helps after what you saw?' She made it a snap. 'I can tell you this much. He's worried, he's anything but happy. I think there's another raid planned, and it could be for early next week – because he won't let me charter a boat until at least next Thursday.' Opening her cabin door, she looked over her shoulder at Carrick again. 'After breakfast tomorrow. Be ready.'

She went in and the cabin door closed behind her. He waited, and in under a minute the computer keyboard was clicking again.

Peter Kee was still aboard. Paul Wilson and Rose Cullar appeared a little later and Kee produced a deck of cards. Resignedly, Carrick let them talk him into a few hands of poker with no particular run of luck for anyone. Then Rose Cullar decideded she wanted an early night, and he made a similar escape.

He lay in his bunk but, even though he was tired, he didn't get much sleep.

He had too much to think about.

Next morning dawned in a squall of rain which swept in over the harbour and briefly misted out the bulk of Torquil's Shield. Then the rain had gone, the sky mostly cleared, and the wind moderated. There was only a light swell. It was the way things had been forecast. The weather low coming in from the Atlantic would still wait a little longer before properly arriving.

Saturday and the start of the weekend meant that there was very little activity anywhere around the harbour. Aboard the *Dirk*, people emerged late and yawning from their cabins while Webb Carrick finished a coffee-and-rolls breakfast. Margaret Steeven, wearing denim trousers and a turtle-neck sweater, was the only other person bustling around. She had recruited Tom Barratt and Martha Edwards to assist in lowering the research boat's dinghy.

'Webb, I'm ready.' She beckoned Carrick.

He helped her into the dinghy, then lowered down a couple of small wooden boxes that she wanted. He followed them aboard, saw Margaret Steeven settled, then fired the outboard engine. Above them, Tom Barratt untied the dinghy's line and tossed it down.

'Enjoy your day, Dr Margaret,' yawned Barratt, then turned away.

They were well down the harbour, heading for the exit, the outboard growling happily, before Carrick asked, 'What did you tell them?' He thumbed over his shoulder at the research boat.

'A few lies. I'd decided to spend a few hours looking at some of the rock-pool life further along the shore, where there's less risk of a contaminated environment. I'd – ah – persuaded you to come along.' She gave a grim little laugh. 'Age and treachery will always baffle youth and skill. You'll find out some day.'

'And the rest of it worked out?' Carrick shaded the outboard's rudder bar, centring the dinghy's bow on the gap ahead.

Margaret Steeven nodded. But she waited until the dinghy was outside the harbour and was bouncing north through the light swell, not much more than a stone's throw from the shore.

'It's based on a computer profile, nothing more,' she warned, then broke off to wave to a couple of small children who were playing on the beach at the end of the village. It was Saturday morning. No one ever did anything that mattered on a Saturday. 'I warned you, I haven't complete data.'

'But on what you've got?'

'Where it might – ' she repeated the word for emphasis ' – might be, is over on the Treshnish Isles. At Fladda, on the north-east shore.'

Carrick stared. Then he nodded.

'That's where I'll try,' he told her.

If Margaret Steeven's computer prediction was accurate, it meant the Noah Pipeline's associated current eventually did a U-turn somewhere past Lannair, even if the salmon using it broke away for the mainland.

The Treshnish Isles were a strange, scattered little group of uninhabited isles a few miles west of the Mull coast. Ironically, they were almost due west of Ulva, where *Puffin* had intercepted *Dirk* the previous day. There were six actual isles, several times that number of rocks and shoals scattered around them.

Except for Fladda. Fladda had a reasonable approach.

Whatever was coming in.

Which might mean the occasional visiting yacht came exploring once or twice in a summer.

Anything could lie there. For a long, long time.

Like some small insect, the dinghy crept on north along the edge of the coast. All the way, they saw not a trace of another craft as far as the horizon. Port Torquil faded behind them then they reached Sanna Head and the hidden inlet where *Tern* was located. Margaret Steeven stared, surprised, as they swung in past the foaming edging of breakers at its entrance and into the quieter water beyond.

'Clever,' she said with a wry appreciation as she then saw *Tern* lying waiting ahead. 'Sneaky, but clever. So – you'll get rid of me first?'

Carrick nodded. That much she'd reluctantly agreed.

It didn't take long. They'd been seen, the patrol launch's diesels were growling to life, and her Zodiac boat was already coming towards them with Clapper Bell aboard.

Carrick turned the dinghy, took it back out of the inlet with Clapper Bell following closely, and they beached both craft on the shingle a little way along the shore. They saw Margaret Steeven and her two small boxes ashore, then they dragged the dinghy well out of the water.

'All set?' asked Carrick.

She nodded, and they left her, pushing the inflatable back out into the water. *Tern* had emerged from the inlet and was idling off shore, waiting on them. In another couple of minutes they were aboard, the Zodiac boat was being swung out on the stern davit, and Carrick had settled into the command chair.

'Where, skipper?' Gogi MacDonnell was in the coxswain's chair, which gave him first right to ask.

'The Treshnishes,' said Carrick. He saw MacDonnell's raised eyebrows. 'That's where she says, Gogi. That's where we go. Fladda.' He glanced round. The rest of the patrol launch's handful of crew were there, listening. So was Russ Donald, the bandage round his head covered over by a blue beret. *Pippin*'s skipper seemed to have had no trouble fitting in as a working visitor. Carrick looked directly at him. 'Any problem with that, Russ?'

Donald looked pleased at the courtesy, but shook his head.

'Steer 310,' ordered Carrick. He reached for the triple set of throttle levers. 'Going to full ahead.'

Tern began moving. He had a chance to look back towards the shore and saw Margaret Steeven standing watching, then the three big V8 diesels below them were beginning their throbbing roar.

At full ahead, the patrol launch streaked out across the blue waters of the Passage of Tiree towards the gradually firming outlines of the Treshnish Isles. All the time, their radar kept watch. All the time, no other craft showed on its screen. Russ Donald had taken over radio watch and combed the main frequency bands, with only some distant jumbles of conversation to break the general silence.

They took a north curve in towards Fladda, because it was the sensible way. Fladda was flat, Lunga, to the south, was terraced rock, what lay between them was fanged trouble and white water. North, beyond Fladda, with clear water between them, were Burg Mor and Burg Beg. All the Treshnishes formed a recognized bird sanctuary and another breeding colony for seals, and Burg Mor and Burg Beg were great unaccessible cliffs of rock. Burg Beg had once mattered – because of its sheer inaccessibility. A stubborn garrison of Clan MacLean had once held it as a fortress for the exiled Stuart kings – for an unbelievable twenty-five years before they had to give in.

Tern made the final approach towards Fladda's northeast shore cautiously, down to barely half speed. Then, except for Clapper Bell, who was still at the helm, every man aboard used bridge glasses or binoculars to check their first north-to-south pass along the foaming line of beach.

They saw nothing. It was left to Sam Pilsudski to give a sudden shout. He had emerged from his engineroom clutching an old brass telescope salvaged from some mysterious corner, and they had crept back from south to north again on a second pass prior to making a landing.

'There, Webb!' He lowered the old telescope and pointed.

At almost the most northerly point of the beach, where a dark line of weed formed its own high-water mark, a gathering of herring gulls clustered like a colony around a low, humped mound on the shingle. It was a strange mound, isolated, unrelated to any nearby rocks. The big, cruel-beaked herring gulls deserted reluctantly when the patrol launch came closer and sounded her klaxon.

'Skipper.' Gogi MacDonnell looked gravely at Carrick. 'I think we should take a wee look.'

Carrick nodded. They anchored in six fathoms of water barely a stone's throw from the shore, then they used the Zodiac boat. He went in with MacDonnell, Clapper Bell and Pilsudski, and once they had dragged the Zodiac ashore they crunched their way over the shingle to the dark line of seaweed then along towards the humped mound. Some hovering herring gulls screamed overhead or swooped low around them. One gull landed on the mound and pecked at something with its beak. Then they saw what was there.

'Damn you to hell, you scavenging devil!' A fury that was Sam Pilsudski hauled out a wrench from his overall pocket as he ran, and threw it at the bird. The herring gull flew off with a scream.

They reached the mound, then stopped, and Pilsudski silently crossed himself. Clapper Bell was swearing under his breath, Gogi MacDonnell's habitually sad face might have been carved from stone, and Carrick fought down a moment's heaving urge to vomit.

A skeletal arm clad in the ragged remains of a fisherman's sweater protruded from the mound. The trunk of a second body, still wearing what had been an oilskin jacket, was further along. The mound was partly weed, partly small pieces of wreckage from a boat, and partly other debris from the sea. They could see the bloated body of a dead seal and a scattering of fish skeletons.

Wrapped round everything like an obscene, drowning packaging were great long swathes of monofilament salmon netting which still had an occasional float attached here and there along its length.

Anyone and anything caught up in the packaging would have had no chance of escape. And Dr Margaret Steeven's computer had got it right. Protruding from one part of the hump, wrapped in netting like everything else, a lifebuoy had *Iris* painted on it.

They'd found the last remains of the missing long-line boat from Skye. The boat that had vanished somewhere near Lannair. Despite the distance it had been carried by the current, despite over a month in time exposed to the sea and the elements, some of the wreckage they could see still showed the black, heat-scorched damage that had to mean an explosion.

The kind of explosion that had almost finished *Pippin* and her crew.

Russ Donald came ashore when they sent the Zodiac back for some of the things they would need. He walked slowly and white-faced round the edge of the mound, then removed his beret for a moment and stood very silently with the white bandage around his head.

'That could have been us,' he said softly.

There were things that had to be done, an order in which they had to be done, and it helped that the weather still held fair. Photographs had to be taken, measurements made. Then, using lengths of driftwood as crude spades, cutting away the nets, they dug into the mound. There was more wreckage but no third body.

Someone else could decide who had been found, who was still missing. The sea often kept something back for itself.

They loaded the two badly decomposed corpses into heavy plastic body-bags, zipped them shut, and felt at least a little better once that was done. They carried the body bags off the beach and laid them gently side by side in a cleft of rock.

The dead fishermen had already waited weeks. A few more hours couldn't harm now – and there might be less dignity in being aboard *Tern* before they could be taken ashore.

No one said very much as the grey patrol boat made her way back to Mull and Sanna Head. On the way, Carrick drafted a first report for Fleet Support, but left it

194

to Andy Grey to log and then radio. Russ Donald read it through with them, barely nodded agreement, and all the rest was in the bright fury in his eyes.

Margaret Steeven was waiting on the beach where they had left her. Clapper Bell ferried Carrick ashore, then left them to splash in through the shallows while he took the inflatable away again in a rasp of its big outboard.

'Well?' asked Margaret Steeven.

'You were right,' said Carrick quietly. 'We found two of them.'

She bit her lip, nodded, and led the way back to where she'd set up a little camp among the rocks. The two boxes she'd brought lay open. One held specimen jars – she'd filled a number during the time he'd been gone. The other held the remnants of a packed lunch.

'I brought for two,' said the small, grey-haired woman. 'If you feel like eating – '

He shook his head.

'Martha made it up for me.' She gave a small, shaky laugh. 'Would you believe smoked salmon sandwiches?' There were tears very close to her eyes, then she drew a deep breath. 'We'd better get back to the harbour.'

He carried the boxes down to the dinghy for her, launched it into the foaming shallows, helped her aboard, then joined her. The outboard fired at the second attempt, and he turned their bow south, for Port Torquil. The sea had become slightly rougher, and they bobbed along in the swell with spray sheeting aboard.

He had an appointment ahead with the Stewarts. Margaret Steeven also remembered. As they sailed in past the start of the little village, she leaned forward.

'What time are you expected at Torquil House?'

He shook his head and raised his voice above the busy popping of the dinghy's outboard.

'All they said was "late afternoon".' What had had to be done at Fladda meant that it was already well after three by his wristwatch. 'I can check by phone from the harbour.'

She nodded. 'Use the direct line – 048.'

Carrick froze, staring at her. A sea heavier than the rest tossed the dinghy and drenched them in another curtain of spray. He hardly noticed.

'What's wrong?' She was puzzled, immediately anxious, looking around her.

'Say it again,' he told her urgently. 'Exactly what you told me!'

'Use the direct line, 048.' She almost yelled it back at him. 'The Stewarts have a listed business number, the one in the directory. It goes through their office. But Torquil 048 is the direct, unlisted number – straight into the living part of the house. Keren gave me it a long time ago. Why?'

'Just the three numbers?'

'Port Torquil isn't big enough to need more,' she shouted.

So everybody had got it wrong. The pencilled scribble on Dr James Kennedy's radio, the numbers that they'd ruled out as a compass bearing or a radio frequency, that they'd thought was a call-up timing or even a code, was something much more simple. Direct Line 048.

Simple and damning.

He told Margaret Steeven.

Tight-lipped, she shrugged.

Then the dinghy had passed through the harbour entrance and the small woman waved at some fishermen on the quayside as they shouted a greeting.

For a moment, as the dinghy slowed and swung in towards her research boat's fat white hull, she let the mask slip.

'Webb, who's left to trust?' she asked simply, very wearily.

Then the mask was back in place again and she was smiling as Peter Kee appeared on the deck above, ready to help them aboard.

7

The research boat had had a visitor in their absence. As soon as they were aboard, they heard. Michael Alder had arrived about mid-morning, had gossiped for a spell, then had departed after leaving the message that he'd be back in the afternoon and would take Carrick across to Torquil House.

'He said at four-thirty,' Rose Cullar told Carrick. She laughed. 'Never tell me that lawyers have no sense of humour. He told me a couple of the funniest cleaned-up blue jokes I've ever heard!'

'Keep them for your next party-piece,' said Margaret Steeven stonily. She waited while the younger woman retreated below decks, then turned to Carrick. 'Four-thirty – what will you do? Will you still go?'

'It could ring alarm bells if I don't.' Carrick leaned on the deck-rail and looked out across the harbour towards the north quay. Inevitably, when he might have been glad to see her, *Puffin* was gone from her berth. But the basic situation hadn't changed as far as going to Torquil House was concerned. He turned to Margaret Steeven. 'I'll go with Alder. Unless you hear something has gone wrong, give me a few hours – then you know who to tell.'

She didn't like it, but she nodded.

The night before, he'd sorted out the list of items he wanted to borrow from the research boat's scuba diving equipment. Most of it was equipment similar to the gear he regularly used, well maintained, and he'd chosen a simple aqualung unit teamed with a big single air cylinder. Carrick packed them in a canvas bag, then went down to his cabin and changed his clothes, emerging again wearing a crisply fresh grey shirt, denim trousers, and Sam Pilsudski's jacket.

'You need a new jacket,' said Peter Kee when they met on deck. 'Can't you get rid of that thing?'

'Not unless someone shoots it first,' said Carrick solemnly.

Then a horn sounded ashore. Michael Alder's Toyota pick-up was coming along the quay and stopped near to the *Dirk*'s gangway.

'Shove your gear in the back,' instructed Alder when Carrick left the *Dirk* carrying the canvas sack with his borrowed scuba equipment. The thin, fair-haired lawyer lazed behind the pick-up's wheel while Carrick did that, then nodded a greeting as his passenger got aboard beside him. 'Where did beloved Dr Margaret drag you to this morning?'

'We were north along the coast,' said Carrick vaguely. 'If she found something that moved, it went into a jar. I was duty slave.'

'Better you than me.' Alder gave one of his chipped-tooth grins, seemed satisfied, and set the Toyota moving.

Chrome glinting, whip aerials quivering, the four-wheel-drive made a tight U-turn on the quay then headed back. Through the village, it snarled its way up the tight, potholed track that led to the top of the Torquil's Shield ridge. Then, suddenly, Alder brought them to a skidding halt on the final bend, a viewpoint with the whole spread of coast down below.

'Ever seen it from here before?' asked Alder.

'No,' lied Carrick. Except it was only a partial lie. The other time had been by night. 'Never had the chance.'

'Like working for Dr Margaret?'

Carrick shrugged. 'You get used to her.'

'True.' Alder smiled. 'How long were you deep-sea before you got this job – on your last ship? You said it was the *Maura*, didn't you? With Captain Henderson?'

'Captain Pendleton,' corrected Carrick, wooden-faced. 'Two years.'

'A big difference.' Alder's deep-set green eyes were almost hooded for a moment. He reached into the pocket of the unbuttoned khaki drill safari-style jacket he was wearing, produced a roll of peppermints, and flicked one into his mouth. 'Well, let's go diving!'

The pick-up began moving again. Around another bend, the track had stopped climbing. Then they were on the run down towards the other, tree-fringed bay and the big, grey bulk of Torquil House.

Once again, the same little fleet of trawlers and other boats was anchored in the bay, most with the white cockade funnel flash which marked a Stewart vessel. They lay in shelter – although for the moment the strong wind of earlier seemed to have vanished. There was blue sky and sunlight and the sea was a flat calm.

But Carrick wondered. Every instinct told him that the picture could be false and brief. The low-pressure system was still roaming the weather map, its edges somewhere near. Given the chance, it could scream and storm its way down and along the West Highland coast.

Alder's Toyota bounced down the final stretch of track towards the ugly three-storey bulk of Torquil House, rounded one side of its overgrown gardens and dilapidated exterior, and crunched to a halt in the gravel forecourt outside the front door, which overlooked both the boathouse and the Stewarts' private pier. There were other cars on the forecourt. A Stewart clam-dredging boat lay at the pier.

Carrick and Alder got out of the Toyota. The front door of the house was open and two figures watched the new arrivals come over.

'We've been waiting on you,' said Keren Stewart, smiling a welcome. She was wearing denim trousers and a close-fitting white shirt. She looked at Carrick with a sparkle in her intense blue eyes. 'Got your diving gear?'

'In the pick-up.' Alder thumbed back at the vehicle. But he was staring at the figure beside Keren Stewart. The portly, round-faced Dr James Kennedy had exchanged his usual tweeds for a casual grey weekend jacket and lighter grey linen trousers. 'Are you coming along?'

'No.' Kennedy shook his head.

'Good.' Alder grinned. 'With you in the water, people might think it was a whale hunt and start throwing harpoons!'

'No chance of that.' Kennedy managed a weak laugh, but his plump face flushed. 'I'm just leaving. I – ' he hesitated, and glanced first at Carrick then, quickly, at Keren Stewart ' – it was a professional call.'

'No problem, is there?' asked Michael Alder slowly.

'None.' Keren Stewart answered for him, curtly. She turned back to Kennedy. 'Thanks for coming. It could have waited until Monday.'

'I – uh – ' Kennedy looked momentary confused ' – I had other calls anyway. But I'll have the evening at home.' Then, with another glance around, he became his usual laid-back self again. 'Well, enjoy your swim-swim fun!'

He gave a final duty smile around then walked away towards one of the parked cars. Getting behind the wheel, he drove rapidly away in the direction of Port Torquil.

'Sorry if I upset him,' said Alder dryly.

'So why do it?' Keren Stewart sighed then brightened. 'Come in, both of you.'

They followed her into the hallway of the big house. Like the exterior, it showed a one-time grandeur that had been neglected. Wood panelling on the walls was stained with damp, a carpet was faded and worn, curtains were threadbare.

'Don't bother to be polite,' she told Carrick. 'The place is a wreck – we know it. When he bought it, our father had delusions of grandeur, without the money!'

She brought them into a vast ground-floor room. It had the great bow window that Carrick had seen from the sea – and although only the area at the curved window was furnished and the rest lay bare, that area had room for a couch, a scatter of armchairs, and some other items.

200

'You could hold a convention in this one,' said Keren Stewart dryly. She gestured towards the group over at the window. 'You know everyone.'

Carrick did. Charlie Stewart was there, a giant host in blue overalls who was clutching a can of beer. Liz Lawson sat in one of the chairs, wearing denim trousers, red fashion boots, and a yellow sweater, her long chestnut hair secured back by a silver clasp. Behind her, looking round from the window, Tom Grant was also wearing denims and, as usual, was sucking an edge of his wispy moustache. He looked pleased to see Carrick – reasonable enough when even a self-proclaimed neutral like Grant found himself deep in Stewart home territory.

Ignoring her brother's beer, Keren Stewart offered coffee in mugs and a pile of freshly made sandwiches. There was some general talk, with even Charlie Stewart showing an affable side to his character.

'Webb. Spare a minute?' asked Keren Stewart suddenly. She waited until he had set down his coffee mug, then led the way over to the far side of the great window. She stood very near to him, and not for the first time he felt the full, raw attraction of this tawny lioness of a woman. She showed her white teeth in a wide smile. 'This dive – can I tell you what we've planned?'

'Go ahead,' invited Carrick. She wore a faint, musky perfume. Their bodies brushed in a tantalizing way, and her eyes showed she knew it. But she gave a slight chuckle of a laugh, telling him it was a game.

'It's only a practice dive – call it playtime. You and I, Charlie and Michael Alder.' She gestured towards Liz Lawson and Tom Grant. 'They want to head off somewhere on their own, their business. What we'll be doing is diving down on a reef just outside the bay. Sixty feet maximum depth, so we can make it an easy forty-minute duration. No need for any decompression stop. Any problems with that?'

'None.' He felt their bodies brush again. This time, it

201

had been deliberate on her part. Almost a challenge. 'That, I can handle.'

'Good.' The same wanton look was in her eyes again. But she wasn't finished. 'We take a break. Maybe we'll go down again later, but if we do, then the usual add-on time applies. Agreed?'

Carrick nodded. It was all by the book. Working at sixty feet, no decompression stops were needed on the way back up provided a dive didn't exceed fifty-five minutes. But the standard tables warned that any second dive within the following twelve-hour period had to be added on.

'I'll go along with it.' He leaned back against the window sill, then managed a lopsided grin at her. 'Keren – that's no islands name.'

'True.' She grimaced a little at the change of subject. 'Simple story. My father had an older brother who was a soldier in World War Two – in a Highland regiment. There was a battle at a place called Keren in East Africa. His brother was killed and they gave him a medal. I'm the family's walking war memorial.'

'It could have been worse,' mused Carrick. 'Suppose it had been Dunkirk?'

'I know.' She gave a dry laugh. 'I made out a list once.'

She left him, managing to brush against him again in the process, the smile still lingering on her lips.

Charlie Stewart had demolished another can of beer by the time the coffee and sandwiches were finished. Suddenly, the big, copper-haired man gave a bellow for attention.

'Right, everybody,' he declared. 'Time we moved – before we dam' well take root!' He lumbered towards Carrick. 'Has Keren told you what we'll do?'

'Yes,' said his sister from the background.

'Not all of it.' Stewart gave a caustic grunt. 'This is only sixty feet – no big deal. But anywhere underwater is dangerous. We keep our eyes open. We remember there's deep water beyond the reef.' He paused, and his blue eyes, so startlingly like those of his sister, seemed to linger on Liz Lawson. Then he came back to Carrick. 'Very deep. With a strong tide and a stronger current. We don't go near it. You understand?'

'I understand,' said Carrick.

But just for a moment he had felt a chill which had nothing to do with the sea or the wind. That he had been presented with something that was both a warning and an answer.

They left the house in a group, Liz Lawson and Grant climbing into an old Volvo and driving away while Carrick and Alder fetched their scuba equipment from Alder's pick-up truck. The sky had dulled over a little and the wind was returning.

'It'll be fine,' declared Charlie Stewart. He beckoned his sister, and they all followed him over to the pier where the clam dredger was still tied to a bollard.

A faint blue haze of smoke was already pulsing from the thin exhaust stack behind the wheelhouse. There was a man to help them aboard, and another figure waiting in the wheelhouse. When the man in the wheelhouse looked their way, Carrick recognized the bald boatman named Willie who had been there when Fred Cormack's body was recovered from the harbour.

'That's everybody. Cast off,' ordered Stewart. The deckhand, a rat-faced little man, scurried to obey, and Stewart nodded at the man in the wheelhouse. 'Move her, Willie. The usual place.'

The clam dredger's engine began thumping, the plume of exhaust thickened and then they were moving. As soon as they were clear of the pier, both Stewarts vanished below to change into scuba dress and Carrick joined Michael Alder who was in the shelter of the little deck-house aft. Alder had already removed his shore clothes and was getting into his grey rubber wet-suit.

'Got all you need?' Alder cleared some space to allow Carrick to spread out his borrowed equipment. Overhead, one of the boat's big steel-ringed bottom dredges clinked and rattled as its purse-like bag swayed with the roll of the hull and for a moment the man hummed to himself, under his breath. He glanced at Carrick's scuba lung, with its big single air cylinder, then thumbed at the twin tanks on his own outfit. 'I still prefer these – more endurance.'

'And more drag,' reminded Carrick.

'Drag doesn't worry me.' Alder watched as Carrick pulled out a black wet-suit with yellow-striped sleeves. He showed his chipped front tooth in a grin. 'Nice style. Prehistoric wasp?'

Each of them went through the usual ritual check list. By the time they had finished and had gone for'ard, the Stewart twins were also back on deck. Both wore black wet-suits, and wet-suits could be clumsy, unglamorous items. Charlie Stewart's was shapeless. But his sister wore a suit which looked as though it had been moulded to her measurements. Carrick knew only one maker who produced so precisely. He was American, and he was expensive.

On Keren Stewart, the expense seemed justified . . . even to the detail touch of the white cockade flash on the suit's left breast. The tall, bronzed, broad-boned woman caught his eye and grinned.

They were already out past the other fishing boats at anchor in the bay and the clam dredger was obviously being lined against some on-shore marks. The boat began to slow, her engine died, then the anchor chain rattled out. She drifted briefly, jerked as the anchor took hold, then swung on it.

'All ready?' asked Charlie Stewart. 'Then let's do it!'

A ladder had been hooked to the boat's port side. But the sea lapped near enough below and, one by one, they simply went in. Carrick was third in line to pull his face mask down, bite on his scuba-lung mouthpiece, and step off. He went under, the sea hit him with its usual first chill, then he surfaced again with water sparkling like diamonds on the face-mask glass as a glimpse of sunlight

204

suddenly escaped between the clouds overhead. He saw Alder about to step off, and duck-dived down.

It was the way Keren Stewart had told him. He reached bottom at a quiver short of sixty feet on his wrist-gauge, and at that depth and in the bay's clarity of water it was like being submerged in a soft twilight. The reef was a jungle of rock and weed inhabited by hundreds of small, darting fish. Briefly, he centred on the clam dredger's angled anchor chain and the black shape of the underside of her hull overhead.

He felt a hard tap on his shoulder, kicked and rolled round in sheer reflex action – and Keren Stewart shaped a query at him through her face-mask glass, bubbles of exhaled air pluming gently above her.

Carrick nodded. Satisfied, she beckoned and led the way in a powerful crawl-beat kick. He followed. To their left, he caught a glimpse of her brother and Alder, black suit and grey suit, swimming in the same direction.

It was simple, it was routine, it should have relaxed him. At another time, it could even have been enjoyable. He followed the supple, black-suited figure of Keren Stewart along and around the reef, seeing that white cockade every now and again as she turned to make sure he was still there.

At one place, she showed him a strange, circular underwater garden where flat slabs of rock had been edged with a low green weed. At another, there were the bare, skeletal ribs of an old wooden hull, scoured thin by the tides. As they passed, a conger eel briefly showed its killer face then quickly drew back into the blackness under a rock. They chased a hurrying lobster but lost it among a forest tangle of wrackweed. A family of big, fat, unexpected bass swept past, large-scaled, blue-backed fish that didn't often come so far north.

Five minutes short of the forty minutes, Keren Stewart signalled that the dive was over. He let her lead the way back along the reef, then they made a gradual, controlled ascent towards the black hull. They broke surface within easy distance astern of the clam dredger, and she pointed towards the ladder on the port side, signalling she would go first. Carrick nodded, then began to swim after her at a more leisurely pace.

Keren Stewart reached the ladder and pulled herself out of the water. Swimming in behind her, Carrick saw her pause, push up her face mask and stare back at him.

Something happening aft on the clam dredger caught his eye. Then, bare moments later, the sky seemed to fill with a great heavy web. It was winging out, it was dropping over him . . . and in the same heartbeat as the big steel triangle of the clam dredge and its jangling mesh of welded steel rings smashed down, Webb Carrick suddenly knew why it was happening, why the salmon raiding off Lannair mattered so much.

It had all been there. For anyone who put it in the right order. One way and another, it had been almost spelled out for him. If he had only remembered more about the St Kilda Mailboat . . .

Then the massive clam dredge, shackled to that long, thick steel bar, was over him and around him and taking him down as it plummeted towards the bottom of the bay.

What had taken minutes coming up took seconds going down. Carrick struggled, he fought to keep the lifegiving mouthpiece between his teeth while his air demand valve fought to cope, he was thrown full length as the dredge hit the bottom in a dense cloud of disturbed ooze and tiny, startled fish.

At the same time, he heard a strange, distant rumble. The clam dredger was upping anchor. He knew what was certain to follow.

It did. Slowly, while he struggled and fought for a way out, the steel trap began moving. The dredge was being dragged over the bottom at a gradually increasing pace.

A first dredged clam was swept into the steel purse. Then another, and a huge grey flatfish followed. Small, snagged rocks broke off and tumbled in. Thrown about,

hauled along, the scuba tank constantly grating and banging against the metal rings cloaked around him, Carrick
wanted to scream, wanted to curse, wanted to call out –
but couldn't do any of them.

Not without losing his grip on that all-important
mouthpiece.

The dredge was being pulled straight towards some
short pinnacles of rock. Carrick saw them coming, then
the metal bars were bouncing and scraping and he was
thrown around again, struck on the head by something
hard, left partly dazed. A few more big clams had been
brought in, along with strands of weed, a large crab, and
a couple of frantic mullet.

Then, when his senses were beginning to give way, the
whole dredge took a sudden lurch to one side. It swung.
It emptied. He was falling, freed like the frantic, fleeing
fish and the sinking, vanishing clams and broken pieces
of rock.

Charlie Stewart had talked of deep water beyond the
reef, part of his mockery of a warning before an audience.
Now the dredge had reached it, had fallen over the edge
of some underwater precipice.

And he had been reprieved from a certain, brutal death.
He could see the metal purse still swinging through the
water like a pendulum, going away. Up above, the people
on the clam dredger would quickly know something had
happened. But what could they do apart from draw in
the dredge and find it empty? What kind of sensible search
could they mount for a man they must presume they had
almost certainly killed already?

It was what he did next that mattered.

Achieving it took the discipline of desperation while he
fought to clear his numbed mind and control his battered,
pain-filled body. Somehow, his scuba lung was still operating, even though his depth-gauge and his wristwatch had
both been torn away. His thick rubber wet-suit had been
ripped to tatters, with one entire leg and most of both

207

arms missing. Now, above all, Carrick knew he must fight down the urge to get back up to the surface.

He had plenty of air. He could guess depth by the light around him and let himself float. He could count seconds to make minutes, add minutes together. He had to use the sea as his friend again, his ally – compared with what might still be prowling above.

It seemed like for ever before he decided it might be safe to start ascending. He swam up to what he decided had to be about twenty-five feet. He waited at that depth for several minutes, then rose and stopped again at ten feet, which panicked a small school of mackerel as he came up in the middle of them.

He swam a little distance, knowing that he was back over the reef. It had reached the time when his air supply should already have given out.

Webb Carrick surfaced into a heavy, chopping swell, spat out his mouthpiece, shoved back his face mask, took several long, deep lungfuls of spray-filled air, then looked around.

He was inside the sweep of the bay, even though he was a long way from the shore. The clam dredger was a faint, stern-on shape in the distance, heading back in towards its pier. At least one of the trawlers had sailed, another seemed to be moving.

Carrick pulled the CO_2 trigger to inflate his lifejacket. Nothing happened, because there was hardly any lifejacket left around him. Wearily, he dumped the scuba weight belt from around his waist then, still treading water, dumped every other piece of scuba gear that remained.

Then he began swimming for that shore. Swimming on and on. Nothing else mattered.

A long time later, a long green wave of water broke white as it reached the shore and threw him the last distance in on sandy beach. Webb Carrick crawled up to where the sand was dry.

Then he collapsed under an overhang of rock, and let the world crash with him.

It was over an hour later before he had recovered enough to realize that something very small was crawling across his arm. He raised his head enough to look, and a tiny green crab scurried off into the sand. After another couple of minutes, he sat upright, rubbed a hand across his eyes, then looked around.

Every one of the fishing boats had gone. The bay was an empty stretch of lumping, angry-looking water, the wind was north-west and was gusting enough to stir small dust-clouds from the sand around him. Overhead, the sun was edging down towards the horizon through a sky streaked with dark, hurrying cloud. The Atlantic weather low was making threats again.

Where he was, he wasn't doing anything.

Wincing at what it did to several different sets of muscles, Carrick hauled himself to his feet. He was maybe half a mile along the shore from Torquil House, which looked empty and deserted.

Between them, Keren and Charlie Stewart had tried to kill him. He'd been cold-bloodedly set up, as far as they knew they had succeeded. That meant they had found out about him . . . or had seen enough to guess.

He cursed, running his tongue over his dry, salt-tasting lips. The blue-eyed copper-haired woman had moved in on him, literally closing for the kill, while he'd been too busy watching everyone else to realize it.

But it didn't need a genius to realize that the timing had mattered, and that now the way the fishing boats had gone also mattered. Yes, Torquil House should be empty. It was also the nearest place he knew with a telephone.

He needed help.

Bitterly, he started walking along the shore, close to the swirls of foam coming in from the steady, crashing waves. He found a thick piece of driftwood that might do as a club. Carrick grimaced at it. It was almost as thick as he had been.

But now, at last, maybe he had the final edge.

Then, suddenly, as he came nearer and nearer to the big, deserted house, taking his chance on being out in the open, a new small miracle made him stop and stare. An unmistakable figure had come running from the house and was racing towards him. Carrick grinned and tossed away the club as Clapper Bell skidded to a wide-eyed halt in front of him.

'Skipper, where the bloody hell have you been?' demanded the burly man happily. 'I'd have given odds you were dead!' He looked Carrick over and shaped a silent, concerned whistle. 'You look like somebody tried hard enough. Alder?'

'Alder and the Stewart twins – both of them.' Carrick gestured at the house. 'Empty?'

'Empty.' Bell nodded. 'When we got here.'

'We?' Carrick stared at him. 'What's going on?'

'Your pal Dr Margaret got worried an' sent for us.' Still hovering close, watching him anxiously, *Tern*'s bo'sun led him towards the house.

'Sent who?'

'Her.' Bell thumbed. 'In their dinghy.'

Martha Edwards was standing in the doorway ahead, her feet placed firmly apart, hands resting on her broad hips, a satisfied beam on her pudgy face, a beam that faded slightly at the edges as she saw Carrick's condition.

'Shit,' she said softly.

She wasn't alone. Russ Donald, his head still bandaged, had appeared behind her.

'Any more of you?' asked Carrick.

'No.' Martha Edwards looked at Bell, grinned at him and shook her head. 'No need.'

There was no mystery about how they'd got in. There was splintered wood where the front door had been kicked in. The clear imprint of a large boot-heel began exactly four fingerwidths below the lock. Exactly four finger-widths. It was one of Clapper Bell's trademarks.

'I'll be back,' said Russ Donald. *Pippin*'s skipper turned on his heel and hurried off.

Martha Edwards and Bell took Carrick into the big front room where he'd met with the rest of the Stewart scuba party only a few hours earlier. He flopped into a chair, and nodded his thanks as the woman found the drinks cabinet and brought him back a crystal tumbler filled to the brim with whisky.

'Medicine,' she said shortly. 'The hell with what doctors say.'

Carrick took a first long gulp, put the glass down on the floor beside the chair, and let the whisky seep new life into him. 'Where's *Tern*?' he asked.

'At Port Torquil,' said Russ Donald, overhearing as he joined them again. He was carrying a bundle of clothes, the clothes Carrick had been wearing when he boarded the clam dredger. 'Yours?'

'Yes.'

'They must have brought them ashore when they came back. Who could mistake the famous Pilsudski jacket?' Donald dropped the bundle into his lap. 'You could use them.'

'*Tern* first,' insisted Carrick. If the patrol launch was openly lying off Port Torquil –

'Relax, skipper,' soothed Clapper Bell. 'There's no problem an' it saved time. We put a canvas bandage on her nose an' covered her name. As far as Port Torquil's concerned, they're looking at *Puffin* as usual.'

'Twins, aren't they?' reminded Russ Donald. Add his own *Pippin* and there had been triplets. 'We'll get away with it. I radioed Johnny Walker to stay clear.'

'So finish that drink and get out of the distressed merman outfit,' ordered Martha Edwards. She shaped a scowl. 'I've seen men before, so don't expect me to be impressed.'

But she still winced as Carrick changed and they saw

211

the many surface cuts and the already visible bruising which covered much of his body.

'How?' she asked quietly.

He told them in a sentence while he finished, pulling the denim trousers up over his shirt tails and zipping the front. His body still ached. But he was gradually feeling better, stronger – wanting answers to a queue of his own questions. Russ Donald met a couple before he could ask.

'Harry Gold's repair yard is shut, empty – we checked. Then we – uh – borrowed a car that was there.'

'Hot-wired it, skipper.' Clapper Bell gave Martha Edwards a glance of admiration. 'She did. Fast and neat.'

'It was my degree-course option,' said Martha Edwards. 'A pleasure.' Her plain, plump face became serious. 'You could have told me earlier – you or Dr Margaret. I wondered about you.'

'Sorry.' Coaxing a dinghy along the coast in that ugly, cross-cutting swell to reach *Tern* could have been no easy task. 'Anyone who knew was at risk, Martha.'

It only partly satisfied her. But she fell silent.

'Webb.' Russ Donald asked it mildly. He could have been discussing the weather. 'Do we know what the hell is going on?'

'Now? Yes.' Carrick drained the last of the whisky from the crystal tumbler. 'Most of it.' Like magic, Clapper Bell had appeared beside him with the whisky bottle and the tumbler had refilled. Carrick nursed the glass. It gave his hands something to do and stopped them from shaking. 'Ever heard of the St Kilda Mailboat – any of you?'

'Skipper?' Bell's big, rugged face showed a struggle as he attempted to understand. Martha Edwards looked blank, shook her head, and sat on the arm of a chair. What might have been the start of a glimmer of understanding showed in Russ Donald's eyes, but he stayed silent. That left it to Bell to try again. 'St Kilda, skipper?'

Anyone who knew the seas of the Hebrides knew St Kilda, three tiny islands falling off the map, isolated more than 110 miles west of the mainland. A tiny, diminishing community of forty men, women and children had finally been evacuated in the 1930s. Their ancestors had been there since prehistoric times, they had reared a unique species of goat-like sheep and had caught fish and sea-birds. Isolated from civilization, most of them only spoke Gaelic and had a way of life that was centuries behind the outside world. On the mainland, some of them had soon died quickly from a broken heart.

'St Kilda was evacuated because of storms. Usually, it was cut off from the rest of the world at least eight months of the year. No ship could get through. Helicopters didn't exist. If you were injured or took ill, the odds were you died.' Carrick set down the whisky glass. 'So – one hundred and ten miles out in the Atlantic, when there wasn't going to be any contact from the mainland for months, how did they send urgent news, what did they do to tell the outside world about disaster, anything?'

'Straight out of the past,' said Russ Donald softly. 'Yes, I remember.'

'Clapper?'

Chief Petty Officer William 'Clapper' Bell gave a slow nod. 'I've heard Gogi MacDonnell on about it. I know.'

'But I'm damned if I do,' scowled Martha Edwards, hunched forward on the chair-arm. 'Forget the ancient legends. Hell, Webb, we're talking about people getting killed – today, here, now!'

'The St Kilda Mailboat was like putting a note in a bottle and throwing it into the sea,' said Carrick patiently. 'Except the people on St Kilda used a hollowed-out wooden tube, an exact size and exact weight. They put their letters inside it, they added their orders for food and clothes and medicine – and they launched their mailboat from a specific spot at a specific state of the tide.'

The plump, aggressive woman stared at him. She moistened her lips.

'They knew where the currents would take it?'

Carrick nodded. 'A lot of the time, their mailboats were washed in on a mainland beach a couple of weeks later.

213

It was one-way, it was primitive. But it was a link. Their only link in the storm months.'

'And we've got the Noah Pipeline,' said Russ Donald softly. 'Mapped out all the way by all-singing, all-dancing, all updated computer graphs. Mapped all the way from – where is it, Iceland?'

'Greenland,' said Carrick.

'So if you launch into the Noah Pipeline, launch something that matters, then – ' *Pippin*'s skipper fiercely massaged his bandaged head ' – then it should come in along probably the same route as the salmon. Except it's crazy! They'd need to cover the whole width of that pipeline!'

'Miles,' agreed Carrick.

'They do, damn them!' Suddenly, Donald understood. 'The salmon nets! Hell, what width is the Noah?'

'Three miles, four at the most,' said Martha Edwards woodenly. 'I'm not supposed to know about it – Dr Margaret keeps any Noah data to herself.' She grinned a little. 'Except that most of us can access her computer. Someday we'll tell her.'

'Pay off the hired peasants with the salmon and a cash bonus, keep the real profit on the other catch they net – ' Clapper Bell caught up and was impressed. He sucked hard and noisily on his strong white teeth. 'We're talking smuggling? Big-time?'

'All the way from Greenland?' Martha Edwards gave an aggressive snort. 'Big-time what? Fairytales?'

'Think on it,' said Carrick softly. He moved a little, and winced as a multitude of bruised muscles protested. 'Suppose it happens a lot of miles away from here, on one of the regular Atlantic shipping routes. You need a ship going direct from A to B, and a crew who will keep their mouths shut. You dump your packages into the sea at an exact location. You send a signal. Please collect!' He paused and sipped the whisky again. 'Somebody does – at this end, courtesy of the Noah Pipeline!'

And a ship that hadn't gone anywhere near land and

hadn't gone anywhere near another vessel had delivered her cargo.

Yet so much of it had been there to see, right from the start. The Noah Pipeline and the attack on *Pippin*. James Kennedy's radio transmitter. Margaret Steeven being able to compute where some drowned fishermen would be washed ashore. The size of rewards that would be needed to persuade Stewarts and Grants to work together.

Even those damned stupid carved fish mounted on the walls of the Pride of Mull might have nudged his mind . . .

'Clever bastards,' said Clapper Bell hoarsely.

'Get it right, bo'sun,' said Russ Donald, his voice like ice. 'Murdering clever bastards.'

Bell was still holding the opened whisky bottle. He nodded, scratched his chin, took a swallow direct from it, then saw Martha Edwards frown.

'Sorry, lady.' Apologetically, he wiped the mouth of the bottle with his sleeve then offered it.

'Thank you.' Almost absentmindedly, she took the bottle, looked at it in some surprise, then nodded, raised it to her lips, and drank. She grimaced. 'All right, I'll take it as real. You think it's happening again, tonight?'

'Yes.' He had one good reason, separate from anything else. 'Give things another week, and the Noah Pipeline will have gone off the boil for the season.'

'Dr Margaret says?'

He nodded.

'Who am I to argue?' She sighed. Then she paused, frowning, looking at each of the three Fishery Protection men in turn. 'Smuggling. Smuggling what, from where?'

'I know who to ask,' said Carrick, standing. He felt fewer pains than he had expected. There were times when whisky could be a good medication. 'We head back to Port Torquil. Russ, can you contact Fleet Support from *Tern*, bring them up to date? Martha, tell Dr Margaret all this – no one else.'

They both nodded.

'That leaves you an' me,' said Clapper Bell. He raised a massive eyebrow in a silent question.

'We're going to visit a medical man,' said Carrick. 'Without an appointment.'

Then, ankles still protesting every step he took, he led them out of the big, drab house and pulled the door shut behind them. The wind, he noticed, was now steady from the north-west – and still gradually rising.

The car that Martha Edwards had hot-wired and taken from Harry Gold's repair yard was a rusty, nondescript Ford station wagon. It had stained, greasy upholstery and smelled of stale cigarette smoke. The suspension had gone. But it fired first time and ran smoothly. She drove with Clapper Bell beside her, Carrick talking with Russ Donald in the rear and giving *Pippin*'s skipper a quick outline of anything helpful that he knew.

Away from the bay, over the great rise of Torquil's Shield, they bumped and bounced along the hill track down towards the fishing village spread out below them. The anonymous grey shape of a patrol launch was lying at anchor just outside the harbour entrance.

To anyone who hadn't lived with them day after day and week after week, she could have been *Puffin* as usual.

When they reached the start of the village, Martha Edwards stopped the Ford briefly while Carrick and Bell climbed out. Then she let it murmur off again, heading for the harbour.

James Kennedy's house was in the next street. Carrick and Bell walked to the corner, then Carrick stopped.

'Two minutes, Clapper. He doesn't know you.'

'Fine.' Bell gave what was meant as a friendly nod to a woman who was passing with two children. She sniffed hard and walked faster, dragging the children along. The Glasgow-Irishman grunted to himself. 'You too, lady! Two minutes is fine, skipper.'

Bell set off alone, just one more man in the standard Port Torquil male outfit of a sweater and denims. From the corner, Carrick watched as the big bo'sun reached

216

Kennedy's house, turned in at the brass plate, walked up the short path, then rang the doorbell. A few moments passed, the Glasgow-Irishman tried the doorbell again, and then, the way Carrick had expected, the curtain twitched at the living-room window and a round face peered out.

Kennedy saw a stranger, and stayed at the window just a moment longer. But there was no one else in sight – just a man who might have been a fisherman. Clapper Bell scowled, pointed a finger at Kennedy, then pointed urgently at the door. Kennedy vanished from the window.

What happened next was quick and fuss-free and Carrick only saw part of it. One moment the house door had opened just a crack. Next moment there was a thud of wood hitting flesh as Clapper Bell used a shovel-like hand to shove the door hard back on its hinges. There was a muffled, partly frightened yelp of pain, then Bell had gone inside the house and the door had almost closed again.

Carrick walked over, past a man working in his garden. The man was busy and didn't look up. Nothing stirred among the neighbouring homes. He reached Kennedy's house, went through the open door and closed it behind him.

'Welcome aboard, skipper,' said Clapper Bell cheerfully.

Carrick locked the door. Bell was standing just inside the little hallway, pinning Kennedy against the wall at full arm's length, one massive hand stretched around the medical man's thick throat. Kennedy's face was pouring blood from a split lip, a gashed forehead and damaged nose. He was moaning – softly. Bell's hand around his throat was making it difficult.

'Let him breathe a little,' suggested Carrick.

Bell obliged.

'This – this animal – ' almost incoherent, taking great gulps of air, Kennedy forced the words out ' – he attacked me!' Then he seemed suddenly to realize who was in front

217

of him. His eyes, already terrified, widened. 'Carrick? I –
I don't understand – '

'If you were told I was dead, don't believe it.' Carrick
ran his hands over the man's clothing. Kennedy was still
wearing his weekend jacket and lightweight linen trousers.
He wasn't armed. 'Anyone else in the house?'

Kennedy gave a small, frightened shake of his head.

'Check,' Carrick told Bell. 'If there's a back door, make
sure it's locked.'

The big man nodded, released his grip on Kennedy's
throat, wiped some blood from his hand by rubbing it
down Kennedy's jacket front, then ambled off. Shakily,
Kennedy took a handkerchief from one of his pockets and
held it like a pad against his injured mouth and nose.

'Listen to me,' said Carrick softly. 'Everyone who matters is out with the boats – everyone except you. Right
now, I don't give a damn what you try to deny. I'm going
to let you go into your surgery. I'm going to let you do
some first aid on that face. Then we go upstairs – ' he
saw Kennedy's eyes flicker ' – upstairs to the radio room.
Try anything, and you'll wish you hadn't. My large friend
likes throwing people through upstairs windows.'

It was a mild libel on Clapper Bell. But the quivering
village doctor swallowed and nodded.

They went into the surgery and Carrick stayed close
while the plump, still shaking figure splashed water on
his face from a washbasin and treated his cuts.

'This is only so you have a chance to start thinking,'
Carrick told him curtly. 'There are no kind words, Kennedy – not any more.'

Clapper Bell returned and nodded that his task was
done. Kennedy in the middle, they went up the stairs and
into the little spare room with its sparse furnishings and
the radio apparatus. The pencilled DL 048 was still there
on the tuning dial above the auxiliary set, handily close
to the telephone extension for reference. The main transmitter was live and humming gently.

'Skipper – ' Bell made it a soft growl of a warning at

the same time as he grabbed Kennedy by the shoulder ' – he's helluva interested in the drawer under that table. Want to check it?'

Carrick had barely noticed the man stealthily easing towards the small table Bell indicated. But, having been stopped, Kennedy had a new fear in his eyes. Carrick crossed over and opened the drawer. There were some spare signal pads and other incidentals at the front, then he opened the drawer a little wider. He reached in and drew out a compact, chrome-finished Walther ·32 automatic pistol. When he checked, it was loaded with a full seven-round magazine clip.

'Every doctor should have one – depending on his patients,' mused Carrick. He squinted down the barrel of the Walther and almost grinned. The bore was thick with dust and ooze. A very long time had passed since it had last been fired anywhere. While Kennedy watched in silence, he dropped the gun into a pocket. Then he swung back to the radio transmitter. It was set to a frequency slightly below the usual fishing setting, being used for the moment only as a receiver. The auxiliary set was monitoring the regular frequency. At last, stony-faced, he turned to Kennedy. 'Well, doctor? Going to tell us about it?'

'No.' Kennedy swallowed hard. He spoke slowly, carefully. 'I don't understand why you're here. I – someone gave me that gun years ago, I just keep it in that drawer.'

'But you'd never dream of touching it,' said Carrick sarcastically. He considered the village doctor again carefully. 'I know someone who wants to thank you for sending that Mayday message after the Fishery Protection patrol launch was bombed – her skipper. He's in Port Torquil right now.'

'I – ' Kennedy dabbed a hand against his damaged, swollen lip. 'I didn't – '

'Don't be so damned stupid,' said Carrick patiently. 'The coastguard tape all Maydays. We identified your voice. Remember a telephone call you had a few days

ago, a medical supplies offer? That was all we needed.'
He saw the horror struggling on Kennedy's face. 'The
Mayday is probably the one sane thing you did, Kennedy
– and we've got you half a dozen other ways.' He paused
and drew in a deep breath of disgust. 'You're the village
doctor, someone people trust. What the hell are you doing
in this kind of a mess?'

James Kennedy seemed too frightened, too stunned to
say anything.

'Tell me one thing,' said Carrick very quietly. 'What
did you do with the old man you shipped off to the
mainland for Alder – old John Hill? Did you kill him?'

'No! They – they wanted to, but I wouldn't let them.
He's hidden away in a safe place.' Suddenly, the plump
man's defences totally disintegrated. He was shaking
again. 'Alder said he was in the way, that he had to go
– that's why I got him out.'

'And fixed it so Alder keeps drawing old uncle's pension.'

'He's not Alder's uncle,' said Kennedy wearily. 'Alder
just sold him on the idea so that Alder had a first foothold
here.'

'All right.' It was a start. Kennedy was the weak link,
the one still so badly needed. But just at that moment,
the white-faced doctor, his smart jacket spattered with
bloodstains, looked near to collapse. Carrick glanced at
Clapper Bell, who had gone back to lounge against the
door-frame. 'Get him a chair.'

The Glasgow-Irishman grunted, ambled across the
room, came back with a straight-back cane chair, and
slapped it down.

'Sit,' he barked.

Kennedy sat.

A whisper of a voice sounded above the low static
coming from the auxiliary set. It was a distant message
from one fishing boat to another, far to the north. A
fainter voice replied, acknowledging, then there was only

220

the static again. Saturday nights were meant for better things.

'Where were you when they attacked *Pippin*?' asked Carrick unemotionally.

'Here.' James Kennedy gave a small shrug. 'They didn't realize it was a patrol launch at first. Then – well, they thought she was sinking, they wanted to get away.'

'Do they know you sent that anonymous Mayday?'

Kennedy shook his head.

'Why did you do it?' Carrick stood over the man, and provided his own answer. 'Was it because you heard what was happening, because you remembered another fishing boat, the *Iris*?'

'Yes.' Kennedy looked down at his feet. He shook his head. 'Charlie Stewart came here about an hour ago, before they all sailed. He said you were dead. We – we knew from last night that you were Fishery Protection.'

Clapper Bell, leaning at his doorpost again, gave a rumble of interest. 'How?'

'Your little runaway deckhand, Torrance,' said James Kennedy. He ran a cautious tongue over his gashed, already swollen lips, moistening them. 'He listens at cabin doors – including Margaret Steeven's. He remembers when a new man stays out late.' He eyed Carrick slyly. 'Torrance turned up at Harry Gold's yard, looking for a job. Harry bought him a couple of drinks – that was all it took.'

'Where is Torrance?' asked Carrick.

'Tucked away on a Stewart trawler.' Kennedy hesitated, suddenly uneasy. 'I – I'm only hired help, right? My being able to front as a doctor is something they like. I do that, I tend this radio – ' He let his voice die away.

'What's coming in tonight?' Carrick's voice was iron hard.

'I – ' Kennedy paused and swallowed. 'Drugs.'

'What kind of drugs?' Carrick's voice didn't change.

'Cocaine. Uncut Colombian.' Kennedy squirmed warily in his chair. 'Shipped out through Venezuela.'

221

'What quantity?'

'This time?' The plump man sighed through his swollen lips. 'Four tons . . . metric.'

Clapper Bell whistled to himself. Carrick stared, his mind suddenly turned to ice. Four metric tons of cocaine, 1,000 kilogrammes to a metric ton.

In street value, it would represent mind-boggling millions – and Kennedy had said 'this time'.

'Once they've netted it, where do they bring it in?' he demanded.

'So you don't know that part?' Kennedy gave a sickly grin, then cringed as he saw Carrick's expression. 'I'm helping. You'll remember that?'

'Where does it come in?'

'It doesn't – not here. That's why it has worked!' Kennedy tried to force his grin again. 'That cocaine travels on! Think – what's the last big up-for-grabs market for hard drugs left in the world? Not North America, not Western Europe – they're tied up. This is new frontiers, Eastern Europe, right? *Glasnost*. That's where the drug cartels see the market place!' Looking at each of them in turn he saw their contempt and finished feebly. 'But – anyway, we're just handling agents.'

'Explain,' said Carrick softly. 'Who runs this end? Alder?'

'Keren Stewart,' said Kennedy simply. 'She's the boss, brother Charlie just does what he's told, Michael Alder keeps an eye on things for the cartel.'

'Bloody hell,' said Clapper Bell softly.

Carrick chewed his lip. Any last faint illusion of doubt that might have remained had just been destroyed. Keren Stewart, the beautiful lioness, was his real enemy – however hard it was to believe.

'Here's how it works.' Kennedy plunged on. 'There's a ship on one of the transatlantic runs, heading for Rotterdam or Hamburg – anywhere but the UK. Right?

'At an exact point off the Scottish coast, at an exact time to an exact schedule, she stops and floats off her containers. They're plastic, with enough negative buoyancy to keep them submerged.' He grew in confidence, telling of things he knew well. 'The delivery coming in now was floated off at dusk three days ago. It's been travelling in with the current ever since. We're talking twenty containers, each holding two hundred kilogrammes. They reach the salmon nets between nine and midnight tonight.'

'Suppose some don't?' demanded Clapper Bell.

'Allowed for.' Kennedy nodded. 'They lost a few last time. But there's a timed self-destruct in each container. They'd sink long before they came ashore.' He was eager to finish. 'When they're collected, all the containers are transferred to Charlie Stewart's *Stargirl*. She's fast. She heads north for maybe a couple of hours – where there just happens to be a Russian trawler plodding along. Twenty minutes together, the containers have been transferred – goodbye, *tovarich*.'

It was smooth, it was simple. Carrick nodded a resigned understanding. The *Stargirl* could be back in Port Torquil before dawn. An unknown, unseen cargo ship was already days away – and a steady flow of fishing boats of all nationalities travelled legitimately between the mainland and the islands. As long as they weren't fishing, as long as they didn't come into a harbour, they weren't troubled.

When that Russian trawler got back to its Baltic home port, its papers would show it hadn't touched land. Probably, by then, four metric tons of cocaine had already been off-loaded to another local boat –

The risks were minimal.

Or had been.

Suddenly, Dr James Kennedy wouldn't stop talking.

Beginning with how he had been recruited by Michael Alder, who knew his past. Alder was already established in Port Torquil and, once Keren Stewart had interviewed and approved Kennedy, they had footed the bill to move their new doctor over from the mainland. The radio transmitter had been secretly installed in the spare room, which was kept locked when the occasional cleaning woman came in.

He talked details, he talked people, he talked radio schedules. He only knew that the cocaine operation was Florida-based, and that Old Charlie Stewart, living in retirement out there, was also somehow involved.

Maybe through reasons of self-preservation, he also wanted to talk about Keren Stewart.

Keren Stewart.

Keren Stewart the manipulator. The copper-haired woman's role as leader went back to when she had heard a first hint about the Noah Pipeline from an unsuspecting Margaret Steeven, who had then gradually, unwittingly, provided other scraps which could be put together.

But not enough. Keren Stewart's next step had been to ease her one-time university friend, Rose Cullar, into the research team when a job as Margaret Steeven's secretary-assistant became available. A second innocent source went into place, to be ruthlessly exploited. Rose Cullar had access to all of Dr Margaret Steeven's records.

The doorbell rang below. Carrick stopped him, went over to the room window, looked down, and saw Russ Donald standing outside. Martha Edwards had come back with him.

'Let them in,' he told Clapper Bell.

Then he stopped at the window for a moment, looking out, while the big Glasgow-Irishman padded downstairs. There were more and more gulls flying over the village and around Torquil's Shield. The white birds could be as good as any barometer when it came to forecasting weather, but the other signs were there in the fading light. There were racing clouds overhead. A gust of wind found gaps in the window-frame beside him and made it rattle.

The Atlantic depression was stalking nearer.

The front door opened and closed, then he heard voices murmuring below. Clapper Bell was giving a brief summary of what had gone on.

'Kennedy – ' Carrick turned on the man again ' – what

about the Grants? Why do they go along with the Stewarts in this?'

'Some Grants, and some Stewarts, the ones they thought would go along with most things. The balance of the crews has been brought in from the mainland,' corrected Kennedy with an almost petulant precision. 'The Stewarts needed the Grant boats as well as their own. Once he was persuaded, Sam Lawson talked a few of his people into it. They don't ask what they're smuggling, they don't want to know – they're happy with the money they're getting.'

'How was Sam Lawson "persuaded"?' asked Carrick grimly.

'His daughter.' Kennedy's round face suddenly looked very old and very tired, like a half-deflated football. 'Out of the blue, they told him where she worked in London, where she lived, named her friends – and said they'd kill her. He was sensible – he believed them.'

'But when she turned up here?'

'How do you think Lawson heard she was coming?' There were footsteps on the stairway. Carefully, Kennedy clasped his hands together on his lap as if preparing himself for anything. 'Keren Stewart telephoned that morning to tell him.'

'Where is Liz Lawson now – right now?' Carrick glanced briefly at the three figures entering the room and silenced them with a gesture. 'Where is she, Kennedy?'

'She's safe enough.' Kennedy made an attempt at an ingratiating smile towards Martha Edwards and Russ Donald. 'They grabbed her this afternoon – and Tom Grant, because he was with her. Both of them are locked in an outhouse at Michael Alder's place.' He hesitated, then made a small additional confession. 'They're – ah – slightly sedated.'

'You bastard,' said Martha Edwards huskily. She took one stride forward and hit Kennedy across the face with the back of her hand. It sounded like a pistol shot. Then she turned to Carrick. 'The rest of it is true?'

225

He nodded but got their news first.

Russ Donald had gone out to *Tern* and had reported to Fleet Support. John Kennan, ignoring it was Saturday, had been at his desk.

'He's stirring the hive,' distilled Russ Donald dryly. 'You've to get to Lannair, fast.'

'And Dr Margaret?' asked Carrick.

'Ready to kill on sight,' said Martha Edwards, remembering.

Carrick grinned. He reached into his pocket, took out the chrome-plated Walther, and handed it to Russ Donald.

'You'd better have this,' he told *Pippin*'s skipper.

'I've got the short straw,' agreed Donald sadly. 'So what's to do?'

It took only minutes to sort out. Then Carrick glanced at Clapper Bell, who had been making a small alteration to one part of the transmitter's wiring circuit under Martha Edwards' critical guidance.

'Ready, skipper,' agreed Bell with some relief. 'You?'

'In a moment.' Carrick turned to the sad slump of a figure that was James Kennedy, now tied to his chair. There was one mind-niggling thing he wanted to know. 'A few nights back, Keren Stewart came here late. You gave her a parcel. What was in it?'

'That?' Kennedy took a moment to understand, then gave a noise close to a hysterical giggle. 'You worried about that? Rat poison, Carrick – they've rats at Torquil House, the four-legged kind. I made up some stuff to kill them off – ' he gave a sudden glare ' – maybe I should have made some extra.' He drew breath. 'My turn. What brought you nosing in my direction?'

'Whisky,' said Carrick.

He gave a small smile to Martha Edwards and nodded to Russ Donald. Then, Clapper Bell at his heels, leaving an open-mouthed Kennedy still staring, he went downstairs and left the house.

226

The wind had strengthened. They headed for the harbour.

Fifteen minutes later the grey patrol launch that had been lying off Port Torquil harbour quietly hauled up her anchor and made an apparently leisurely departure into the deepening dusk and the chopping, heaving swell.

Carrick was in the command chair, Clapper Bell beside him in the coxswain's seat. They had walked through the Saturday-night empty harbour in that same half light to where Bell had left a rubber dinghy. They had seen no one, and the research boat *Dirk* had been one of the few patches of light on the two long quays. When they had boarded *Tern*, Carrick still made sure nothing was done at a rush.

Everything had to seem normal. One gossiping fishing boat skipper using his radio might be enough to alert the salmon-net boats.

'How many of them, skipper?' asked Andy Grey.

'A maximum of eight boats, maybe thirty-five men.' That much Carrick had been told by Kennedy. It matched the boats he'd seen earlier off Torquil House plus some of the gaps around the harbour. He glanced round at Grey, who was checking their radar screen. 'Anything around?'

'Clear, skipper,' confirmed the dark-haired Second Officer.

Carrick looked back at the great bulk of Torquil's Shield as *Tern* muttered slowly away from the little harbour. The raw face of rock was crowned by heavy ribbons of thick, fast cloud. The barometer was still falling, and the heavy swells around were becoming tipped with white. He used the engineroom intercom.

'Sam – ' he heard a grunt of a reply ' – we'll start winding them up.'

'Hi-ho, hi-ho,' said Pilsudski brightly. 'Off to work!'

That left Gogi MacDonnell, who had gone aft to unpack the weapons that had been sent aboard. He had other tasks waiting when that was done. Carrick closed the intercom switch.

'Clapper, come round to 270 degrees.' He watched Bell feed the big, thin-rimmed steering wheel, could imagine the big triple rudders biting underwater, then saw the compass card wing under its dull binnacle light as the patrol launch turned. His right hand reached for the throttle levers. 'Going to two thirds ahead, all engines.'

In a moment, *Tern*'s three big V8 diesels had gone from a murmur to a roar. Her wake astern began building, spray lashed at her bridge windows. Bucking along, her hull vibration increasing, she seemed to come alive, to be in her real element.

She had an appointment to keep, off Lannair Island.

'Skipper – ' Andy Grey had come for'ard from the radar screen, his thin young face questioning ' – you reckon they're out there now?'

'Exactly now.' Dusk was giving way to dark, the moon was occasionally breaking through the clouds still sweeping overhead. He was going by James Kennedy's timings. 'Nets going down, then waiting.'

'What happens when they radio Kennedy?' persisted Grey.

'Clapper fixed that – with a little help.' He thought of Martha Edwards frowning, instructing, and grinned. In the background, he noticed that Gogi MacDonnell had returned and was listening. 'All they're going to hear back is some squashed electronic noises.'

'Guaranteed,' confirmed Clapper Bell cheerfully, nursing the wheel.

'This Kennedy – ' Gogi MacDonnell made it a protest from behind them ' – can you trust him, skipper?'

Carrick nodded. 'Because we've got him by the dangling bits.'

'Aye.' Satisfied, MacDonnell shoved back his woollen cap. 'A Kennedy – strange. I know a few Kennedys. One is about the most decent man I know – even though he's from Coll.'

With the judgement delivered, Chief Petty Officer Gogi MacDonnell headed aft again.

Tern bucked on through the steady swell. The barometer steadied briefly – and as it did, the bridge radio tuned to Fishery Protection's private frequency coughed to life with their call-sign. Switching in the scrambler circuit, Carrick answered and found the caller was John Kennan, from his Fleet Support desk.

'Mother says you've to stop playing rough games,' said Kennan dryly. 'Russ Donald made it sound interesting. How do you feel?'

'Fine.' He was still discovering new aches every time he moved.

'Good.' Kennan was satisfied. 'Found *Puffin* yet?'

'Any time now.'

'If Walker hasn't got lost,' said Kennan flatly. There was a moment's pause when static ruled. 'Here's an update, our end. Two fishery cruisers heading your way as promised – *Blackfish* and *Marlin*. They're coming at you from the west, they'll need a couple of hours. You've got *Lapwing* trying to get into the act from the north, but no promises.' They could hear him draw breath. 'There's a Royal Navy frigate on her way up from the Clyde, our Irish friends are watching their side, I've an American nuclear submarine that wants in on the act, and there's air search-and-rescue support on standby. Enough?'

'Enough.' Carrick swallowed, glanced over at Clapper Bell, and winked. *Marlin* had been their last ship, still ruled by a fire-and-sword Captain James Shannon. He maintained a personal feud with *Blackfish*'s captain – neither of them would be slacking. *Lapwing* was different, the latest addition to the patrol launch nest, still officially finishing her sea trials. But he had one question left unanswered. 'Any new word from Port Torquil?'

'Not yet.' Kennan understood. 'I'll get back to you when they find the Lawson girl. Out.'

'Out.' Carrick flicked switches back to standby.

He saw the barometer. It had fallen again, and *Tern*

was bucking through a new set of wave troughs that were the wrong size for her length.

The Stewarts had picked a bad night for their containers to arrive. But Atlantic weather never did give a damn for anyone, anytime.

Five minutes later they had *Puffin* on radar, coming up from the south. Another eight minutes, and Johnny Walker had swung his small command in a curving turn which brought her plunging and thudding almost parallel with *Tern*, their broad washes blending astern under the fitful moonlight. A signal lamp clattered from *Puffin*'s bridge, *Tern* flashed back an affirmative, and both patrol launches reduced speed to little more than steerage way, keeping bow-on to the heavy seas.

They had met about a mile east of the Sula Rocks, a white line breaking water in the blackness ahead. Lannair Island was beyond that, a few miles to the north. There was movement inside *Puffin*'s enclosed bridge, then a figure in oilskins and clutching a loud-hailer scrambled out on the heaving, water-lashed deck. Johnny Walker waved briefly as Carrick similarly emerged on *Tern*. *Puffin*'s pudgy skipper clipped a safety harness to a line, then raised his loud-hailer.

'Helluva night for it, Webb,' his voice rasped across the heaving gap between them. 'I'll save time. Fleet Support briefed me. So what now?'

Carrick used his own loud-hailer. 'The net-line should be west of Lannair. We'll go round by the north. Stay visual – no lights, no radio except in emergency. Half speed.'

'Sneak up on them.' Walker's voice rasped back. 'Understood. What's the chance they've a new lookout on Lannair?'

'Every chance,' replied Carrick briefly.

'Helps to know.' Walker's loud-hailer briefly developed a squeal then barked again. 'Question. What's the price tag on four thousand kilos of cocaine?'

Carrick grinned and used *Tern*'s loud-hailer again. 'Not

230

certain, Johnny. At least enough to keep you in new boats for ever!'

A metallic crudity of a curse came back from Walker. Then both men got back into shelter. Once again the sea began to churn astern of the two patrol launches as their diesels gathered power. *Tern* in the lead, *Puffin* tucking in close astern, they got under way on what had to be their final lap.

A brief, fierce squall of rain lashed down. When it cleared, the bulk of Lannair Island was already beginning to grow ahead. But if there was a new lookout posted up there, would he have much chance of spotting the two small, unlit patrol launches – in that broken moonlight, on that mad expanse of white-capped waves and wind-whipped spray?

'No,' said Carrick aloud. Then he glanced round at his crew, all at their duty stations. Clapper Bell might have heard. But he was the only one.

The diesels were rumbling hoarsely. But the sounds of the sea, the thunder of those waves breaking along Lannair's shore, should be loud enough to muffle that problem. He hoped.

Just as he knew Johnny Walker would be hoping.

Andy Grey's radar screen showed they were almost into the magnetic problem area round Lannair when, with only a squeal as a warning, the Fleet Support radio channel called them again. John Kennan automatically used the scrambler circuit.

'Your priority, *Tern*,' his voice snapped out from the bulkhead speaker. 'Affirmative. We have recovered the girl, and her companion. Both well. I repeat, the Lawson girl and her companion. Both found at Alder's house, both well. Did you read?'

'Received,' confirmed Carrick. The patrol launch's propeller blades screamed for a moment as she fell into a trough and, momentarily, there was no sea beneath them. Then the blades bit again, with a shudder. That didn't matter. *Tern* was built for that. The relief at Kennan's news brought a fierce grin to his lips. 'I have *Puffin*, we have Lannair between us and the net-line location.'

'There's some extra update from Port Torquil,' crackled John Kennan's voice from the snug Headquarters office in Edinburgh. 'Some police have filtered into Torquil House. They found a couple of what look like container modules – both empty. There have also been two radio check calls, unidentified, on the special frequency on Dr Kennedy's set. They got the transmitter carrier-only reply.'

'Any reaction from them?' asked Carrick.

'They didn't like it,' said Kennan. He didn't elaborate. 'They could be nervous. If it helps, *Marlin* and *Blackfish* should now reach you in one hour.' A sudden chuckle entered his voice. 'Tell your bo'sun we're running a book – it's even money on Shannon by a neck. Good luck with it – ' the signal was breaking and fading ' – and whatever you do . . . ' The rest vanished in a wail of static.

Tern and *Puffin* had entered the problem area around the island. Then, briefly, there was also the benefit of being under the weather lee of the sea-cliff island and the swell faded a little. Carrick made his way back to the navigation space, where the Admiralty chart for the Lannair sea area was already taped down. Whatever happened at the net-line, there wouldn't be time for doubts or second-call decisions. Peering at the outlined rocks and soundings, he felt a hand on his arm.

'Skipper.' Gogi MacDonnell solemnly handed him a mug of coffee. 'Medicinal.'

It reeked of whisky. He didn't argue. He also noticed that MacDonnell seemed to have distributed the pack of weapons they'd taken aboard. The ex-fisherman had a Savage twelve-gauge pump-action shotgun swinging from its sling over one shoulder and had left Andy Grey looking startled at the automatic rifle placed beside him.

Coffee and whisky, whatever the blend, it had already started to hold down the muscle-ache pains again as he clambered back into the black padded leather of the command chair.

Then, suddenly, they were clear of the lee of the island, and moments later it was the way they had hoped. Ahead of them, a series of pinhead mastlights marked a line of fishing boats. At the same time, the radar clutter cleared.

'Seven of them, skipper,' yelped Andy Grey, staring at the sweeping screen in front of him. 'Two groups – three dead ahead, a singleton, then the other three to your port. Range, two miles!'

'Two miles,' repeated Carrick automatically. He used the patrol launch radio channel, straight into their private call-signs. 'Black Label, we have them.'

'We have them, Whisky Straight,' confirmed Johnny Walker laconically. 'Call it.'

'A sheepdog run, Black Label,' said Carrick. 'Stay close.'

'Close,' suggested Clapper Bell in a hoarse aside. 'But not too bloody close!'

Carrick chuckled. 'Going in, Black Label – wind them up!'

Then he palmed the trio of small brass throttle levers wide open and nodded to Clapper Bell. The Glasgow-Irishman began swinging *Tern*'s big, slim steering wheel exactly as her diesels started into their full-throated thunder. As the deck vibrated and the patrol launch began racing forward, Carrick glanced back and to starboard. *Puffin* was already there, in wing position, maybe six lengths back, slamming through the swell, keeping exactly on station.

When it came to a show, Johnny Walker always did well.

They had more than halved the distance to the line of slow-moving, apparently unsuspecting fishing boats when there was a panic-stricken squawk from the fishing band radio, the first time they'd heard it do more than whisper since Port Torquil.

Within seconds, the first voice was joined by other

clamouring warnings as other boats spotted the two charging patrol launches, bow-waves like phosphorescent white arrowheads cutting through the night.

A siren yelped, moving lights showed on decks, a shower of sparks rose from an exhaust stack, a plume of oily black smoke coughed from another – and still the two patrol launches slammed over the waves, thundering nearer. Until, at the last possible moment, at under two hundred yards distance, still in formation, they went into a lurching, startling ninety-degree curve of a turn which had their portside bridge windows almost kissing the sea.

When they recovered, they were racing across the front of the entire line of boats.

'Searchlight!' ordered Carrick.

The big, glaring beam flared to life. Behind them, *Puffin*'s searchlight did the same. Then, together, the white lances of light sought out each fishing boat in turn as they passed down the line. Four were trawlers, one was a converted motor-drifter, the other two were clam dredgers. The lights of an eighth boat showed some distance to starboard, on sentry duty at one end of the vast span of nets. But for the moment, Carrick ignored it.

He was seeing white Stewart cockades on some of the boats, identifying others by their dark paintwork as Grant boats. The first trawler he passed was Sam Lawson's *Coral*. Another, further down, flaunting its white cockade, was Charlie Stewart's *Stargirl*. One of the clam dredgers was probably the boat which had almost killed him.

'Skipper!' He heard a yell from Clapper Bell. 'Look at this one!'

Andy Grey had moved their searchlight's beam to play on the motor-drifter. She had been caught with men busy on her deck and a length of net hauled clear of the water, a net glistening with thirty or forty struggling salmon – and among them a big, grey, inert shape like a fat torpedo.

Except that in its own way it was more deadly.

There was one voice still yelping in panic on the radio. One of the boats ahead had men on deck, frantically

234

freeing a swathe of net she'd either been hauling in or re-laying – more than one curtain of net would be in use this night. If there was panic, it was time. Carrick used the fishing band radio, transmitting at *Tern*'s full power.

'Sam Lawson on *Coral* – Lawson, this is Fishery Protection. Hear me. Your daughter is safe. I repeat, Sam – your daughter has been found and is safe.' Carrick paused, counted to five, then went on. 'Sam – and anyone else who doesn't know – whatever they told you they're smuggling in, it's cocaine. I say again, cocaine.' He paused again, signalled to Clapper Bell at the helm, then braced himself as *Tern* bucked and thrashed round in another tight turn to come back up the line. 'Sam, don't get in any deeper. You or any skipper who has had enough, break off now. Break off now. Return to Port Torquil. Direct to Port Torquil. The police will meet you there.'

He put down the handset. *Tern*'s searchlight was already sweeping up the line as she started her return run. *Puffin* was into her stage of the sheepdog routine, completing a wider turn, starting to bellow her way up along the other side of the fishing boats with her search-light stabbing its own tracery along the silhouetted hulls.

A figure ran out on one deck, knelt, aimed a rifle, and fired a string of shots. A bullet smashed a hole in one of the bridge windows. Others smacked somewhere aft, then the fishing boat broached in a big swell, water deluged along her decks, and when it cleared the man had lost his weapon and was dragging himself back into the shelter.

The radio was babbling. Johnny Walker was whooping his siren on the far side, and Carrick reached to do the same.

He didn't. Because it was happening.

Sam Lawson's *Coral* was the first to break line and get under way. Her own, deeper siren sounded a series of short blasts at the same time as her decklights came on. Another of the trawlers and a clam boat followed, their lights also switched on – and the sentinel boat over to starboard was doing the same while a new squall of wind and rain swept in across everything.

'Whisky Straight – ' Johnny Walker shouted exultantly over the private frequency, only his searchlight's glare visible in the dark chaos ' – that cuts it better!' Suddenly, his voice faltered then switched to a yell of warning. 'Webb, port bow – heading for you!'

Carrick saw the dark shape of the raider boat a moment later. It came out from behind the Stewart trawler *Stargirl*, bouncing and falling as it began racing through a patch of sea where the waves were eerily green under the overhead moons of the searchlights. Big twin outboard engines howled at her stern and two figures crouched aboard. Both wore scuba wet-suits, one in black hugging the tiller, the other a man in grey who was clutching something close to his chest.

'Andy – get on her,' yelled Carrick, and saw *Tern*'s searchlight beam swing round.

It took the raider boat head on. The figure at the tiller threw an arm up as a shield against the glare, but the speeding little craft didn't slow and at *Tern*'s own closing speed the gap was vanishing.

'Stand by!' Carrick knew he had one chance to call it right. 'Clapper, she wants to shave our starboard. We'll take her portside.'

'Portside,' acknowledged the Glasgow-Irishman, his hands knuckle-white on the wheel.

'Gogi – '

'Portside, skipper,' said Gogi MacDonnell from just behind him.

They counted the seconds as the two craft rushed towards each other. The little raider boat's bow angle suddenly, fractionally altered and Carrick knew he had been right. It was coming in to run along their starboard side, risking the dangers of the swell and *Tern*'s foaming bow-wave. He could see the two men very clearly now.

Recognize them. Charlie Stewart and Michael Alder together.

'Now,' he snarled.

Clapper Bell spun the patrol launch's wheel in an ultimate test for her hydraulic system. Underneath, the three big spade rudders bit at a new angle – and where the raider boat had been almost on their starboard bow she was now to port. The man in the grey scuba suit, already half-straightened, ready to hurl his satchel charge, lost moments to adjust to it.

As he hugged the charge for the throw, Gogi MacDonnell leaned out of the opened port door of the cockpit bridge, calmly sighted the long barrel of the Savage pump-action, and fired twice.

One solid shot, able to penetrate an engine casing, smashed into the raider boat's hull. The second hit the satchel charge, went through it, then tore a gaping hole in Michael Alder's chest. A fraction of a second later, the satchel charge exploded aboard the raider boat. Another fraction of a second later, there were two more explosions aboard the stricken raider boat – searing, volcano-cored blasts as at least one other satchel charge aboard exploded and the fuel tanks blew up.

They felt the blasts hard aboard *Tern*. Sam Pilsudski was thrown across his engineroom and was left half dazed across a generator casing. On the bridge and aft, anything loose was sent crashing and tumbling.

'*Tern*, are you all right?' demanded Johnny Walker urgently over the radio.

'Fine, Johnny,' answered Carrick. 'Nice back-up.'

They circled round and came back. What was left of the raider boat's hull was lying upside down in the water, already being lapped by a thin line of abandoned salmon net. There was no sign of either Alder or Stewart. But their bodies were under there somewhere.

Maybe under the net.

Carrick looked round. Gogi MacDonnell grimaced at him and shrugged.

Clapper Bell didn't leave it. He cleared his throat.

'Next time, you win a bloody teddy bear,' he said gruffly.

They had come down to half speed agin. *Puffin* was about a quarter mile away, herding three boats. All had the white Stewart cockade on their paintwork.

But there should have been four . . . *Stargirl* had gone.

He grabbed for the bridge glasses, and scanned the night without success while the patrol launch completed a giant circle.

'Found her, skipper,' said Andy Grey from the radar screen. 'South-east, about two miles – and cutting corners. She's damned near the Sula Rocks.'

Carrick told Johnny Walker to stay with his three captive boats and once again *Tern* began slamming through the night sea and those great, long, widowmaker grey swells. There was broken glass everywhere beneath their feet and one propeller shaft had developed a strange whine, but she was still answering all her controls and Sam Pilsudski was cursing healthily down below.

Yet there was something wrong. The blip on the radar plot that was *Stargirl* had slowed then was drifting, obviously out of control. It merged into the clutter that was the Sula Rocks. Then, ahead, two distress rockets soared and burst under the fierce cloudrace sky.

They went on through the broken, angry seas, came down to a slow crawl as they neared the harsh line of the rocks, and used the searchlight. It swept along the white, frothing reef, where green and brown algae clung to wet, waiting fangs, then they found the trawler.

Dr Margaret Steeven had sworn that Charlie Stewart would force his *Stargirl* too hard one day. Now someone else had done it.

Those steady walls of water had swept the boat along then had thrown her sideways into the reef. How often she had been slammed that way was impossible to guess. But her back was already broken. Her stern wheelhouse was torn separate from her for'ard section by a cauldron turmoil of dark, deep water, bow and stern sections shuddering with each new surge of swell that came in, both starting to sink.

Three fishermen were clinging to the wreckage of a hatch cover jammed at an angle among the wreckage on the bow section. A torch waved another appeal from the wheelhouse.

'We could go away,' said Clapper Bell. He looked around his audience, and scowled. 'Joke, right? So who else gets his feet wet?'

They needed his strength on deck. Gogi MacDonnell took over the helm, Sam Pilsudski dropped into the command chair to nurse his engine throttles. Then, with infinite care, the patrol launch came in, inch by battling inch.

Out at the bow, lifejacket harnesses clipped to safety lines, Carrick and Bell crouched under each incoming deluge of spray and whole water while the rock and the broken bow section in front of them seemed to rise and fall every few seconds. The three fishermen by the hatch cover had seen them.

'Wait,' yelled Carrick as one man started to move.

His voice was lost under a roar of incoming sea. Then two of the men had gone – until the next sea threw one back again, past Bell, who grabbed a leg, hauled, and physically dragged him aboard.

Tern backed off and came in again while Andy Grey pulled the man back on a shared safety line and into the shelter of the bridge.

The next time they came in, the remaining man literally took a simple running jump across, landed in Carrick's outstretched arms, and nearly took them both overboard in the process.

But the torch was still waving from the wheelhouse section of what had been *Stargirl*.

Manœuvring round to make a fresh approach, *Tern* was struck broadside by very large sea. She rolled as if she would never recover, then lurched back with the propeller shaft that had been off-key now screaming and another sounding sick. As they backed away, her starboard hull was clawed by rocks they couldn't see.

'I can see two of them in there,' yelled Clapper Bell through cupped hands close to Carrick's ear. 'Maybe we could float in a line – '

'No time.' Carrick wiped another drenching curtain of salt spray from his face. He could see them too, each time the heaving, shaking patrol boat steadied long enough for its searchlight beam to probe. A scared, white-faced John Torrance was clinging to part of the gap where the wheelhouse door had been. Keren Stewart was the other figure beside him, standing tall, holding some other support, still defiant, the white Stewart cockade clearly visible on the breast of her black scuba suit. 'There's only one other way, we can try – '

He stared at the gradually sinking stern section, lying partly on its side, most of her rudder already out of the water as she slid further and deeper down the savage slope of glistening wet rock. Over there, inside the wheelhouse was the only shelter. Over there, tangled wreckage also partly blocked the only way out, where that missing door had been. It needed someone on the outside.

'No chance, skipper!' Bell seemed to read his mind.

'We'll try.'

Looking round at *Tern*'s bridge windows, Carrick hand-signalled – then had to hand-signal again before Sam Pilsudski either understood or accepted what he wanted. The patrol launch's damaged propeller shafts slowly increased their protesting revolutions and she began to creep in – and in – then hard in on the next swell.

Until her starboard bow grated on rock and wreckage and hung there, held while her diesels sobbed on and her stern rose and fell.

Clumsy in his harness and lifejacket, Carrick jumped on to the trawler's splintered remnant of quivering deck. Two strides through thigh-deep, foaming sea took him to the wheelhouse entrance. He clung there while another sea briefly engulfed him, then John Torrance was being

240

thrust out by Keren Stewart. He pulled the young run-away deckhand free like a cork from a bottle. Two strides back, and he threw Torrance up to be caught by Clapper Bell, then turned and fought his way back to the wheel-house again.

Another wall of water hit. He clung to wreckage, splut-tering, then hauled himself to the wheelhouse entrance as the sea poured back. Keren Stewart was struggling to free herself and Carrick made to help her. She glared, she spat in his face – then she let him haul her clear.

The next wave left them clinging to each other. As it receded, he struggled to wade them both back across the broken deck towards *Tern*.

Then he saw the next great grey wall of water coming. He shouted. The copper-haired woman he was holding tried to shout back – and then the wave had struck.

Stargirl's wheelhouse was sliding and slipping, he was being tumbled through breaking sea – and Keren Stewart had gone, had vanished.

Clapper Bell and Andy Grey hauled him back aboard *Tern*. There was only the foaming sea and the reef to be lit by the searchlight, and on two sick engines, the third shut down, *Tern* hauled herself clear. Her pumps were fighting the water pouring in through two underwater gashes on her starboard side.

Wet, cold and exhausted, Carrick left Sam Pilsudski in the command chair and slumped down with Bell in front of the navigation space. The big Glasgow-Irishman didn't look any better. They barely stirred as the private fre-quency radio squeaked to life.

'Just shut up, Johnny,' willed Carrick softly. Next moment, he blinked.

'Whisky Straight, this is Whisky Sour,' said a voice he knew. 'Can't I trust you to go anywhere without getting into trouble? We thought we'd better be around!'

Whisky Sour had always been the third private call-sign, used by Russ Donald on *Pippin*. Carrick hauled himself to his feet, and looked out.

Lit like a Christmas tree, the fat white-hulled research boat *Dirk* was thumping down towards them. As she came nearer, he could see Russ Donald on her bridge, and the small, grey-haired figure of Margaret Steeven. She held up a hand in a simple greeting. But just to be there, the *Dirk* must have thrashed and fought every inch of the way.

In the far background, a display of signal rockets in the night showed that *Marlin* and *Blackfish* had arrived in a dead heat. They could hear their captains begin arguing on the private frequency.

Johnny Walker could take care of it.

They floated a line across to the research boat for a tow.

It was a long, slow haul through those battering seas. It was nearly three a.m. when *Tern* entered harbour at Port Torquil and tied up.

Three weeks later, on another Saturday afternoon, Webb Carrick stood in the warm sunlight outside the Pride of Mull bar. His bruises and his aches had faded. He wore a sweater and denims, two six-pack cartons lay at his feet, and he was there to meet Russ Donald. They had an escape planned for the afternoon.

Where he stood, he saw the whole stretch of Port Torquil harbour. There were still gaps here and there. Boats and people.

Boats had been impounded.

Some people – like Dr James Kennedy – were in jail. Although an old man had been found safe and well.

Some people – like Sam Lawson – were out on bail. Lawson was likely to face some kind of prison sentence, but was content that his daughter was safe.

Some people – like a subdued young Torrance – had been left licking their wounds.

The bodies of Keren Stewart and the trawlerman who had died with her had been found washed on to the Sula Rocks. The bodies of Charlie Stewart and Michael Alder had still to be recovered. Maybe on that beach on Fladda. Maybe in another week.

Out of the anticipated twenty incoming container-loads of cocaine, only six had been recovered – five seized aboard fishing boats, one later washed up on Lannair. The others had been still coming in when the netting operation was disrupted. Their self-destruct mechanisms meant they weren't expected to be recovered.

Carrick hadn't been in Port Torquil on the day that Keren Stewart's body had been recovered and brought in by *Blackfish*. It had been one of several days when he had been in a helicopter, shuttling from Mull to Fishery Protection headquarters in Edinburgh to meet people, talk with people, explain to people. But on one trip he also visited the proud, sad widow of a man named Fred Cormack who had died trying to do his job. On the next, he had delivered a particular bottle of whisky and his father's birthday card. That had its own priority.

Many of the days seemed to merge. A joint task force of US, Soviet and British customs and drugs enforcement teams had arrived to work on the Noah Pipeline operation. Among other things, a Panamanian-registered freighter, newly arrived from Venezuela, was being held in Rotterdam and her crew of eight had been arrested.

A dozen Russian trawlers had been found in an extensive sweep-search north of Mull. But if one of them was the one that mattered, it couldn't be identified. Even so, some East European possibilities had been discovered in other ways, and might matter.

If James Kennedy was to be believed, it would have been the second full-scale run after two pilot trials.

In the same way, some facts and some possibilities were being uncovered on the other side of the Atlantic. Particularly in Florida, where Big Charlie Stewart and his wife, their planned life in retirement shattered, were still being questioned.

That was where it had begun, when Keren Stewart went out to visit her parents in their new home looking out at the Gulf of Mexico. Where she met with people, then sold an idea.

A name had emerged to work on.

But back on Mull, Webb Carrick had visited the crumbling, empty Torquil House. He had seen decaying rooms where Victorian wallpaper was peeling off damp walls. He had seen a banqueting hall, large enough to host a Rotary dinner but where there were old, bare floorboards and a wormed, abandoned piano.

Then he had been shown the background report being assembled on Charlie Stewart's long trail of petty frauds and clumsy embezzlements, of assaults and gambling debts.

And, still even then a surprise, the similar report being pulled together on Keren Stewart. Her frauds, her manipulations had been careful, complex and often cruel. But they both covered things up, for her brother had financed a high-spending, second, very different lifestyle that she stepped into any time she visited the mainland.

Carrick drew in a deep breath, enjoying the warmth of the sun on his back. There was a lot to sort out, even locally. Nobody was ready to guess what would happen now between the Grants and the Stewarts. The old hatreds had been fading away. Now that both sides were dulled with shock, the hatreds might never return. Or they might suddenly smoulder back again.

Behind him, he could hear shouts and laughter from inside the Pride of Mull. *Tern*'s crew were there, along with a trio from *Puffin* and some men from the two big coastguard cutters now in harbour.

For the moment, *Tern*'s stay in Port Torquil was nearly over.

Russ Donald had already taken over as relief skipper on *Puffin*, while Johnny Walker went off on leave. Tomorrow, the shiny new *Lapwing* with a shiny new skipper was due to arrive, her sea trials completed, ready for duty. *Tern* had been repaired enough to head down to the Clyde for a full dockyard overhaul.

Carrick would go with her.

The voices behind him in the Pride of Mull were getting fiercer and louder. He grinned – but for another reason.

Russ Donald was ambling along the street towards him. Only Russ Donald could have gambled on the weather and found a small sail-boat they could use for the rest of the day. Only Russ Donald could have talked the two women who walked with him into also coming sailing. They were both in their late twenties, slim and smart and cool, one blonde and one brunette. The blonde was Russian, the brunette was American. They were both members of the customs investigation team drafted to Port Torquil.

Both considerably outranked Carrick and Donald. Maybe that was why he saw they had brought their own beer.

He straightened up, then froze for a moment.

Behind him, the argument had crystallized into an intellectual debate between Clapper Bell and Gogi Mac-Donnell. As debates, they were famed.

'See you?' yelled MacDonnell. 'Man, you're stupid as well as ugly!'

'Stupid?' Clapper Bell digested that for a moment. Then his bellow sounded back. 'But if I had a face like yours, I'd paint my arse and walk on my hands!'

A table crashed over.

Carefully, Webb Carrick picked up his two six-packs. With something better to do, he walked away.

POSTSCRIPT

The Noah Pipeline is fictional in its location. The channels travelled by salmon between Greenland and Scotland, called 'tramways' by the Scottish Fishery Protection Service, are charted but secret. Illegal, highly organized salmon raids in off-shore waters, using miles of nets each strike, are an extremely profitable criminal activity. The small trawlers involved can be accompanied by a larger deep-freeze storage ship.

Separately, numbers of bales containing drugs have been washed ashore at different times at certain locations around the British coast. Their origins and intended destinations are in the main unknown.

On the West Highland coast, in one of several recent anti-drugs operations, customs officers boarded a small yacht off Dunstaffnage, in the Firth of Lorne, and 1,400 kilos of drugs was seized. In another raid, 4,000 kilos of drugs was seized as they came ashore.

Finally, given a time and location after a tragedy at sea, fishermen who know tides and currents can often forecast when and where bodies and wreckage will be washed ashore. Churchyards at many fishing villages on many coasts provide mute evidence of the great distances which can be involved.

B.K.